The CMS User's Guide

Prentice Hall Mainframe Software Series

Essential Resources, Inc. (ERI) with Jan Diamondstone, *Using VAX/VMS*

Gildersleeve, *The CICS Companion: A Reference Guide to COBOL Command Level Programming*

Hoffman/Hicks, *The CMS User's Guide*

Inmon, *Optimizing Performance in DB2*

Lee, *CICS/VS Command Level Programming with COBOL Examples*

Lee, *CICS/VS Online System Design and Implementation Techniques*

Lee, *IMS/VS DB/DC Online Programming Using MFS and DL/1*

Lee, *IMS/VS DL/1 Programming with COBOL Examples*

Lee, *VSAM Coding in COBOL and VSAM AMS*

Martin, *Fourth-Generation Languages: Principles,* Volume I

Martin/ARBEN, *Fourth-Generation Languages: Representative 4 GLS,* Volume II

Martin/ARBEN, *Fourth-Generation Languages: 4 GLS from IBM,* Volume III

Martin/ARBEN, *SNA: IBM's Networking Solution*

Martin/ARBEN, *VSAM: Access Method Services and Programming Techniques*

Narayan, *Data Dictionary: Implementation, Use, and Maintenance*

Rindfleisch, *OS and VS Job Control Language and Utility Programs, second edition*

Roetzheim, *Structured Computer Project Management*

The CMS User's Guide

Paul E. Hoffman
and G. Mack Hicks

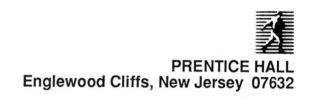

PRENTICE HALL
Englewood Cliffs, New Jersey 07632

Library of Congress Cataloging-in-Publication Data

HOFFMAN, PAUL (date)
    The CMS user's guide / Paul E. Hoffman and G. Mack Hicks.
      p. cm.
    Includes index.
    ISBN 0-13-187725-9
    1. VM/CMS (Computer operating system) I. Hicks, G. Mack (date).
    II. Title.
QA76.76.063H643 1989   89-15687
005.4'429--dc 19

Cover design: Ben Santora
Manufacturing buyer: Mary Ann Gloriande

© 1989 by Prentice-Hall, Inc.
A division of Simon & Schuster
Englewood Cliffs, New Jersey 07632

Prentice Hall Mainframe Software Series

The publisher offers discounts on this book when ordered
in bulk quantities. For more information, write
        Special Sales/College Marketing
        Prentice-Hall, Inc.
        College Technical and Reference Division
        Englewood Cliffs, NJ 07632

Printed in the United States of America

10 9 8 7 6 5 4 3 2

ISBN   0-13-187725-9

Prentice-Hall International (UK) Limited, *London*
Prentice-Hall of Australia Pty. Limited, *Sydney*
Prentice-Hall Canada Inc., *Toronto*
Prentice-Hall Hispanoamericana, S.A., *Mexico*
Prentice-Hall of India Private Limited, *New Delhi*
Prentice-Hall of Japan, Inc.*, Tokyo*
Simon & Schuster Asia Pte. Ltd., *Singapore*
Editora Prentice-Hall do Brasil, Ltda., *Rio de Janeiro*

Dedication

To Alan Tippy

Contents

6   Introduction to XEDIT   111

7   Introduction to REXX   155

8   Advanced CMS Topics   169

9   Different Versions of CMS   191

Appendices

Preface

This book explains CMS in a simple, straightforward manner to beginning- and intermediate-level CMS users. For beginners, this book deals with the basics of what an operating system is and what CMS can do for you. For more advanced readers, the book tells you how to use all of CMS's important features without burdening you with details you won't use.

Most readers will find this book a useful complement to IBM's documentation for CMS. Due to CMS's flexibility and wide-ranging uses, IBM's one-size-fits-all manuals often do not introduce CMS concepts in a logical fashion for many readers. IBM's reference manuals are complete guides to CMS and thus don't differentiate between frequently-used commands and lightly-used commands. This book covers what we feel most users need to know to use CMS and to explore its power on their own.

One problem with IBM's manuals is the jungle of acronyms and strange names for the parts of the operating system. Although technically precise, these names can intimidate people learning CMS or make them think that learning to use CMS is more difficult than it really is. This book uses names that are logical and easy to remember, while still being accurate.

WHO SHOULD READ THIS BOOK

Almost any CMS user will find clear, useful information in this book.

- Beginners will find the tutorial style of the beginning chapters especially useful. The book explains things in one place that a reader would normally have to look for in many different manuals. New terms are explained as they are used, and there are many examples throughout the book.

- Intermediate users will appreciate that the book does not contain every CMS command in minute detail. Commands that are rarely used by most people (such as those for specific types of programmers) have been purposefully left out of the book. There are highlighted sections that compare CMS to other operating systems on other computers; since many intermediate users work with more than one computer, these comparisons will help them absorb the material quicker. Chapter 8, which covers advanced CMS topics, will be of special interest to intermediate users.

- Advanced readers will find the later chapters serve as good brush-up courses on the details of XEDIT and REXX. These chapters will also be able to point other users to parts of the book which explain CMS concepts that are not clearly introduced in the IBM documentation.

This book is also quite useful for system administrators, customer service personnel, and other people who are often asked for help. Instead of having to refer confused users to IBM's reference guides which may explain commands in very technical language, they can show them the section in this book that explains both the command and the concepts behind using it.

WHAT IT IS LIKE TO LEARN CMS

People learn to use CMS at different speeds. Some pick up CMS skills rapidly, while others have a hard time with them. This book is meant to help the entire range of readers. The material in this book does not pretend that learning CMS is a snap for users.

If you are familiar with microcomputer operating systems like MS-DOS, you will find that many CMS commands in this book are quite easy to learn since many have English names. If you have used other mainframe operating systems, it is very likely that you will be impressed with how fast CMS can be learned compared to other operating systems.

Advanced users and system administrators will find that this book does not pull any punches when it comes to teaching the difficult portions of CMS. Certainly, CMS is given credit where credit is due; however, the tricky aspects of CMS are all identified as such to help prepare readers and to show when they may need to spend more time and effort.

Many people find CMS to be the most powerful system for personal computing in use today. Its flexibility and maturity have attracted an ardent following. This can lead to beginners being both excited and overwhelmed. The occasional irreverent tone in this book is meant to help beginners over the rough spots so that they can both appreciate and use the vast powers of CMS.

WHAT IS IN THIS BOOK

The first two chapters of the book introduce you to CMS and explain the basics of using it. They show how you interact with CMS at your terminal and why it is important to know how to use CMS commands. You are shown how to log on and use the most common CMS commands.

Since disks and files are very important in your work, Chapter 3 explains them in detail. The chapter also covers many of the different types of disks and files you may encounter as you use CMS. This chapter also shows you how to use other common CMS commands.

Chapter 4 covers the rest of the CMS commands that you are likely to use. It is arranged by type of command so you can see the relationships between CMS commands. After you finish the chapter, you will know how to use all the common (and many of the not-so-common but still useful) CMS commands and understand how they relate to your work.

Of course, your work involves much more than just giving CMS commands: You want to run real applications. Chapter 5 gives you an overview of what many of the IBM applications do and why you might be interested in them. After reading this chapter, you will have a much better understanding of what CMS can do for you in your business.

One of the most useful and powerful programs on CMS is the XEDIT file editor (sometimes called the *System Product Editor*). With XEDIT, you can create your own documents and text files. You will see in chapter 6 that XEDIT's parts make a great deal of sense if you learn them step by step. Even if you already know a bit about using XEDIT, the organization of chapter 6 will help you see the connection between various XEDIT commands and thus become a more proficient user.

Chapter 7 gives you a thorough introduction to CMS's command processing language called REXX (sometimes called the *System Product Interpreter*). Almost anyone can write simple REXX programs, and users find its powerful features useful in their daily work. You will see how learning a bit of programming will help you solve common CMS problems. The chapter also describes EXEC2, an antique cousin of REXX that some people used before REXX was available.

When IBM developed CMS in the late 1960s, most people who used it knew a fair amount about computers. Many of the underlying concepts of CMS are heavily based on theories taught in computer science departments at colleges. Of course, now most CMS users do not have that background. Chapter 8 describes some of CMS's advanced topics in language most people can understand. The material in this chapter is not necessary for everyone, but knowing it will give you a good sense of the other powerful and interesting facets of using CMS.

This book describes Release 5 of CMS. Since IBM releases new versions of CMS every few years, readers of this book may not have all the features described. Chapter 9 discusses previous releases of the operating system as well as some variations on Release 5.

The appendices are reference guides to using CMS. Since many companies do not do their own programming, Appendix A describes some of the commercial software that you can buy to use under CMS.

Appendices B and C are quick references to the parts of CMS. They contain concise descriptions of commands. You will find these appendices useful when you are using CMS and want a short reminder on how to use it. Appendix B covers CMS; Appendix C covers XEDIT.

Appendix D describes the IBM manuals that relate to CMS. You can use this chapter as a guide to finding other information on CMS. Appendix E is a collection of all the checklists (described in the next section) from the book.

FEATURES OF THE BOOK

There are many examples of actual CMS commands. The examples are designed so that you can replicate most of them on your CMS computer. Many examples build on each other so you can get a feeling for how CMS commands relate.

Comparisons to Other Computers

Since many readers have used other computers, there are special boxes with comparisons between CMS and other systems. These are especially geared toward readers who have used microcomputers like the IBM PC and Apple Macintosh, as well as larger UNIX computers. The boxes look like this:

> **If You Are Familiar With Other Computers**
>
> CMS commands are often similar in structure to commands on micro-computers.

Keeping Track of Your Configuration

There are many ways to set up your CMS system. For example, you might have CMS automatically link disks of other users when you log on. Since these setup options affect the commands you can give and CMS's responses to commands, it is important to keep track of the special settings.

As you read the book, you will find that system settings that affect the way you work with CMS are indicated by checklists. Fill in the checklists with the information for your CMS system so you can refer to them as needed when you are reading this book or the IBM manuals. If you are unsure of the information requested in a checklist, you should ask your system administrator or system consultant. For example, a checklist might look like this:

Disks that are linked when you log on:

☐ Mine
☐ System
☐ Another user's (named _____)

Appendix E is a compendium of all the checklists; this will help you bring all the relevant information about your system together in one place.

Commands To Be Used with Care

A few of the commands described in this book should be used with caution, since they can cause changes to your disk. These commands are safe in normal use, but extra care should be taken when you use them. These commands are marked with a ⓦ sign.

Your System Administrator

Throughout this book, we refer to someone called the *system administrator*. This is the person who can give you access to the computer, solve mysterious problems that come up when using it, answer questions about how to get tasks done, and so on. At your site, this person may be called something like "system consultant," "service operator," or "customer service representative."

Your system administrator is:

Whatever they are called, it is a good idea to get to know them and to show them this book so that they know what you are using to learn CMS.

WHAT THIS BOOK DOES NOT COVER

Since it is a user's guide, this book does not try to be everything to everybody. For example, it does not contain the highly-technical information needed by programmers who are writing programs to run under CMS. It does, however, give you a good beginning for becoming proficient at the parts of CMS which all programmers use in their daily work.

CMS is a broad-based operating system used by beginners and advanced users. There are some CMS commands used by so few people that they have been left out. There are some technical commands that you need to run CMS: They are covered in the most friendly fashion possible within the constraints of clarity. Also, some reasonable commands have a few very technical options; those have been left out as well.

In other words, the book covers everything for which most people use CMS, but purposefully tends toward understandability and usefulness rather than completeness.

ACKNOWLEDGMENTS

This book would not have been possible without the help of many people. We had a great deal of help from our initial reviewers who gave us advice and guidance on the content and tone of the book. These reviewers include David Susarret, Don Erbel, Patty Neill, Frank Muth, and Rich McConnell. We are especially grateful to our dear friend Austin Shelton for the incredible amount of time he spent reviewing and criticizing the book.

1

Introduction to CMS

This chapter gives you an introduction to the whole of the CMS operating system. Learning about CMS involves learning first about its underlying concepts (which are covered in this chapter, Chapter 2, and Chapter 3) and learning about how you can operate it (covered throughout the book).

Many CMS concepts are quite advanced, but these parts of CMS are not commonly used by beginning users. Thus, they are covered later in the book. The first few chapters cover ideas and actions that are basic to understanding CMS.

OPERATING SYSTEMS

CMS is a piece of computer software. This means it is a program that runs on a computer; it is not the computer itself. You might hear people say, "We run CMS on our 9370," or, "I used a 4300 with CMS the other day." CMS looks the same to you regardless of the computer on which it runs.

There are many different kinds of computer software. CMS is an *operating system*. Operating systems are software that control the way you deal with the computer and the way the computer coordinates its hardware. Other types of software are *applications*, which let you perform specific business tasks like accounting, and *utilities*, which help you control the computer better.

(A minor point: CMS by itself is not really an operating system. *CP*, the control program for the hardware, combined with CMS, the part you deal with, makes up an operating system. Some people refer to this combination as CP/CMS. Also, IBM documentation sometimes calls CP *VM*, and might call the combination VM/CMS. Much of this is ambiguous in the computer world, so this book talks mostly about CMS, even though it is connected with another program.)

An operating system is like the instruments in the cockpit of an airplane. Without the instruments, there is no way to control all of the complex parts of the airplane. But the instruments cannot control the airplane by themselves; they need you to tell them what you want to do and where you want to go. If you imagine the computer hardware as the airplane and CMS as its instruments, you are the pilot. The computer jargon for the pilot in this case is user (which doesn't sound nearly as exciting as being a pilot).

CMS, then, lets you control what your computer does. You use CMS to run applications, to store information in the computer, to communicate with other users, and so on.

If You Are Familiar With Other Computers

Most computers have operating systems. For example, the name of the operating system for the IBM PC is PC-DOS. Other IBM operating systems you may have heard of are MVS/TSO and OS. Some other operating systems are VMS, Wang/VS, CSS, UNIX, Macintosh, and Pick.

2

What CMS Does for You

If you are like most CMS users, you are much more concerned about what CMS can do for you, not how it does it. This book shows you how to talk with CMS to get your work done. However, you might be curious about some of the things that go into CMS and how it controls the computer.

The CMS operating system controls the flow of data in your computer. For example, suppose there is some information on a disk that you want to see on your terminal. The three steps in Illustration 1-1 show some of the basic features of CMS.

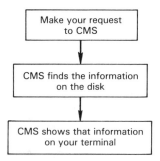

Illustration 1-1

For step 1, CMS needs to have a way to interact with you. As you will see in Chapter 2, you will type instructions on the terminal's keyboard and see responses on the terminal's screen. In CMS, as in most operating systems, these instructions are called *commands*.

For step 2, CMS needs to be able to control the hardware that is attached to the computer (in this case, the disk drive). To get the information from the disk, you don't need to know anything about disk platters, heads, rotation speeds, and so on: CMS handles that for you.

For step 3, CMS needs to be able to turn the data from the magnetic impulses on the disk into something meaningful to you. It also needs to know how you want the data displayed on your terminal. CMS is very good at converting data and remembering how you like things displayed. The information displayed on your terminal is often called CMS's *response*. If you make a mistake in your command, CMS will respond with a message (sometimes called an *error message*).

This discussion may have made CMS's task sound easy. In fact, it is not. The computer's hardware is incredibly complex, and CMS has to know how to act at every moment and in every situation for the hardware to work correctly. The bigger the computer and the more different pieces of hardware attached to it (these pieces are often called *peripherals*), the harder it is for CMS to do its job.

In addition, CP/CMS has to perform these tasks for every person on the system. It wouldn't be so bad if there was only one person using the computer. But CP/CMS is a *multi-user* operating system. This means that CP/CMS has to juggle requests from dozens (and often hundreds) of people at a time. In this sense, CP is like the air traffic control system of an airport. Not only does it have to respond to the actions and requests of each pilot (the CMS systems), it needs to keep the airplanes from crashing into each other.

> **If You Are Familiar With Other Computers**
>
> Most microcomputers have *single-user* operating systems. Only one person uses the computer at a time. For example, PC-DOS is a single-user operating system. Most large computer operating systems, like UNIX, are multi-user, allowing many users to operate the computer simultaneously.

The CMS operating system, then, takes care of a huge number of details while you do your work. Most people, even programmers, do not care in the least about the intricacies of how a communication line works or the electronic signals necessary to make a tape drive go forwards. They want to make a simple statement about what they want done, not all the little steps it takes to do it.

Why Operating Systems Are Important

One of the most frustrating aspects of using a computer is learning how to use it. If you are using an accounting program, it is bad enough that you need to learn all the intricate ins and outs of the program: Having to also learn to use "the computer" (or, more accurately, the operating system) adds insult to injury.

If you are like most people, you don't really want to learn how to use the operating system. However, most programs expect you to understand the operating system before you start to learn the program. Even though you just want to use the accounting program (or the design program, or the word processing program, etc.), you need to know a fair amount about the operating system to use the program effectively.

There are two major areas of the operating system that are important to using all programs. First, you need to know how to give commands so you can know how to start the program. Next, since most programs store information and results in files on the computer's disks, you need to know how to handle files. Commands are covered in Chapter 2, while files and disks are covered in Chapter 3.

In addition to commands and files, there are other important parts of operating systems that are useful in your daily work. Some include:

- Communicating with other users
- Using an editor to create your own files
- Simplifying repetitive processes
- Printing files on a printer

Thus, even if you really just want to run one or two application programs, you need to know a bit about the operating system. Up to a point, the more you know, the more efficiently you can use the computer. This book takes you to that point for CMS.

HARDWARE THAT RUNS CMS

IBM designed CMS to run on a wide variety of hardware. Originally, it only ran on the System/360-67 mainframe computer. Over the years, however, other models of computers have been developed, and CMS has been modified so it can run on them. As stated before, CMS looks the same on different types of hardware.

One of the ways IBM is making CMS available on many types of hardware is their recently announced Systems Application Architecture, more commonly called *SAA*. The concept behind SAA is that it would make life easier for users if they only had to learn one way of talking to computers, and it would also make it easier if programs running on different computers could communicate.

While IBM is committed to SAA, some people feel IBM is overstating the value of SAA and the extent that it will be adopted. Note, however, that many people were skeptical of IBM's commitment to their Systems Network Architecture (called *SNA*), and IBM proved them wrong by making it the standard for almost all large-system networks. It took SNA ten years to mature, but it proved to be of great importance to IBM's users.

System/370

System/370 computers (sometimes called *370* computers) are the most common mainframe computers in use today. They are used in businesses, colleges, and governmental agencies throughout the world. The largest System/370 computers can handle hundreds of users at the same time. Smaller versions of the System/370 (often called *4300* or *43xx* computers) are common in large organizations.

9370 Minicomputers

In late 1986, IBM introduced the 9370 line of minicomputers. The smallest is an inexpensive computer that can handle around five users comfortably. The largest can handle dozens of users at the same time. Computers in the 9370 series are also quite different from standard mainframes in that you do not need to keep them in specially air-conditioned rooms with raised floors. The peripheral hardware you attach to 9370s is also different, and often less expensive. It also attaches to Ethernet using the common TCP/IP protocol.

XT/370 and AT/370 Microcomputers

When IBM introduced the XT/370 computer in 1984, many people dreamed of having a personal computer running CMS sitting on their desks. Many people found the computer underpowered and it never became popular. The AT/370, which was introduced in 1986, was much faster and more powerful than the XT/370, but was still not widely accepted. Both models have been made obsolete by the introduction of the IBM PS/2.

Plug-compatible Computers

IBM is not the only company that makes computers that run CMS. Many other companies make computers that are so similar to IBM's that they can run CMS. These computers are called *plug-compatible machines* (or *PCMs* for short) because you can plug the same peripherals into them that you can plug into IBM computers. Some manufacturers of PCMs that run CMS are Amdahl and National Advanced Systems.

> Your computer hardware is (check one):
>
> ☐ System/370
> ☐ System/370 Extended
> ☐ 9370
> ☐ XT/370 or AT/370
> ☐ Plug-compatible (non-IBM)

VM

The CMS operating system runs under control of a software program known as *VM*. CMS is part of a product which IBM calls *VM/SP*. VM stands for *virtual machine*, and SP stands for *system product*. You can think of VM as the core software of the computer, while CMS is the way you talk to the computer and get it to do useful work.

You do not need to know how VM works to use CMS. The people most concerned with VM are programmers who are writing applications. Your interactions with VM are through CMS, so you just need to know CMS commands.

> **If You Are Familiar With Other Computers**
>
> VM's relationship to CMS is similar to the ROM BIOS's relationship to PC-DOS on the IBM PC.

History of VM and CMS

In the late 1960s, IBM developed a timesharing operating system called CP/67, which only ran on the IBM 360/67 (CP stands for *control program*). It became popular due to its central feature: When running under CP/67, each user could pretend he or she was the only user of the computer. Their programs did not need to know about what other users were doing or what computer resources they were using. Although it looked to each user that they had a full machine, they only really had the illusion of a full machine. This illusion was called a *virtual machine* (the illusion was so complete it even seemed the computer had buttons and knobs like an old-style computer).

CMS was developed to give CP/67 users a method to get the system to perform normal tasks. CMS stands for *conversational monitor system*, which means "a program that you can talk to." CMS, then, is like an operating system that works under another operating system (that is, under CP).

In the early 1970s, IBM developed the 370 series of computers. These computers had special hardware called *virtual memory* built into them. This hardware enabled the operating system software to give users virtual machines much faster and smaller. IBM completely redesigned CP/67 and called it VM/370 (remember that VM and CP are the same thing). Although IBM marketed software systems other than VM, it was nonetheless very popular.

By the early 1980s, many users had become devoted VM fans. Since the most common operating system under VM is CMS, this made CMS all the more popular. Since CMS is a popular operating system in colleges and universities, many students entering the job market know CMS and can use CMS systems at their companies.

A more detailed history of VM and CMS is given in Chapter 9.

VM and Hardware

The classes of computers that run VM are the same as those listed earlier in this chapter for the types of computers that run CMS. The hardware in each class of computers is very different from the hardware in other classes, but each class of computer has special capabilities built in to help it run VM.

Since CMS runs under VM, CMS is less dependent on the differences in the hardware architecture. For example, even though the disk drives and printers on a 9370 are completely different from those on a System/370, the CMS commands you give to use them are the same, and the information you see is also the same.

There are different "flavors" of VM, but CMS looks the same on each. Currently, the three predominant flavors of VM are VM/SP, VM/SP HPO, and VM/XA SP. Your system administrator chooses which one to use based on the type of hardware your site is running.

When IBM developed VM in the early 1970s, they saw the difficulties the operating system market was having were due to incompatibilities of computer hardware. This was one of the driving forces behind the development of VM: Make it run on different computers so the users don't see the hardware differences.

Many companies with growing data processing needs buy more than one mainframe computer. The mainframes can be connected in a *network* of computers that can share information. Each computer on the network is called a *node*; each node has a unique name so you can identify each computer. Some networks have mini- and microcomputers coexisting with the mainframes.

The type of hardware also affects the use of SAA. One of the best uses of SAA is to allow different computers to communicate in ways that do not affect the users. To do this, there must be hardware connections between the computers. IBM's SAA protocol specifies how these different computers can be linked. Since VM and non-VM computers can be running SAA, the hardware connections between computers allow users of non-IBM hardware to run CMS.

No one knows how people will attach mainframes and other computers together. Most people who deal mostly with microcomputers will have different ideas from mainframe administrators of what a network should look like. Certainly, IBM is stating their opinion on the direction they would like to see networking take. However, users have surprised IBM in the past about their networking choices and may do so again.

This means that networking at your site may be very different from that at another company. The system administrator must juggle many options when designing a network. These options often affect the way you gain access to CMS facilities. Thus, if you have a network at your company, you should probably learn more about how it is set up and how that affects your use of CMS.

Other VM Operating Systems

CMS is only one of the operating systems that can run under VM. Other IBM-supported operating systems that run under VM include DOS/VSE, MVS/SP, MVS/XA, VM/IX (UNIX), and even VM/SP itself. Illustration 1-2 shows the relationship between the hardware, VM, and other operating systems. Many people prefer CMS to these other operating systems because CMS is easier to use and more flexible.

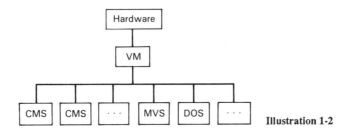

Illustration 1-2

If You Are Familiar With Other Computers

Very few other operating systems allow you to run other operating systems under them. Although some operating systems give the impression that you have a second operating system running under it (such as MS-DOS running under UNIX), these are usually highly modified to make the two coexist.

WHAT YOU SHOULD HAVE

Terminal

There are three types of terminals used with CMS:

- 3270-compatible (such as IBM 3278 or 3279 terminals, personal computers running 3270 emulation, or terminals from other manufacturers which are advertised as "3270 compatible")
- ASCII screen terminals (such as IBM 3101 or DEC VT-100)
- Printing terminals (with paper)

The majority of users communicate with CMS via a 3270-compatible terminal (often simply called a 3270). Many CMS commands (such as XEDIT) are specifically written for 3270 terminals, and using these commands without such a terminal is often slow and cumbersome. On a printing terminal, these commands are indeed difficult.

The material in this book assumes you are using a 3270 terminal. If you are using an ASCII terminal connected either directly or by phone line to a computer running CMS, it is likely that your terminal can act very much like a 3270. For example, even though you may not have all the keys on your keyboard that a 3720 has, there are key combinations you can use to *emulate* (that is, look like) 3270 keys. Your system administrator will tell you more about how your terminal can emulate a 3270. Using terminals is covered in much more detail in Chapter 2.

You may be using more than one terminal. For example, you may have a 3270-compatible terminal on your desk at work but log on to the computer on an ASCII terminal from home. Although switching from one to another may be a bit confusing, you will probably get used to the differences over a short period of time.

Your terminal is:

☐ 3270-compatible
☐ ASCII terminal
☐ Printing terminal

User Identification and Password

Before you can use CMS, you need a user identification (called a *userid*) and a password. You will get much more out of this book if you try out some of the examples instead of just reading them. For instance, reading about sending and receiving messages is just not as useful as actually doing it.

CMS requires that you have a valid userid and password combination. That is, each userid has one password. These are generally assigned by the system administrator. When you start using your terminal, the first thing CMS does is ask you for your userid and password. If you don't have one, CMS won't let you do anything else.

If You Are Familiar With Other Computers

Microcomputers don't usually have userids and passwords: you turn them on and start working. Most computers which allow more than one person on them have userids and passwords.

For security reasons, do *not* write your password in this book. In fact, you should not write your password anywhere where someone else might find it. Chapter 2 discusses more about password security.

Your userid is (do *not* write your password):

2

Giving CMS Commands

In this chapter, you will learn the form in which all CMS commands are given and see some examples of CMS commands. You will also learn about logging on to the computer and getting help if you need it.

COMMAND STRUCTURE

Even though there are dozens of them, every CMS command has a similar structure. When you type a command, you always type the command name first, then you type other information about the command. All CMS commands are like verbs in English sentences: They convey an action. For instance, the CMS command to copy a file on your disk is COPYFILE.

When you give a CMS command with extra information, you always put the command name first. The information, called *arguments*, is given in a specified order; this order is called the command's *syntax*. The syntax for CMS commands is often simple, but some CMS commands have quite complex syntaxes.

If you think of the commands as verbs, you can think of the arguments as nouns, adverbs, and adjectives. In English, you must put the parts of a sentence together in one of many predefined orders, such as subject-verb-object. You have some freedom of the arrangement of the words. For example:

```
The boy and the girl saw the red house.
```

You can rearrange the sentence to be:

```
The girl and the boy saw the red house.
```

You can even change some words slightly to change the word positions:

```
The red house was seen by the boy and the girl.
```

You can't just jumble the word parts, however:

```
The boy saw and the girl the house red.
```

CMS commands have a defined structure and less flexibility. You always start a command with the command name (the verb) and you almost always have to put the arguments in specific order.

```
Shut the door and the window.
```

Some CMS commands have optional arguments, called *options*, which are arguments that can be included but do not have to be for the command to be understood. Options are like adjectives; if there was only one story in a house, you might consider these two sentences to be the same:

```
Shut the front door and the tall window.
```

12

If You Are Familiar With Other Computers

Most operating systems have the same rules for their commands: verb first, then arguments. UNIX and PC-DOS are two examples of this structure. Some operating systems have no typed-in commands; instead, you use a pointing device to indicate what you want to do; the Macintosh operating system is the best known of these.

You give CMS commands one at a time. Each command is executed in order. When you give a command, it is executed immediately; when it is finished, you can enter the next command.

TERMINALS FOR CMS

When you use CMS commands, you enter them at your terminal. In Chapter 1, you saw the different types of terminals you can use with CMS. They were:

- 3270-compatible
- ASCII terminals
- Printing terminals

This section discusses the specifics of how you use these terminals with CMS.

IBM's mainframe line is one of the few series of computers that until recently was designed to use anything other than industry-standard ASCII terminals. Most other mainframes and minicomputers allow you to perform all tasks equally well on ASCII terminals.

In the past few years, ASCII terminal controllers and emulation programs have become available from IBM and other vendors. These allow you to communicate with CMS on ASCII terminals in much the same way you would with a 3270 terminal.

If You Are Familiar With Other Computers

Most microcomputers built since 1985 do not have terminals: instead, they have the keyboard and screen built into the system. This is true for micros like the IBM PC, the IBM PS/2, and Apple Macintosh. Many minicomputers (such as UNIX systems) allow you to use a wide variety of ASCII terminals in a straightforward fashion.

Although it is possible to use CMS with a printing terminal or an ASCII terminal that is not emulating a 3270, it is often much more difficult. Many commands, such as the help facility described later in this chapter or the editor described in Chapter 6, can be awkward to use on non-3270s. This is the main reason the vast majority of CMS users use 3270s or compatibles.

If you are using an ASCII terminal that emulates a 3270, you may want to skip forward in this chapter to the section titled "ASCII Terminals that Emulate 3270s" before you read the following two sections. This book always discusses 3270 keys and keyboard actions; your emulator may require you to use different combinations of keys to get a particular action.

A very fundamental concept in using the 3270 terminal is that it is a *block-mode* terminal (sometimes called a *synchronous* terminal). This means that the terminal does not transmit information to the computer until you tell it to. Block-mode terminals were developed so the mainframe would not be kept busy watching terminals for characters.

If your site has many 3270 terminals, it is likely that they are connected to *cluster controllers*. Cluster controllers make more efficient use of the mainframe by handling the simple interactions with a group of terminals to let the mainframe spend its time computing instead.

3270 Screen

The CMS screen of a 3270 has three main areas:

```

                          ... Output display area ...        (1)




    _    User input area   (2)
                                                Status area    (3)
```

1. Data that the computer displays appears in the *output display area*. This area is usually 22 lines high by 80 characters wide, although some terminals have more area.
2. Below the output display area is a line where you type instructions to CMS; this is called the *user input area*.

3. In the lower right corner of the screen is the *status area*. The status area has short
    messages about what is happening in CMS. (Actually, the user input area is the whole
    23rd line plus most of the 24th line up to the status area, but you will probably only
    use the 23rd line when you use CMS.)

Some 3270 terminals have a 25th line that gives the terminal's status. This line often
contains little pictures and terse messages. Some ASCII terminals that emulate 3270s also
have this line, but most don't.

    You may wonder why your screen has these different parts. The 3270 was originally
designed as a terminal for airline reservations. It was meant to resemble a paper form: You
can type in some areas, but not others. It became the standard terminal for CMS use. Much
of the difficulty with learning to use CMS is not in learning the operating system, but in
learning the intricacies and idiosyncrasies of the 3270.

    When you type on a 3270, you need to know where you are typing. On a typewriter,
you can see where the next letter will go by looking at the gap. On a 3270 screen, the next
letter you type appears where the *cursor* appears. The cursor is the small underline or solid
block on your screen. Most people prefer using a block cursor; for convenience, however,
this book uses an underline to show the location of the cursor on the screen. On the previous
picture, the cursor is shown as the underline at the left of the user input area. Most terminals let you select whether your cursor is an underline or a block with a key marked ALT
CURSR.

3270 Keyboard, Part I

This section explains the basics of how to use a 3270 terminal effectively. There are different
types of keys for different purposes, and many different areas of the screen to watch.
Although you might think that learning about an operating system should not require you
to learn much about a terminal, CMS is different. Many of the operations you will perform
are dependent on you knowing how to use a 3270. This section covers the basics, and the
rest is covered later in this chapter.

    The 3270 family has circuits that can process your keystrokes and save information
in the 3270's memory about what you type. There are two types of keys on a block-mode
terminal: those that cause the computer to know they were pressed, and those that don't.
You will see in this chapter why this distinction is important.

    The 3270 keyboard has many keys with which you may not be familiar. The keyboard
for a 3278 and 3279 (the most popular models) is shown in Illustration 2-1.

    The labels shown below the thin lines are the actions you get when you hold down
the ALT key and press the key shown. Thus, holding down the ALT key and pressing 1
causes the action of PF1 (described soon).

    An older, much less popular model of the 3270 is the 3277. Its keyboard is shown in
Illustration 2-2. Note that the 3277 has no ALT key.

    Other 3270 terminals may have the keys in different locations. If you are using a
different 3270 terminal, you should look at your keyboard while you read this section to
learn where the keys are.

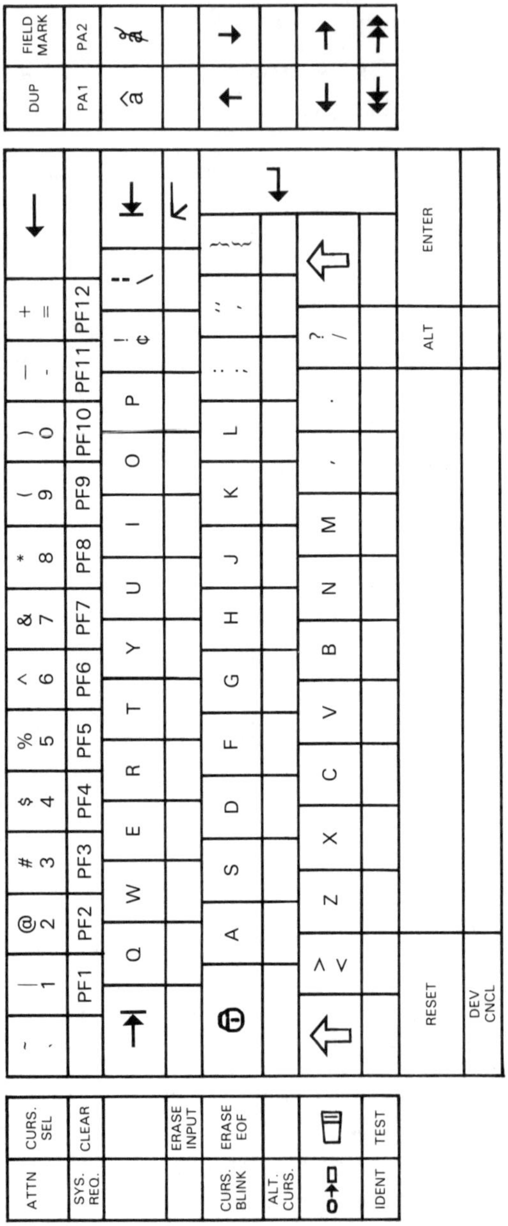

ATTN	CURS. SEL
SYS. REQ.	CLEAR
ERASE INPUT	ERASE EOF
CURS. BLINK	ALT. CURS.
IDENT	TEST

DUP	FIELD MARK
PA1	PA2
←	→
↓	↑

| RESET | ALT | ENTER |
| DEV CNCL | | |

Illustration 2-1

16

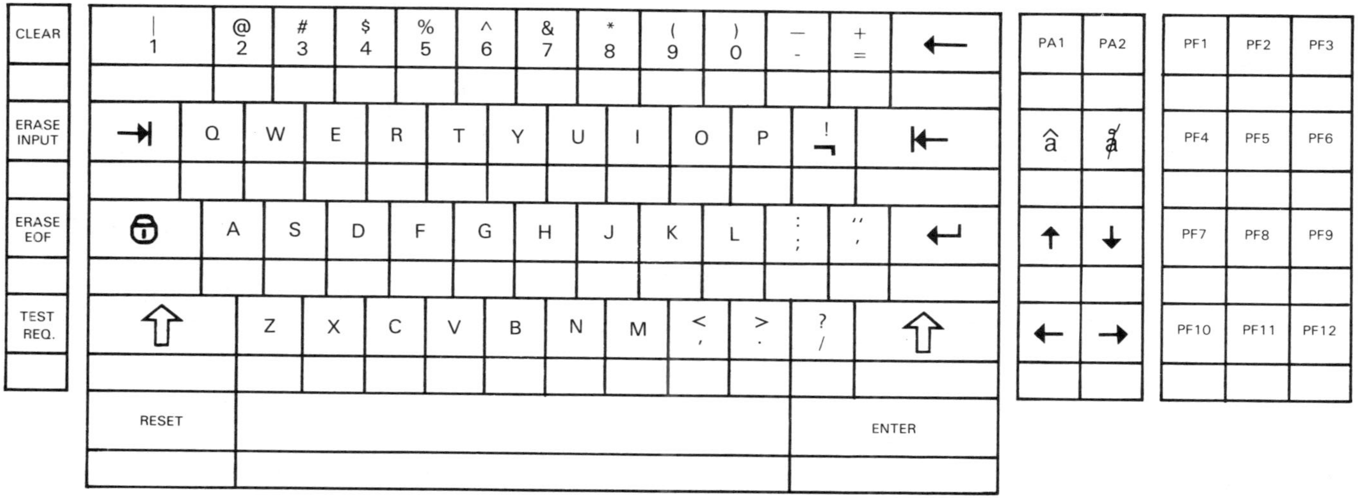

Illustration 2-2

PF1 PF2 PF3
PF4 PF5 PF6
PF7 PF8 PF9
PF10 PF11 PF12

PA1 PA2

CLEAR
ERASE INPUT
ERASE EOF
TEST REQ.

1	2	3	4	5	6	7	8	9	0	-	=
Q	W	E	R	T	Y	U	I	O	P		
A	S	D	F	G	H	J	K	L			
Z	X	C	V	B	N	M				

ENTER

RESET

The keys in the sections on the left and right of the keyboard are keys that control how characters are sent to CMS, while the keys in the center of the keyboard are similar to the keys on a regular electric typewriter.

Probably the most important key on the keyboard to communicate with the computer is the ENTER key, which is at the bottom of the keyboard near the right side, as shown in Illustration 2-3.

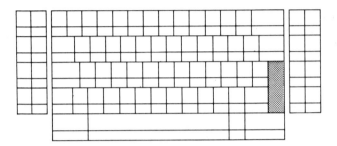

Illustration 2-3

When you type a command to CMS, the computer does not know you have typed until you press the ENTER key (or another special key like the PF keys or the CLEAR key). Every CMS command you give is followed by the ENTER key.

If You Are Familiar With Other Computers

The ENTER key has a very different function than the RETURN key on most computers. The key marked ⏎, which is found where the RETURN key on an ASCII keyboard is usually found, is the NEW LINE key and does not transmit any data to the computer. The NEW LINE key only moves the cursor to the beginning of the next line on the screen.

Many of the keys on the keyboard will be familiar to you. You should recognize the letters, numbers, and punctuation marks from regular typewriters. In addition, the spacebar, SHIFT, and SHIFT LOCK keys, shown in Illustration 2-4, act as they do on regular typewriters (the SHIFT keys are often marked with the hollow up-arrows and the SHIFT LOCK is marked with a lock).

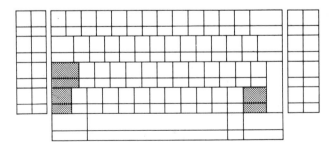

Illustration 2-4

Since no one is a perfect typist, the 3270 keyboard has keys that make it easy to correct mistakes. Two such keys are the ⬅ and ➡ keys which are to the right of (and maybe below) the ⏎ (NEW LINE) key, as shown in Illustration 2-5.

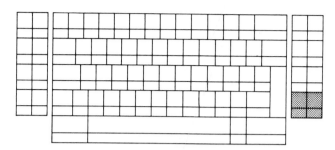

Illustration 2-5

As you type, you can use these keys to move the cursor back and forth. If you move the cursor back one position over another character and type a different character, the first character disappears.

For example, assume that you just typed:

```
This has a mistakr_
```

(Remember that the underscore indicates the cursor). If you press the ← key, you see:

```
This has a mistakr
```

If you now press the "e" key, you see:

```
This has a mistake_
```

You can use the ← and → keys to move anywhere in the line so that you can type over your errors. You will see later in the chapter how to use other editing keys on the 3270 keyboard.

Another valuable set of keys, whose location is shown in Illustration 2-6, is the *PF keys* ("PF" stands for "program function"). PF keys are quick ways of sending instructions to the computer. Instead of having to type in a command and pressing the ENTER key, you can press a PF key that corresponds to the command. The PF keys make using many CMS programs quicker and much easier. Notice on some of the keyboard drawings that "PF1" is written on the front of the "1" key.

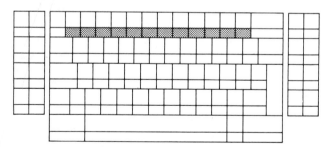

Illustration 2-6

This means that the "1" key has two uses. To type the number "1," simply press the key. To get the key to act like PF1, you must hold down the ALT key (at the right of the spacebar) and press the "1" key while you are holding down the ALT key. "ALT" is an abbreviation for "alternate."

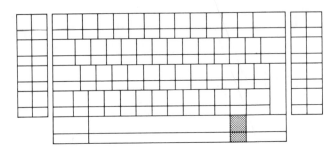

Illustration 2-7

The ALT key is like the SHIFT key: you hold it down and press another key to get a different action out of the other key. Newer terminals usually do not make you use the ALT key to get PF keys.

The ALT key by itself doesn't do anything; you always use it in combination with other keys. Anytime you see a key label on the front of a key (as compared to the top of the key), you can get the action of the label on the front by holding down the ALT key and pressing that key. For example, if you want to press PF9, you would hold down the ALT key and press the "9" key.

If You Are Familiar With Other Computers

The ALT key acts like the CONTROL key on many terminals; however, it does not transmit control codes. For example, holding down the ALT key and pressing the "C" key does not send a CONTROL-C character.

These keys are sufficient to get you started working with CMS. The other keys you see on the keyboard are explained later in this chapter.

ASCII Terminals that Emulate 3270s

If you are using an ASCII terminal that emulates a 3270, the procedures you will use are very similar to those in the previous section. The major difference is usually that your ASCII terminal has fewer keys than a 3270 and you must somehow compensate for that. The screen of most ASCII terminals is very similar to that of a 3270 (usually only omitting the last line).

You should get explicit instructions about how to operate your ASCII terminal as a 3270. These should have come with your terminal, and may be available from your system administrator. Read those instructions before you continue with this section.

On many ASCII terminals, there are no "PF" keys like there are on a 3270. To emulate a 3270 key such as PF3, you might have to press and release the ESCAPE key then the "3" key. Or, you might have to hold down one key (such as the CONTROL key) while pressing the "3" key. Some keys on the ASCII keyboard may directly represent 3270 keys: for example, the RETURN key on an ASCII keyboard often emulates the ENTER key on a 3270 instead of the ⏎ key.

You should note that the two actions described in the last paragraph are very different. On an ASCII terminal, pressing one key then pressing another has a very different effect than holding down one key and pressing another. Be sure you understand which you are supposed to do when you emulate 3270 keys.

The following checklist includes all of the keys which you should be able to emulate; fill in the keys you must type, and specify if you type them or hold one down while you press the other.

```
Equivalent keystrokes for ASCII terminals:


3270 key                              Your keystrokes

ENTER
PF1
PF2
PF3
PF4
PF5
PF6
PF7
PF8
PF9
PF10
PF11
PF12
Up              [↑]
Down            [↓]
Left            [←]
Right           [→]
Tab             [→|]
Back tab        [|←]
Return          [↵]
Home            [↖]
Delete          [i]
Insert          [a]
ATTN
CLEAR
ERASE INPUT
ERASE EOF
RESET
PA1
PA2
```

THE CLEAR KEY AND THE MORE... MESSAGE

One of the most commonly used keys on your keyboard is the CLEAR key, shown in Illustration 2-8. You use it to clear the screen when it is full.

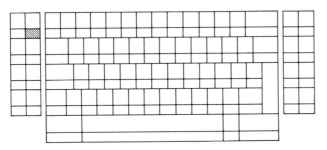

Illustration 2-8

When CMS fills your screen with information (such as after it has put many messages on the screen), you must tell it that you want to see the next screen. When the screen is full, you see the message in the status area change to "MORE...":

```
—
                                                                    MORE...
```

The system does not stop, but it doesn't put any more messages on the screen, either. Instead, one of three things happens:

- You press the CLEAR or PA2 key to clear the screen.
- You don't do anything for 60 seconds. The screen clears automatically.
- You press the ENTER key to put the screen into indefinite hold.

After either of the first two events, the screen clears and you can see the other information that CMS is displaying.

If you press ENTER, however, CMS then changes the status area to "HOLDING":

```
—
                                                                    HOLDING
```

This causes CMS to hold the information on your screen indefinitely. To get out of the holding state, press ENTER again. This clears the screen, allowing you to see the next screen.

There are many ways of making your keyboard "lock up" or not respond. For example, if you attempt to type in an area of the screen only meant for display, your terminal becomes inoperable. If you have a 25th line on your screen, you may see an "X" near the middle of the line when it is locked up. To clear this condition, press the RESET key if you have one. If that doesn't work press the CLEAR key. This often clears up the problem.

> **If You Are Familiar With Other Computers**
>
> Most terminals do not purposely lock up when the user makes a mistake. Instead, they simply prevent you from making the mistake.

Some CMS commands may end up displaying more information on your screen than you wanted to see. You can halt the typing of such commands when the status area has "MORE..." in it. To halt typing, enter:

```
HT
```

and press the ENTER key, then press the CLEAR key. CMS does not type the rest of the output.

SIGNING ON

You are finally ready to log on. When you turn on your 3270, you see a message indicating VM is ready to start. It may be a simple one-line message like:

```
VM/370 online
```

At many installations, the VM message is an elaborate logo that takes up the full screen, such as:

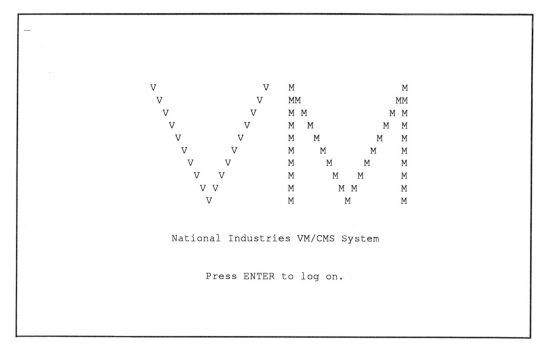

Press the ENTER key on your terminal. Your screen now shows:

```
Enter one of the following commands:

LOGON userid          (Example: LOGON VMUSER1)
DIAL userid           (Example: DIAL VMUSER2)
MSG userid msgtext    (Example: MSG VMUSER2 GOOD MORNING)
LOGOFF





_



                                                    CP READ      BANK2
```

In this screen, you can see the cursor near the lower left corner of the screen in the user input area. As you saw earlier in this chapter, this is where you type in your commands.

The first command you want to give is the LOGON command (you can ignore the other suggested commands for now). The LOGON command is followed by one word: your userid. Thus, if your userid was CHRISJ, you would type:

LOGON CHRISJ

Press ENTER to have VM accept your command. VM next prompts you for your password:

ENTER PASSWORD (IT WILL NOT APPEAR WHEN TYPED):

You type your password and press ENTER. You do not see the characters you type when you enter your password. This is a security feature to prevent someone from looking at your screen over your shoulder and seeing your password. If you are on a printing terminal, VM types some characters before you can type your password to make it difficult to see the password on the paper.

If you entered your userid and password correctly, you will probably see a few messages on your screen; these are described soon. If you get an error message (that is, a line of text that says you did something wrong), see the section later in this chapter to determine what to do.

Once You Have Logged On

When you have logged on successfully, you are in *CP mode* (sometimes called the *CP environment*). CP tells you the time and date, and may also give you other messages (depending on whether your system administrator has put in general logon messages). Then, one of two things happens:

- You are left in CP mode and you must tell CP that you want to run CMS.
- You are automatically moved into CMS mode.

You can tell which mode you are in by looking at the status area in the lower right corner of your screen. After you log on, if the status area says:

```
CP READ
```

you are in CP mode. If the status area says:

```
VM READ
```

or:

```
RUNNING
```

you are already in CMS mode.

If you are in CP mode, you can get into CMS mode by giving the command:

```
IPL CMS
```

You may wonder why some people end up in CP mode while others go directly to CMS. If you use more than one operating system under VM, you want to be in CP mode so you can choose the operating system to run (with the IPL command). IPL stands for *initial program load*, which is a technical way of saying "start a program." Thus, when you are in CP mode, you can start any operating system you want; of course, if you are reading this book, you are most likely concerned with running CMS.

If You Are Familiar With Other Computers

IPL is like turning on a computer. If you are familiar with IBM PCs, it is like pressing CTRL-ALT-DEL.

You can get your system administrator to make CMS come up automatically for you when you log on. This feature is called *automatic IPL*, and it is what most CMS users have. If you do not currently have automatic IPL set, you should ask for it.

You have automatic IPL:

☐　Yes
☐　No

What You See When CMS Has Started

When you are in CMS mode, your screen may look something like this:

```
LOGMSG 16:10:59 03/19/87
* New HELP screens available for accounting programs

* Welcome to National Industries VM/CMS System!
* For assistance with using the system, call x-9140.

FILES: 000 RDR, 000 PRT, 000 PUN

LOGON AT 10:15:27 PST WEDNESDAY 11/18/87

CMS RELEASE 5 -- 9/12/87

Ready; T=0.01/0.01 10:15:32




_
                                                                    RUNNING
```

The first messages are set by the system administrator. These are often important messages that tell you about planned maintenance of the system or any known problems. You should read them every time you log on.

The "FILES" message tells you about your virtual devices. You can ignore it for now. The last message looks something like this:

```
Ready; T=0.01/0.01 10:15:32
```

This is CMS's *ready message*: It tells you that CMS is ready for you to give it commands. If you are using CMS Release 4 or earlier, you see:

```
R; T=0.01/0.01 10:15:32
```

The "Ready;" or "R;" means that the last thing that you did (in this case, logging on) did not have any errors. The "T=" part tells you how much CPU time the command took; you can generally ignore this. The time at the end of the line is the current time of day.

Every time CMS finishes executing a command, it displays a ready message. If the command had errors, you see a number (called a *return code*) in parentheses after the "R", such as:

```
R(00001); T=0.03/0.03 10:17:12
```

A return code indicates that the command may not have worked the way you expected it to. The return codes mean different things for different commands.

Even when you can see them, these messages are often cryptic and of little use. For example, the first time you log on, you may find that your disk is not "formatted" (this is explained in Chapter 3). Instead of an error message that says "Your disk has not been formatted yet," you see CMS's error message:

```
DMSACC112S 'A(191)' DEVICE ERROR
```

Clearly, this does not tell you what is wrong. The more you use CMS, the better you will get at guessing what the error messages mean.

If You Are Familiar With Other Computers

Most microcomputers have very explicit error messages that give you information about what to do about the errors. Some, like the Macintosh, can have almost unlimited amounts of information. Many minicomputer operating systems, such as UNIX, have short or mysterious error messages like CMS.

Error Messages You Might Get When Logging On

If you typed your userid incorrectly, you see:

```
DMKLOG053E userid NOT IN CP DIRECTORY
```

or:

```
DMKLOG020E USERID MISSING OR INVALID
```

Check to see that you typed the correct userid.

If you entered your password incorrectly, you get the error message:

```
DMKLOGO50E LOGON UNSUCCESSFUL--PASSWORD INCORRECT
```

This is followed by the same suggestions about command syntax. Most of these choices are not useful to you: You simply want to try to log on again. Repeat your LOGON command and type your password very carefully.

If you are using the same userid and password as another person (which is generally a bad idea), and that other person is logged on, you get the error message:

```
DMKLOGO54E ALREADY LOGGED ON ...
```

with some other information at the end of the message.

If you see:

```
DMKLOG067E COMMAND FORMAT NOT VALID
```

it means that you typed the word LOGON incorrectly.

Password Security

Suppose you went to a neighbor's house during the middle of the day and saw a sign on the front door that said, "I'm not home right now. The key is under the mat." The security afforded by such a sign is, of course, minimal. Why lock the door if you are going to tell everybody where the key is?

This scenario is similar to users who write their password on a slip of paper and post it on their terminal. Since most users on a system know the userids of everyone else, it is quite easy for them to figure out which userid goes with the password. Writing your password down in a place where others can see it is essentially no security at all.

Beginning users often ask why they should keep their password secure at all. "Why would anyone want to log on with my userid?" If someone can log on with your userid and password, they can do many things that you probably do not want:

- They can read your files. For example, if you have private letters or notes or confidential files such as personnel information, they can easily read these without your knowledge.
- They can alter your files. Suppose you have kept employee records or production reports. Someone with access to your userid can change these without you noticing.
- They can send messages that the recipient assumes came from you. As you will see in Chapter 4, you can send notes to other users on your system, or on other systems that are attached to yours. If someone receives a note from your userid, they assume that the note came from you. A false or inflammatory note can cause a great deal of ill will.
- They can use costly system resources that will be attributed to you. If your system bills individuals or departments for time on the computer or resources used, someone with your password can cause you to be billed for their computer use.

Clearly, then, you don't want people logging on with your userid. The best way to prevent this is to not tell your password to anyone.

If you are concerned that you may forget your password, don't write it in a place where anyone else can find it. For example, if you write it on a piece of paper in your wallet, don't identify it as your password.

It is a good idea to change your password every so often, depending on the level of security at your company. In fact, some sites prevent you from logging on if you do not change your password frequently.

Unfortunately, there is no standard way to change your password. At many sites, it must be done for you by the system administrator. You should ask how you can change your password and feel free to change it whenever you are concerned that someone else may have learned it.

You should talk to your system administrator about how to change your password. Your site might be using an IBM program such as DIRMAINT or RACF, or you may be using a program from a commercial company such as VMSECURE from VM Software, Inc. These programs also let you set other features of CMS, such as passwords for your disks and the method that you log on.

> To change your password:

EXAMPLE CMS COMMANDS

Now that you have logged on, you are probably itching to start using CMS commands. This section gives you a few simple commands so you can get familiar with the process of giving commands.

As you just saw, the standard ready message includes the return code, the amount of CPU time, and the time of day. If you want to see only the return code, you can use the SET command to change the ready message format from long to short. The command is:

```
SET RDYMSG SMSG
```

In this case, "RDYMSG" is the first argument and "SMSG" is the second argument to the SET command. When you enter a CMS command, it is put up on the screen, followed by the ready message after the command is complete.

After entering this command, note the difference in the two ready messages:

```
Welcome to National Industries VM/CMS System!

For assistance with using the system, call x-9140.

Ready; T=0.01/0.01 10:15:32

SET RDYMSG SMSG

Ready;








—                                                        VM   READ
```

To change the ready message back to the long form, use the command:

```
SET RDYMSG LMSG
```

You see the longer form of the ready message again.

If you have your ready message set to short and want to know what time it is, you can use the QUERY TIME command. Enter the command:

```
QUERY TIME
```

The response is:

```
TIME IS 10:45:26 PDT WEDNESDAY 11/25/87
CONNECT= 00:00:10 VIRTCPU= 000:00.05 TOTCPU= 000:00.15
```

These two commands are typical of the CMS commands you use. The QUERY command gives you information, and the SET command changes the way you relate to CMS. Many of the CMS commands you will learn about in Chapter 4 have similar uses.

When you use the SET command (such as in the SET RDYMSG SMSG command), the setting remains in effect until you change it with another SET command or until you log off.

Abbreviations

CMS allows you to abbreviate some CMS commands and arguments. You can type in as little of a command as you need to make it unique. For example, since there are no other

CMS commands that begin with the letter "Q," you can abbreviate "QUERY" to "Q"; since the QUERY command has no other arguments that begin with the letter "T," you can abbreviate "TIME" to "T." Thus, the previous command would be:

```
Q T
```

You can also use any length of abbreviation, such as:

```
QU TI
```

Although this might save you a few keystrokes, it is harder to remember. Throughout this book, all commands are shown at their full length. Appendix B shows the shortest abbreviation you can use for each command.

Resources Allocated to You

When you are assigned your userid, the system administrator also assigns limits to what you can do on the computer. For example, one limit is the amount of storage on the disk that you can use. These resources are said to make up your virtual (imaginary) machine.

The most important of these resources is your disk space. Under CMS, you are given a fixed amount of disk space called your *minidisk*. (Disks and disk concepts are discussed in much more detail in Chapter 3.) If you need more than the amount you are initially allocated, you must ask for more from the system administrator.

Disk space is measured in cylinders. It is common to be allocated two to five cylinders when you get your userid.

If You Are Familiar With Other Computers

Most computers measure disk space in thousands of bytes; a thousand bytes is called *1K*. One cylinder usually (but not always) contains 600K of disk storage.

To find out how much minidisk space you have, use the command:

```
QUERY VIRTUAL DASD
```

You see something like:

```
DASD 190 3380 CMSA54 R/O     60 CYL
DASD 191 3380 CMSA44 R/W      2 CYL
DASD 19C 3380 CMSA52 R/O      4 CYL
DASD 19D 3380 CMSA76 R/O     40 CYL
```

The amount you have allocated is listed under "DASD 191"; in this case it is 2 cylinders.

```
┌─────────────────────────────────────────────────────────────┐
│                                                               │
│  Amount of disk space you have been allocated:               │
│                                                               │
│                                                               │
│                                                               │
│                                                               │
└─────────────────────────────────────────────────────────────┘
```

Another resource that you are assigned is the amount of *virtual storage* you can use at any one time. This is not usually important since most CMS commands run in a small amount of virtual storage. However, some CMS programs require a great deal of virtual storage and cannot run without it. Virtual storage is also measured in thousands of bytes. It is common to be allocated 512K or 1024K when you get your userid. To find out how much virtual storage you have allocated, use the command:

```
QUERY VIRTUAL STORAGE
```

You see something like:

```
STORAGE = 01024K
```

```
┌─────────────────────────────────────────────────────────────┐
│                                                               │
│  Amount of virtual storage you have been allocated:          │
│                                                               │
│                                                               │
│                                                               │
│                                                               │
└─────────────────────────────────────────────────────────────┘
```

When you log on, your virtual storage amount is set for that session. The amount at which it is set may be lower than the maximum you have been allocated. You use the DEFINE STORAGE command described in Chapter 4 to increase your virtual storage to the maximum you have been allocated.

CP

For mostly historical reasons, CMS has two types of commands: CMS commands and CP commands. You can use both types of commands when you are in CMS mode without worrying about which type is which. Since this book is about running CMS, and many CP commands are very useful when running CMS, both types of commands are presented together.

There are a few reasons why you might want to know the difference between the two types of commands:

- CP commands are often described in different IBM manuals than CMS commands. For example, the *CMS Command and Macro Reference* (SC19-6209) does not list CP commands, even though they are used all the time by CMS users. Some IBM manuals, such as the *Quick Reference* (SX20-4400) list both types of commands together.

- Some CP commands have the same names as CMS commands. If you look up a command in a CMS manual and can't find an argument that you are sure works, you should know to also look in the CP manuals.

- Although you can use CP commands in CMS mode, you cannot use CMS commands in CP mode. It is unlikely that you will spend much time in CP mode, but if you do, you need to know which commands you cannot use.

- The HELP facility (described later in this chapter) does not mix CMS and CP commands. If you want help on a CP command, you must state that it is a CP command.

When you use a CP command in CMS, CMS normally executes it even if you don't identify it as a CP command. This is because the default setting of CMS is to search through the CP commands if you use a command that is not a CMS command.

You want to stay in CMS mode almost all of the time. If you end up in CP mode (you can tell by your status line reading "CP READ"), enter the BEGIN command. You can end up in CP mode through a program error or by accidentally pressing the PA1 key.

For example, the QUERY TIME command you learned earlier is actually a CP command. When you enter the command, CMS first decides that QUERY TIME is not a CMS command; it then checks to see if it is a CP command. Since it is, it executes it for you automatically.

This automatic checking is almost always what you want to happen. If, for some reason, you don't want CMS to always check whether an unknown command is a CP command, use the CMS command:

```
SET IMPCP OFF
```

The default for IMPCP (which is short for *implicit CP*) is ON.

If you have used the SET IMPCP OFF command, you can still give CP commands fairly easily. Instead of just typing the command, precede it with "CP." For example, for the QUERY TIME command, you would type:

```
CP QUERY TIME
```

You can always precede any CP command with "CP" regardless of the mode that you are in.

Most of IBM's manuals are different for CMS and CP, even though this difference is not important to many users. In this book, CP commands are not differentiated in the text. The list of commands in Appendix B includes all the commands together in alphabetical order. CP commands are marked so you can identify them.

GETTING HELP

So far, the commands discussed have easy-to-remember formats. You may find some CMS commands are much more complex and have many options. Remembering them, especially the ones you use only occasionally, may be harder until you become more familiar with them. Fortunately, you can easily get help from CMS.

The HELP command gives you information about all of CMS's commands, as well as CP commands and general usage of CMS. Many sites add information to the HELP command that relates to a particular site, such as how to use a program that was developed at that site.

The syntax of the HELP command is quite simple. If you want to see general help, give the command:

```
HELP
```

If you want help on a particular command, give that command as an argument to HELP. For example:

```
HELP SET RDYMSG
```

You can get three kinds of help: brief, detailed, and related. Brief help shows you a few lines of information, while detailed help gives you much more information. Related help tells you what other CMS commands are related to the command you are viewing. Generally, you are most interested in brief and detailed help.

This section shows you how to use the HELP command so you can start using it right away. The HELP command is based on the XEDIT editor that you will learn about in Chapter 6. Chapter 6 tells you more about XEDIT so you can use HELP even more effectively. When you read Chapter 6, you will find out even more handy things you can do.

The HELP Screen

The HELP command is a full-screen command. This means it uses all of the area on your 3270. For example, enter the command HELP QUERY. Your screen shows:

```
  COMMANDS QUERY         ALL Help Information        line  1 of 193
(c) Copyright IBM Corporation 1980, 1986
    (adapted from IBM Form SC19-6209)

QUERY

Use the QUERY command to gather information about your CMS virtual
machine.  You can determine:

*   The state of virtual machine characteristics that are controlled
    by the CMS SET command

*   File definitions (set with the FILEDEF and DLBL commands) that are
    in effect

*   The status of accessed disks

*   The status of CMS/DOS functions

 PF1= Help     2= Top      3= Quit     4= Return     5= Clocate   6= ?
 PF7= Backward 8= Forward  9= PFkeys  10=            11= Related  12= Cursor
Requested HELP section unavailable; ALL option assumed.
====>
                                                 Macro-read 1 File
```

The information at the top tells you that you are running HELP. The cursor is to the right of the "====>" arrow. This is where you type any commands.

Most commands you want to execute in the HELP command are available on PF keys. The list of actions is shown in the bottom two lines of the screen. You can often find all the help you need by moving the cursor around the screen and using the PF keys.

The PF keys for the HELP command are:

PF1   HELP — Gets you help on the topic you have selected. To select a topic, use the cursor movement keys to move the cursor to any part of the topic on which you want help.

PF2   TOP — Move to the top of the help information.

PF3   QUIT — Leave the HELP command.

PF4   RETURN — When you use the PF1 key to get further help on a subject, this gets you back to where you started.

PF5   CLOCATE — Search for a word in the help information. If you enter the word you want in the input area (next to the "====>") and press PF5, HELP shows you the next place where that word is used.

PF6   ? — This causes the last line that you entered in the input area to be redisplayed there.

PF7   BACKWARD — Move back one screenful. If you have moved forward
          in the help text, you use this key to move back one screen at a time.

PF8   FORWARD — Move forward one screenful. You use this key more than
          any other as you read the information in the help text.

PF9   PFKEY — Reassign PF keys (not recommended for most users).

PF10   BRIEF — Switches between brief and detailed help.

PF11   RELATED — Switches between related and detailed help.

PF12   CURSOR — Switch the cursor from the command line to the last position
          on the screen, or vice versa.

Typically, you run the HELP command and use mostly PF8 (forward a screen) and
PF7 (backward a screen) to read text. If there is a great deal of information, such as in the
help for QUERY, you can enter a word you want to find and use PF5. To leave HELP,
simply press PF3.

Figuring Out Where to Start

Sometimes you do not know what you want help on. If you want help on a CMS command
but cannot remember its name, enter the HELP CMS command. You see the following:

```
  CMS MENU       Menu Help Information       line  1 of  35
(c) Copyright IBM 1980, 1986 (adapted from IBM Form SC19-6209)

A file may be selected for viewing by placing the cursor under any
character of the file wanted and pressing the ENTER key or the PF1 key.
A MENU file is indicated when a name is preceded by an asterisk (*).
A TASK file is indicated when a name is preceded by a colon  (:).
For a description of the HELP operands and options, type HELP HELP.


*BORDER    CONVert   EXECIO    HT         MOVEfile  READcard  SSERV
*CMSQUERY  CONWAIT   EXECLoad  HX         N         RECEIVE   START
*CMSSET    COPYfile  EXECMap   IDentify   NAMEFind  REFresh   STATE
*DEBUG     CP        EXECOS    IMMCMD     NAMES     RELease   STATEW
*EDIT      CURsor    EXECStat  INclude    NOTE      Rename    SVCTrace
*EXEC      D         EXECUPDT  ITASK      NUCEXT    RESERVE   SYNonym
*EXEC2     DDR       F         L          NUCXDROP  REStore   TAPE
*GROUP     DEBUG     FETch     LAbeldef   NUCXLOAD  RO        TAPEMAC
*REXX      DEFAULTS  FIledef   LANGADD    NUCXMAP   ROUTE     TAPPDS
PF1= Help     2= Top      3= Quit     4= Return    5= Clocate   6= ?
PF7= Backward 8= Forward  9= PFkeys  10=           11= Relate  12= Cursor

====>
                                        Macro-read 1 File
```

When you determine which command you want help on, use the cursor control keys
to move the cursor to any letter in the command's name and press the PF1 key. The cursor
control keys are the ⬅ and ➡ keys that you saw before, and the ⬆ and ⬇ keys. As you
probably guessed, the ⬆ and ⬇ keys move the cursor up and down. You can usually find
the ⬆ and ⬇ keys near the ⬅ and ➡ keys on your keyboard.

For example, if you want to get help on the NOTE command (which you will see more about in Chapter 4), use the ⬆ key to move up 7 lines and the ➡ key to move over to the word "NOTE" (you can also use the ⭢ key, described later in this chapter):

```
==> CMS MENU <=====> HELP   INFORMATION <=====>line ===> 1 of 27
(c) Copyrighted IBM 1980, 1986 (from IBM Form SC19-6209)

A file may be selected for viewing  by placing the cursor under any character
of the file wanted and  pressing the ENTER key or the PF 1  key. A MENU file
is indicated when a  name is preceded by an asterisk  (*).  A TASK file
is indicated when a name is preceded by a colon  (:).  For a description
of the operands and options type HELP HELP.


*DEBUG    CONWAIT   EXECDROP  HELPCONV  MAKEBUF   RDRList   START
*EDIT     COPYfile  EXECIO    HI        MODmap    READcard  STATE
*EXEC     CP        EXECLOAD  HO        MOVEfile  RECEIVE   STATEW
*EXEC2    DDR       EXECMAP   HT        NAMEFind  RELease   SVCtrace
*GROUP    DEBUG     EXECOS    HX        NAMES     Rename    SYNonym
*REXX     DEFAULTS  EXECSTAT  IDentify  NOTE      RESERVE   TAPE
*XEDIT    DESBUF    EXECUPDT  IMMCMD    NUCEXT    RO        TAPEMAC
:SRPI     DISK      FETch     INclude   NUCXDROP  RESRV     TAPPDS
ACcess    DISKID    FIledef   LAneldef  NUCXLOAD  RT        TE
1= Help     2= Top     3= Quit   4= Return      5= Clocate     6= ?
7= Backward 8= Forward 9= PFkey 10= Backward 1/2 11= Forward 1/2 12= Cursor

====>
                                                   Macro-read 1 File
```

Then press the PF1 key to get help on this topic.

This gives you another *help level*. When you are done looking at the help for that command and press PF3, you go back to the HELP CMS screen instead of back to CMS. You can enter many levels of help, each time returning to the previous level when you press PF3.

The HELP command gives you access to more than just information about commands. If you want a list of other tasks you might have, give the HELP TASKS command. Like the HELP CMS command, the first screen is a menu of choices. Move your cursor to the choice you want and press the PF1 key to get to the next level.

Getting Help About Error Messages

A feature of the HELP command that can be very useful to CMS users is its ability to give you more information on CMS's cryptic messages. If you know the message's number, give the HELP command with the number as the argument. (Note that the message number is different than a return code.)

The message number is not just the number you see in the ready message. It is a "number" consisting of three or six letters, followed by a three-digit number, followed by another letter. You saw examples of these error numbers earlier in the chapter. For instance, in the message:

DMKLOGO50E LOGON UNSUCCESSFUL--PASSWORD INCORRECT

"DMKLOG050E" is the error number. If you give the command:

```
HELP DMKLOG050E
```

you can find out more about the error.

Normally, no error messages are displayed; you only see a return code in the ready message. To see error messages and their numbers, give the command:

```
SET EMSG ON
```

From then on, any error messages you see include their error numbers. You can then use the HELP command to explain the error messages in greater detail.

If You Cannot Figure Out Where to Go

CMS is a complex operating system with many diverse parts. No help system could ever help everyone with all tasks. If you can't figure out what to do, even after looking through the manuals and using the HELP command, you can always ask the system administrator.

3270 KEYBOARD, PART II

So far, you have seen how to use the 3270 or emulators to do simple tasks with CMS. There are many other keys on the 3270 keyboard that you will find useful.

As you read this section, remember that some keys cause CMS to perform tasks, while others only affect your 3270 screen. Of the keys you have learned about so far:

- ENTER, CLEAR, and the PF keys cause CMS to take action.
- The ⊖, ⬆, ⬇, ⬅, and ➡ keys only affect the screen.

Other Cursor Movement Keys

Earlier in this chapter, you learned about using the ⬅ and ➡ keys to move the cursor around on the input line. You also saw how to use the ⬆ and ⬇ keys. There are three other cursor position keys you will find useful when using CMS. The key marked ➡, whose location is shown in Illustration 2-9, is the TAB key.

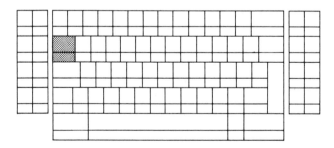

Illustration 2-9

Pressing this key moves the cursor to the next "tab" position of the screen. (Tab positions are also called *fields*; this is a remnant from the airline-terminal days.) If there are no more tab positions on the current line, the ➡ key moves the cursor to the first field of the next line.

The ⊡ key is very useful when using XEDIT or utilities based on XEDIT (such as HELP). For example, give the HELP CMS command again. If you want help on the SENDFILE command, move up 12 lines. Next, instead of pressing the ⊡ key, you can press the ⊡ key to skip from column to column. This is clearly quicker than using the ⊡ key.

The key marked ⊡, whose location is shown in Illustration 2-10, is the BACK TAB key.

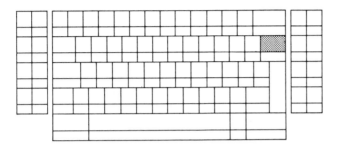

Illustration 2-10

It acts just like the ⊡ key in reverse. It moves the cursor to the previous tab position, or the last tab field on the previous line.

The HOME key (usually marked ⊡), shown in Illustration 2-11, moves the cursor to different places, depending on the program you are running.

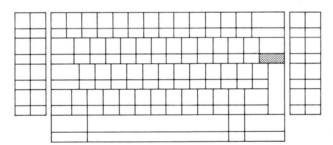

Illustration 2-11

Most programs have the ⊡ key move the cursor to either the beginning of the first line or to the upper left corner of the screen. On 3278 and 3279 keyboards, the ⊡ key is on the front of the ⊡ key (so you must use the ALT key to get it to work).

Incidentally, many 3270 keyboards repeat the cursor control keys if you hold them down instead of pressing them over and over. For instance, if you want to move across a long line of text, you can hold down the ⊡ key instead of pressing it repeatedly.

Some 3270 keyboards have keys marked ⊡ and ⊡. These keys move the cursor left and right at twice the normal rate when used with the ALT key.

Inserting and Deleting Characters

When you learned how to enter CMS commands, you were shown how to correct typing errors with the ⊡ and ⊡ keys. The major disadvantage of using these keys is that you can only type over mistakes. If you leave out a letter, or have an extra letter, the ⊡ and ⊡ keys don't save you much time.

You can use the ⊡ and ⊡ keys, shown in Illustration 2-12, a to insert and delete letters in the input line.

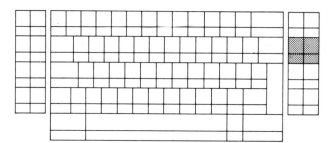

Illustration 2-12

The Ⓐ key is the *insert mode* key, and is sometimes marked INS MODE. The Ⓘ key is the delete key, and is sometimes marked DEL.

When you press the Ⓐ key, you are put into insert mode. When you are in insert mode, typing characters causes them to appear at the cursor position, not written over the other characters on the line. For example, type the following line in the user input area:

```
This is a short example._
```

Use the ⬅ key to move the cursor to underneath the "s" in "short":

```
This is a short example.
```

Now press the Ⓐ key and type "very" followed by a space:

```
This is a very short example.
```

Notice how the characters you type appear at the cursor while the text over the cursor and to the right of it moves to the right as you type. To leave insert mode, press the RESET key.

To see how the Ⓘ key works, press it once. The line now looks like this:

```
This is a very hort example.
```

It erases the character under the cursor and moves the rest of the line one character to the left.

If you want to delete all the characters from the current position to the end of the line, you can use the ERASE EOF key (EOF is computer jargon for "end of field").

In this case, the "field" is the entire line, so pressing ERASE EOF erases from the cursor to the end of the line:

```
This is a very _
```

Now that you are done with this example, you may want to erase the line from the user input area (since it is not a CMS command). You could move to the beginning of the line and press the Ⓘ key many times (or hold it down, if your terminal will repeat the key). A faster method is to press the ERASE INPUT key as shown in Illustration 2-13. This clears the entire user input area in one keystroke.

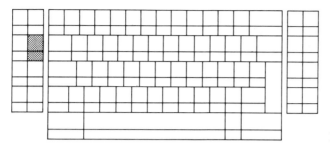

Illustration 2-13

Retrieving Previous Commands

The default setting for most users is to have the PF1 key retrieve the previous CMS command. For example, if you issue a long CMS command and make a typing error, you can press PF1 to have CMS put that command in the user input area, leaving the cursor at the end of the line. You can then use the cursor control keys to edit the line and make your correction. When you have corrected the line, simply press ENTER to give the command. This is also useful if you have a command you must give many times but you need to make a small modification each time.

CMS keeps many of the previous commands for you. For example, if you want to reexecute the command you gave three commands ago, simply press the PF1 key three times.

COMPUTERS AND NETWORKS

A few CMS commands require you to know which machines other CMS users have their userids on. If your site has a network, it is easy to determine both your computer's name and the names of all the other computers (nodes) on the network.

Most systems display the node name in the lower right corner of the 3270 display. For example:

```
                                           CP READ     BANK2
```

BANK2 is the node name. If your node name is not on your screen, you can use the following command:

```
QUERY USERID
```

The result might be:

```
CHRISJ AT BANK2
```

Name of your node:

You cannot find out the node name for another user in any easy fashion (other than asking them directly). Some sites have special commands for getting a list of all nodes. If you need to know the name of other nodes, ask your system administrator how you can get the list.

```
To get a list of all nodes:



```

LOGGING OFF

When you are finished using CMS, you should always log off to prevent someone else from using your CMS account while you are away (this is also called *logging out*). There are many security advantages to logging off when you are leaving your terminal, and it only takes a moment.

When you log off, your virtual machine vanishes, although the files on your disk remain intact. Thus, only changes that you have made to your minidisk or to tapes remain after you log off.

To log off, simply enter the LOGOFF command. The system shows some information about your CMS session:

```
CONNECT=01:26:48 VIRTCPU=000:27.31 TOTCPU=000:35.92
LOGOFF AT 11:42:20 PST WEDNESDAY 11/18/87

PRESS ENTER OR CLEAR TO CONTINUE
```

If you press ENTER or CLEAR, you see the logo you saw before you started your CMS session.

3

Introduction to Disks and Files

One of the fundamental parts of any operating system is the way it handles disks and files. As a user, disks and files are very important to you since that is where all of your data is kept. You need to know a fair amount about CMS's disk and file system to use it effectively.

When CMS was developed, most CMS users were programmers. This is still reflected in some of the aspects of CMS's disk and file system. For example, if you run out of disk space, you cannot simply ask for more; your system administrator has to allocate different disk space and move all your current files to the new space. As you read this chapter, you will find out how CMS's file system is important to your work.

DISKS

For the past 20 years, disks have been the primary medium for storage of often-used data. Disks have many properties that are easy to understand since they are based on technologies with which most people are familiar.

A disk is a flat round platter that is covered with magnetic media. The media is similar to the coating on audio tape. When you record on an audio tape, your tape player passes the tape over a head that pulses a magnet. The pulses realign the media on the tape and are thus recorded. When you play the tape, another head senses the magnetic pulses on the tape and turns those pulses into sound.

On a disk, the magnetic media covers the entire surface. The disk is constantly spinning. As can be seen in Illustration 3-1, the head is positioned over the disk and can be moved in and out along a radius by the disk arm.

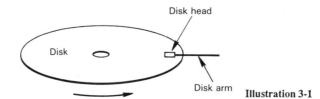

Illustration 3-1

The disk head stores information with magnetic pulses. Like the audio tape, these pulses change the media on the disk.

The largest difference between audio tape and computer disks is the method by which data is located. On a tape, you can only specify location of a piece of music in a linear fashion. For example, you might tell your tape player to start playing at the spot 20 minutes into the first side of the tape. The tape player would then start winding the tape from one reel to the other until it reached that location.

Minidisks

In CMS, each user is given a *minidisk* which is an area on the disk for your files. As shown in Illustration 3-2, your minidisk is actually a doughnut-shaped ring on the disk.

You are the only person who has access to that area of the disk (unless you give someone else access, as you will see in the next chapter). This means that no one can accidentally or maliciously harm your area of the disk.

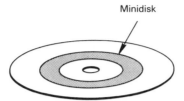

Minidisk

Illustration 3-2

As you saw in Chapter 2, IBM measures disk space in cylinders. The cylinders are tubes of different diameter that fit inside each other. The size of your minidisk is determined by the number of adjacent cylinders you are allocated.

A very common problem among CMS users is that of running out of disk space. If you fill up your minidisk with information, you cannot simply use more disk space because the cylinders further out and further in from yours may be already allocated to other users. You need to get a bigger group of cylinders somewhere else on the disk (or on another disk).

If You Are Familiar With Other Computers

Most other operating systems let you use as much or as little disk space as you want. On almost every other multi-user system, each user's files are distributed over the disk with every other user's. Some operating systems allow the system administrator to restrict the amount of disk space a single user can have; however, if the system administrator gives a user more space, that user can add more files.

It is important to note that you will use more than just your own minidisk. All CMS's programs are stored on other minidisks. These are often called *system disks* or *shared disks*. You are normally not allowed to save files on these or even modify the files already on them.

In some offices, people also share minidisks; for instance, your department may keep a large database on a shared minidisk. At most sites, however, you are usually restricted to storing your files on your own minidisk.

The information on your minidisk is only available to you and the system administrator. Most sites have automatic backup programs that copy all of the files on your minidisk onto tape at regular intervals. Ask your system administrator for more information on backup procedures at your site.

Formatting Your Minidisk Ⓦ

A minidisk must be *formatted* before it can be used. Formatting prepares a minidisk to store data. When your system administrator first allocates your minidisk space, it may or may not be formatted for you.

You may wonder why you have to prepare a minidisk. A minidisk is like a parking lot for data. When a parking lot is first paved, there are no lines on the parking lot, and cars have no idea where to park. Cars would park in a jumble and would not efficiently use the lot's space. Formatting a minidisk is like painting lines in the parking lot and numbering each parking space. When you format your minidisk, CMS puts markers on the minidisk that specify where data can go.

If there is already data on your minidisk and you format it again, all the data already on the minidisk is lost. Thus, it is very unlikely that you ever want to format your disk once you start using it. Reformatting your disk is like painting the parking lot black, then putting down new lines. Any information in the old lines is lost.

Disk Names

When you want to access information on a minidisk, you need to know the minidisk's name. Minidisk names are single letters. Using minidisk names is necessary because some programs require you to be very specific about the files they handle. Thus, you must specify not only a file's name, but the name of the minidisk it is on as well.

Your own minidisk is named your A-disk. If you have more than one minidisk assigned to you (which is not common), the second disk is probably your D-disk. The system disk is labelled S, and there is almost always a second system disk called the Y-disk.

If You Are Familiar With Other Computers

The single-letter name for CMS is similar to that used in MS-DOS and CP/M. Some operating systems, like Macintosh and UNIX, do not have disk names.

You will see in Chapter 4 how to access other users' minidisks.

When you format your minidisk, you can also attach a label to the disk (you will see the command for this in Chapter 4). Disk labels are useful reminders of what your minidisk is used for. A disk label can be 6 characters long. For instance, if you have a separate minidisk for your memoranda, you might label that minidisk "MEMOS".

FILES

Up to this point, files have been discussed as objects that hold things. Files hold "information"; this information might be text that you typed in, data in a database, a report that was created by a program, the instructions which make up a program, a picture, and so on.

The best way to think of a file is as a box. Some of the unusual properties of this box are:

- It starts off very small, but can be effortlessly stretched to hold gigantic objects.
- It can hold almost any kind of stuff you can imagine. The two most common types of contents are information (data, memos, and so on) and instructions (programs).

- You can easily examine the outside of the box to find its size, the type of contents, and when the contents were last modified. If the contents are information, you can usually examine the contents and often change them.
- You can easily compare the contents of two boxes.
- The boxes reside in a storage area (your minidisk). You cannot stretch the accumulated size of the boxes to be larger than the storage area.
- Each box has a unique name on it. No two boxes in one storage area can have the same name. However, it is easy to change the name of the box.

Probably the most important concept to remember about files is that they can contain anything. Many files on the S- and Y-disks contain CMS commands and programs; the files that you store on your A-disk usually contain information.

How Files Are Created

Files are created in many ways. You can create and modify your own files with XEDIT, as you will see in Chapter 6. When you start the XEDIT program, you tell it the name of the file you want to work with. If that file does not already exist, XEDIT lets you create it. This is how you can create a file from scratch. Once a file exists, you can use XEDIT to change it; you can easily add information to, or subtract information from, the file you are editing.

Other programs can also create and modify files. For instance, if your department uses a database management system, the program creates and modifies data files. Most accounting programs create files to hold data as well as files to hold reports. Programming languages also create files, namely the programs themselves and listings of their contents.

As you use CMS, you will find that there is an incredibly wide variety of files, created by an equally wide variety of methods. It is not usually important to know what created a file. The more important things to know are how a file is used and how can you modify it if you need to.

File Names

CMS file names have two parts: the *filename* and the *filetype*. Don't get confused by the two terms, "file's name" and "filename." The filename is only the first half of a file's name; the filetype is the second part. Each is a separate, distinct label. Every file has both a filename and a filetype.

In some cases, you want to specify the name of the minidisk on which the file resides. To do this, you include the disk name (the single character) after the filetype. This is called the *filemode*.

The filename or the filetype can each be one to eight characters long, and can include any of the following characters:

- The capital letters A to Z
- The digits 0 to 9
- The punctuation marks $ (dollar sign), + (plus sign), - (minus sign), : (colon), _ (underscore), # (pound sign), and @ (at sign). The # and @ are rarely used since these characters have special meaning on printing terminals.

CMS also lets you use lowercase letters (a to z), but some commands do not work with files that have lowercase letters in their names, so you should avoid them.

If You Are Familiar With Other Computers

CMS's naming rules are similar to those used in MS-DOS. Note, however, that the filetype in MS-DOS can only have three characters; CMS's filetypes have eight. Many operating systems like UNIX and Macintosh have only filenames and no filetypes.

Some examples of CMS file names are:

```
PROFILE EXEC
RODNEY MEMO
TO_DO SCRIPT
FAMILY:B PROGRAM
```

As you can see, CMS gives you a fair amount of leeway in naming your files. It also puts some restrictions. There are many filetypes that are used for special purposes. When you name files, you should only use the special filetypes for files that match the purposes.

The most common reserved filetypes that you might use are EXEC, FORTRAN, NAMES, NETLOG, NOTEBOOK, SCRIPT, SYNONYM, and XEDIT. You will see the CMS commands that work with files with these filetypes throughout the book. If you are a programmer, there is a much longer list of reserved filetypes; see your programming documentation for a list.

When you create files, you should follow some general rules about naming them:

- Use names that mean something to you. After a few months of using CMS, you will have dozens of files on your minidisk. If you use cryptic names, you probably won't remember what is in the files, and will have to examine them to determine their contents.

- Try to keep consistent names. For instance, you might call your status report for June 1 "88-06-01 STATUS"; the status report for June 15 would then be "88-06-15 STATUS". Putting the year first in the dates makes sorting files by filename also sort the file by date.

- Use only a few punctuation marks. You can usually differentiate files adequately with the minus sign and the underscore.

Using File Names in CMS Commands

When you use a CMS command that has a file name for an argument, you often have many choices about how much of the name you use. Almost every CMS command allows you to type in the whole file name. Some commands only require that you use the filename because the command only works with files that have a specific filetype. Other commands require that you give both the filename and filetype.

For example, if you accessed both your minidisk and the department's minidisk, and you want to view a file that is on the department's minidisk, you need to tell CMS on which minidisk to look. Assume that the file's name is "NEW ACCOUNTS" (that is, the filename is "NEW" and the filetype is "ACCOUNTS") and you have attached the departmental minidisk as "B". You would use the name "NEW ACCOUNTS B" for the file.

Most CMS commands assume that if you don't list a filemode, you mean that the file is on your A disk. Thus, in the previous example, if you only specified "NEW ACCOUNTS", CMS would assume that you meant "NEW ACCOUNTS A". You should therefore be careful when you give the file name for files that are not on your own minidisk.

Looking at a Text File

Now that you understand what a file is and how you get at its contents, it is a good time to take a look in a simple file. As you saw before, there are many kinds of files. Files that you can examine and modify with the standard CMS commands are *text files*. (Note that CMS programmers use files called TEXT files that are nothing like text files described in this book. This may cause some confusion.)

To see the contents of a text file, use the TYPE command (for now; you will see a much better way in chapter 6). The argument to the type command is the name of the file you want to see. For instance, give the command:

```
TYPE PROFILE EXEC
```

This types on your screen the contents of the file on your A disk called "PROFILE EXEC." This file is usually created for you by the system administrator when you get a userid. You will see later in this chapter what this file is used for. (If you get an error message that says "FILE NOT FOUND," you either typed the file name incorrectly or you do not have a PROFILE EXEC file.)

If You Are Familiar With Other Computers

The TYPE command is very similar to the TYPE command in MS-DOS.

There is no "standard" PROFILE EXEC file, so the contents you see on the screen will probably be different from the file that follows. You might see something like this:

```
TYPE PROFILE EXEC

/* Sample PROFILE EXEC */
SET BLIP OFF
SET EMSG ON
SET PF1 RETRIEVE
SPOOL READER CLASS A NOHOLD NOCONT


Ready; T=0.01/0.01 10:48:48




                                                                    RUNNING
```

On the first line, CMS copied your command from the user input line and put it on the screen. It then typed the contents of the file PROFILE EXEC A, then put up the ready message.

Your PROFILE EXEC file may be many dozens of lines long. In this case, CMS stops when the screen is full, as you saw in Chapter 2. The status message is "MORE...". It appears that nothing is happening. To see the next screen, press the CLEAR key. Do this until the entire file has been typed (CMS has displayed the entire file when it displays the ready message at the end). You can stop the TYPE command with the HT command.

If there are files that are not text files on your minidisk, you should not try to display them with the TYPE command. Although this does not harm anything, you will not see any information of any use in non-text files. You can assume that all files whose filetypes are EXEC or XEDIT are text files. In fact, it is likely that most of the files on your minidisk when you first get your userid are text files.

Listing the Files on Your Minidisk

To get a list of the names of all the files on your minidisk, use the LISTFILE command. The LISTFILE command with no arguments lists all the files on your A disk. For example, enter the LISTFILE command:

```
LISTFILE
```

CMS might display:

```
PROFILE   EXEC    A1
PROFILE   XEDIT   A1
USER      DATA    A1
```

This indicates that there are three files. (Of course, since all systems are different, you may have fewer or more files than are shown here; this list is just an example of what you might see.)

If You Are Familiar With Other Computers

The LISTFILE command is very similar to the MS-DOS DIR command.

The files are shown in sorted order, first by filename, then by filetype. The LISTFILE command also shows the filemode (for now, you can safely ignore the number after the disk letter).

The LISTFILE command is useful for checking whether or not a certain file resides on your minidisk. For instance, before you enter the TYPE command, you might want to check whether the file you want to type is there. Reviewing the output from the LISTFILE command can tell you that.

If you have dozens of files on your minidisk, searching through a long list for just one file can get tedious. If you want to see whether a particular file exists on your minidisk, you can give its name as an argument to LISTFILE. The list printed will then only include that file if it exists; if the file does not exist, LISTFILE reports an error.

For example, assume that you have the three files from the preceding list on your minidisk. Enter the command:

```
LISTFILE PROFILE XEDIT
```

CMS responds:

```
PROFILE   XEDIT   A1
Ready; T=0.01/0.01 10:53:12
```

This indicates that the file exists; LISTFILE lists the file that matches the argument. If you gave the command:

```
LISTFILE PROFILE XXXX
```

you would get the message:

```
DMSLST002E FILE NOT FOUND
R(00028); T=0.01/0.01 10:53:25
```

The message (accompanied by a return code) indicates that CMS could not file the file called "PROFILE XXXX" on your minidisk.

If you wish, you can include a filemode in the argument. To see whether the file called "DEPART DATA" exists on your B minidisk, use the command:

```
LISTFILE DEPART DATA B
```

(Incidentally, almost every CMS command that takes a file name as an argument lets you include the filemode.)

So far, you have seen how to get LISTFILE to list all the files on your minidisk, and how to get it to list just one file. There are many times, however, when you want something between these two. For example, you might want to use the TYPE command on a file whose filename is PROFILE, but you can't remember the file's filetype. You want to see a list of all the files that match these criteria so you can give the TYPE command correctly.

Essentially, what you want is a way of saying "List all files with the filename PROFILE; I don't care what the filetype is." For CMS commands that can take file names as arguments, you can use an asterisk (*) to indicate the parts that you want to have any value. For example, to list all the files that have the filename PROFILE and any filetype, use the command:

```
LISTFILE PROFILE *
```

The name "PROFILE *" indicates that the filename must be PROFILE, but the filetype can be anything. This causes CMS to respond:

```
PROFILE   EXEC     A1
PROFILE   XEDIT    A1
```

Similarly, you can use an asterisk to indicate a filename when you want to list all files that have a particular filetype. To list all the files on the S disk with the filetype "EXEC", give the command:

```
LISTFILE * EXEC S
```

You can even use an asterisk as part of a filename or filetype. For example, if you want to list every file on your disk whose filename starts with the letter "J" and whose filetype is "EXEC", you would give the command:

```
LISTFILE J* EXEC
```

This is very useful if you only partially remember a file's name.

The percent character (%) is similar to the asterisk. The percent character matches any one character in a file name (instead of the asterisk matching any number of characters). For example, the command:

```
LISTFILE J% EXEC
```

lists files whose filename is two letters long, the first letter being "J". You might want to list all the files whose names are five characters long, the first three characters being "VOW", with any filetype; the command would be:

```
LISTFILE VOW%% *
```

The asterisk and percent characters are often called *wildcard* characters since they have a similar function to wild cards in poker.

Some CMS commands let you use an asterisk instead of a filemode, such as "REPORT SCRIPT *." This indicates that the command will find that file on any minidisks you have available (including the system minidisks). CMS first looks on your A disk, then the B disk, and so on, up to Z. This is called the *search order*.

If You Are Familiar With Other Computers

Most operating systems have wildcards. MS-DOS uses the * and % characters in the same fashion as CMS.

Record Formats

One bit of technical trivia that you should be aware of is the concept of *record formats*. In some cases, files must have a specific record format to work with certain commands. If you know what the possible formats are, you can probably work with the appropriate commands.

A *record* is a part of a file. In text files, a record is the same as a line. In other files, the definition of a record is often more complex. A good way to think of it is a record is part of a file as a page is part of a book.

There are two basic record formats: *fixed* and *variable* (abbreviated "F" and "V"). In a file that is in fixed-length format, each record has the same number of characters.

The number of characters in each record is called the LRECL (which stands for "logical record length"). The LRECL of files with variable-length record format is the length of the longest line in the file. You can see the LRECL by using the LISTFILE command.

THE PROFILE EXEC FILE

You saw earlier in this chapter how to cause CMS to type out the contents of a text file. The file you viewed was the PROFILE EXEC file. This file is a special file every user should have on his or her minidisk. When you log on, CMS looks on your minidisk for a PROFILE EXEC file; if it is there, CMS executes the commands in it.

Generally, you use the PROFILE EXEC file to run three kinds of commands:

- Commands that set up your working environment so that CMS is easier for you to use.
- Commands that tell you the status of your CMS environment.
- Commands that show you system news and personal messages that have been sent to you.

Since CMS executes the commands in the PROFILE EXEC automatically when you log on, you don't have to enter them by hand. Thus, if you have some commands that you give each time you log on, you should include them in your PROFILE EXEC file. This file is called your profile since it gives a profile of how you want the system to look to you.

There are many different types of commands you might have in your PROFILE EXEC file. A simple PROFILE EXEC file consists of CMS commands on separate lines. For example, the sample PROFILE EXEC file you just saw was:

```
/* Sample PROFILE EXEC */
SET BLIP OFF
SET EMSG ON
SET PF1 RETRIEVE
SPOOL READER CLASS * NOHOLD NOCONT
```

This is simply three SET commands, followed by a SPOOL command (described in Chapter 8).

The file your system administrator set up for you might have complex commands that you don't understand. There might be commands that don't look like CMS commands at all; you will find out more about these in Chapter 7. For now, don't worry about understanding what each command does.

In this section, you create a new PROFILE EXEC file. To do this, you will walk through some commands you have not seen before. These commands are explained here only very briefly; all of them are described in much more detail later in the book.

Since you are going to alter the PROFILE EXEC file that was set up by your system administrator, you should first make a *backup copy* of the file. A backup copy is an identical copy of the unaltered file; if you make a mistake while altering the file, or want to see what the file looked like before you altered it, you can use the backup copy.

The copy of the file has a different name, since no two files on your minidisk can have the same name (if they did, you wouldn't be able to tell them apart). The backup copy of the file is called PROFILE OLDEXEC. To copy the file, give the command

```
COPYFILE PROFILE EXEC A PROFILE OLDEXEC A
```

As you might guess, the COPYFILE command copies files. It takes two arguments: the name of the file you want to copy (in this case, PROFILE EXEC A), and the name of the newly created copy (in this case, PROFILE OLDEXEC A). You can verify that the COPYFILE command worked with the LISTFILE command:

```
LISTFILE PROFILE *
```

CMS responds:

```
PROFILE    EXEC      A1
PROFILE    OLDEXEC   A1
PROFILE    XEDIT     A1
```

You are now going to change the contents of the PROFILE EXEC file. You will be using the XEDIT file editor, but only in a very limited fashion. Chapter 6 goes into much more detail about using XEDIT. For now, you will use it to simply add lines to the end of the file. Give the command:

```
XEDIT PROFILE EXEC A (NOSCREEN NOPROFILE
```

The NOSCREEN option indicates that you want to use your terminal as a line editor; this is easier until you learn more about XEDIT. The NOPROFILE option indicates that

XEDIT should ignore any profile you have for XEDIT. During this process, if your screen fills up, remember to press the CLEAR key to continue.

After you give the XEDIT command, you see:

```
DMSXSU587I XEDIT:
```

This indicates that XEDIT is ready for your first command. The next set of commands you give are XEDIT commands, not CMS commands. The XEDIT program takes commands the same way that CMS takes commands: you type them in and press the ENTER key.

Since you want to add commands to the bottom of the file set up by your system administrator, use the BOTTOM command:

```
BOTTOM
```

XEDIT responds:

```
*
```

Next, give the INPUT command so you can add new text to the file:

```
INPUT
```

XEDIT tells you that you are in input mode:

```
DMSXMD573I Input mode:
```

Now, type the following lines exactly. Press the ENTER key after you type in each line. If you make any mistakes, skip to the end of this section, which shows you how to start over.

```
/* Sample PROFILE EXEC */
SET BLIP OFF
SET EMSG ON
SET PF1 RETRIEVE
SPOOL READER CLASS * NOHOLD NOCONT
```

When you have entered these lines, press the ENTER key again (with no text in the user input area); this tells XEDIT that you are finished inputting lines. XEDIT responds:

```
DMSXMD587I XEDIT:
```

Now give the FILE command to tell XEDIT that you are done with this file. XEDIT saves the changes you have made and shows you the ready message to indicate you are now back in CMS.

If you made any mistakes when inputting the lines for the file, press the ENTER key to get out of input mode. Give the QQUIT command; this tells XEDIT to ignore whatever you have done. This leaves you in CMS. You can simply start the process over again.

4

More CMS Commands

This chapter introduces you to most of the CMS commands that you will use in your daily work (other than those you have already seen in Chapter 3). The commands are grouped by their use; for example, all commands you use for communicating with other users are in a group.

As you read this chapter, you should try out some of the commands for yourself. Most of the commands are harmless, although the ones that can change information on your disk are marked with the Ⓦ character.

When you finish this chapter, you will be able to use a wide variety of CMS commands. In addition, you will have seen enough commands to understand more of the logic of CMS. This will enable you to learn more about CMS from IBM's manuals.

As stated earlier, many of the options for CMS commands are rarely used. They are often intended for programmers or system administrators. The best IBM manual for seeing a brief summary of all the options for CMS commands is the *Quick Reference* (SX20-4400). Remember that you can get help at any time by using the HELP command described in Chapter 2.

Note that this chapter covers both CMS and CP commands. The CP commands are not marked as such, since you do not need to know the difference when you give the commands. However, if you want to look up the commands in either the *CMS Command and Macro Reference* (SC19-6209) or the *CP Command Reference for General Users* (SC19-6211), you need to know which manual to use. The tables in Appendix B show which commands are CMS commands or CP commands.

COMMAND STRUCTURES

The examples of CMS commands you have seen so far have all been very specific. This chapter shows you general ways of using CMS commands. For example, instead of only giving specific file names, this chapter will show you how to use any file name as an argument to CMS commands. Similarly, most commands have options; this chapter describes them to you. The structure of a command is called its *syntax*. It is useful to know how to read command syntaxes so you can also refer to IBM's CMS manuals, not just read this book.

In order to give all CMS users power and capabilities, the syntaxes for some CMS commands can get very complex. Some users might be unnecessarily intimidated by just learning about command syntaxes. However, learning the syntaxes for commands is your key to using CMS effectively.

If You Are Familiar With Other Computers

In the last few years, many computers have started using methods to make it possible to use operating systems without having to learn command syntaxes. For example, the Macintosh uses a pointing device called a *mouse* and a system of menus so you don't have to learn about options and arguments. The Microsoft Windows system on MS-DOS uses similar concepts.

General CMS Command Syntax

There are two types of arguments to CMS commands: *operands* and *options*. The differences between these two are subtle and are generally unimportant.

For most users, the only important difference is that, in CMS commands, operands go between the command name and a left parenthesis, and options go after the left parenthesis. Thus, the general syntax is:

```
COMMANDNAME OPERANDS ( OPTIONS
```

(If you know Latin, you might recognize the verb-object-adjective style of CMS commands.)

Some operands are required; as you saw in Chapter 3, the TYPE command requires you to give the name of the file you are typing. If you include any options in a command, you must include the left parenthesis (as you saw in the XEDIT command near the end of Chapter 3).

If You Are Familiar With Other Computers

This style of command syntax has been adopted by most computer operating systems. For example, MS-DOS and UNIX use commands with operands and options. In UNIX, the options are often only one character long, and are usually preceded by a dash.

Special Symbols in Syntaxes

There are two conventions used in IBM manuals (and, in fact, in most computer documentation) for showing generic and optional parts of commands. Generic information is shown in lowercase letters; optional parts are shown in square brackets. Generic information is information you fill in when you give the command.

For example, since the TYPE command can take any file name, and can optionally take the file mode, its syntax would be shown as:

```
TYPE fn ft [ fm ]
```

In this case, "fn" is the generic indicator of "filename," "ft" is the generic indicator of "filetype," and "[fm]" is the generic indicator of "filemode" (and the square brackets mean you can either include it or not in the command). Note that you must specify the filename and filetype before you are permitted to specify the filemode.

The following list shows you the names of the generic indicators:

fn	Filename
ft	Filetype
fm	Filemode
fileid	A file name with all three specifiers: fn ft fm
nnnnn	A number in decimal notation
c	A single character

xxxxxxxx   A group of characters; the length of the group can be from one character up to the number of x's

hhhhh   A number in hexadecimal notation (don't worry if you don't know how to count in hexadecimal)

In general, if a command's syntax has:

```
fn ft [ fm ]
```

and you do not include the filemode, CMS assumes you mean the A-disk, your personal permanent storage area.

The general syntax of a CMS command is:

```
COMMANDNAME OPERANDS [ ( OPTIONS ]
```

This means that if you have options, you must include them after the left parenthesis. This also means that if you include a left parenthesis, you must include at least one option. Options are usually listed like this:

```
COMMANDNAME OPERANDS [ ( options ]
options:
[ option1 ]
[ option2 ]
```

Some commands let you pick only one out of a group of options. This means you can use any of the options in that group, but you cannot use the command with more than one option. The syntax for these commands separates singular options by a vertical bar (|).

The vertical bar means "or." You can specify only one of the choices shown, but not both. It is similar to a restaurant that lets you have soup or salad, but not both.

Curly braces indicate that you must include what is inside the braces. These are not often used for operands before the left parenthesis. The TYPE command can be specified as:

```
TYPE { fn | * } { ft | * } [ fm | * ]
```

This means that you must specify either a filename or an asterisk as the first argument, and you must specify a filetype or an asterisk for the second argument. If you wish, you can specify a third argument: either the filemode or an asterisk.

In options, one of the choices is usually already chosen for you even if you don't give the option in the command. This is like ordering "a glass of the house red" wine in a restaurant: The waiter chooses one of the brands on the wine list for you. Even though that brand is probably listed as an option in the menu, you don't have to order it by name. This is called a default choice. In CMS syntaxes, a *default* choice in an option is shown underlined.

Hopefully, this discussion hasn't scared you off. You will see through the rest of this chapter that most of the commands only have a few arguments and options listed, so the syntaxes generally are easy to follow and understand. To see the syntax of a command while you are logged on, use the HELP command described in Chapter 2.

USING FILES AND MINIDISKS

Since all of your information is kept in files on minidisks, it makes sense that the most common type of CMS commands you use are file and minidisk commands.

The commands covered in this section are:

- COPYFILE — Copies files Ⓦ
- ERASE — Removes files from the minidisk Ⓦ
- RENAME — Changes the names of files Ⓦ
- TYPE — Displays a file on your screen
- LISTFILE — Lists the names of files on a minidisk
- FILELIST — Lets you interact with the list of contents of a minidisk; this command is much more convenient than LISTFILE
- FORMAT — Prepares your minidisk for use; erases all files on your minidisk Ⓦ
- SORT — Sorts the lines in a file
- COMPARE — Checks to see whether two files are the same or how they differ

You have already seen some of these commands in Chapter 3. This section gives you more information about the commands you have already learned to use.

If You Are Familiar With Other Computers

Most operating systems have commands nearly identical in use to CMS's COPYFILE, ERASE, RENAME, TYPE, and LISTFILE. In MS-DOS, they are COPY, ERASE, RENAME, TYPE, and DIR; in UNIX, they are cp, rm, mv, cat, and ls.

COPYFILE Command Ⓦ

The COPYFILE command copies and modifies files. You saw the COPYFILE command briefly in Chapter 3 when you made a backup of the PROFILE EXEC file. The COPYFILE command was used to make an identical copy of a file with a different file name.

The simple form of the COPYFILE command is:

```
COPYFILE fn1 ft1 fm1 fn2 ft2 fm2 [ ( options ]
```

This copies the first file (the *source* file) into the second file (the *destination* file). The COPYFILE command does not affect the source file; it simply creates a new file. For example, to make a new copy of the file JERRYBOB MEMO on your A-disk and call it PHILBILL MEMO, you would use the command:

```
COPYFILE JERRYBOB MEMO A PHILBILL MEMO A
```

The COPYFILE command has a special way of reducing your typing for files that have the same filename, filetype, or filemode. The equal sign (=) can be used in the destination file identifier in place of a part that is the same as the source file name. In the previous example, the filetype and filemode of the destination file are the same as the source file (namely "MEMO" and "A"), so the command could be given as:

```
COPYFILE JERRYBOB MEMO A PHILBILL = =
```

You can use wildcards in the file name of the source file. For example, to make a copy of every file whose filename is "SALES87", regardless of the filetype, and call the new files "OLDSALES", use the command:

```
COPYFILE SALES87 * A OLDSALES = =
```

The COPYFILE command is also handy for copying a large group of files at once to another disk. For instance, if you have a second minidisk (identified as your B-disk) and you want to copy all of your files from your A-disk to your B-disk, you don't need to know anything about the names of the files. You would give the command:

```
COPYFILE * * A = = B
```

You can also use the COPYFILE command to combine two files into a new file. The syntax for doing this is:

```
COPYFILE fn1 ft1 fm1 fn2 ft2 fm2 fn3 ft3 fm3 [ ( options ]
```

In this case, the first two files are the source files, and the third file is the destination file. You can even combine many files into one; all the file identifiers before the last one are the source files, and the last is always the destination.

For instance, you might have two parts of a report called "DRIVE1 SCRIPT" and "DRIVE2 SCRIPT" that you want to combine into a single file called "DRIVEALL SCRIPT". Use the command:

```
COPYFILE DRIVE1 SCRIPT A DRIVE2 SCRIPT A DRIVEALL SCRIPT A
```

When you copy multiple files, you can still use wildcards and equal signs where appropriate. The previous command can be shortened to:

```
COPYFILE DRIVE1 SCRIPT A DRIVE2 = = DRIVEALL = =
```

You don't often use options in the COPYFILE command, but there are three options you will find occasionally useful. These options are:

```
[ NEWFILE | REPLACE ]
[ NOTYPE | TYPE ]
[ NEWDATE | OLDDATE ]
```

Normally, COPYFILE does not let you destroy a file on your minidisk by writing the destination file over it. Imagine if you had an important file called "VALUABLE DATA" on your minidisk and you gave the following command:

```
COPYFILE SANDY MEMO A VALUABLE DATA A
```

You would receive this error message:

```
DMSCPY024E FILE 'VALUABLE DATA A' ALREADY EXISTS -- SPECIFY 'REPLACE'
```

It is likely that you don't want COPYFILE to eliminate the "VALUABLE DATA" file with the contents of "SANDY MEMO". Thus, the default option is for COPYFILE not to replace files. If you use the REPLACE option, COPYFILE creates the destination file whether or not there is already one there with the same name (it is thus a bit dangerous, and shouldn't be used unless you are sure).

The TYPE option lets you see the file names on the screen as they are copied. This is useful when you are using wildcard characters and want to see which files matched the specification.

CMS keeps track of the date and time that each file was last modified. When you create a file, this date is set to the current date. When you modify the file with a CMS command or an application program, the modification date and time are updated. The OLDDATE option in the COPYFILE command specifies that the modification date and time on the destination file should be listed as the source file's modification date instead of using the current date.

ERASE Command Ⓦ

It is easier to remove files from your minidisk than it is to create them. Simply use the ERASE command with the name of the file as an argument. Once a file is erased, there is no way to get it back.

The general syntax is:

```
ERASE fn ft [ fm ] [ ( option:
options:
[ NOTYPE | TYPE ]
```

Every ERASE command must specify a filename and filetype and can optionally specify a filemode. The filename and filetype must be either a full name or a single asterisk (*): You cannot use other wildcard specifications.

The TYPE option tells the ERASE command to list all the files erased as it erases them. This is especially useful when you erase a group of files.

For example, to erase all the files on your A-disk whose filename is "TEMP", use the command

```
ERASE TEMP *
```

Be very careful with the ERASE command, especially when using wildcard characters. Do *not* use "* *" since that will erase everything from your disk.

RENAME Command Ⓦ

You may not want to keep the name you give to a file when you create it. You may think of a better filename or want to change the filetype to match the filetype of other related files, for example. Use the RENAME command to change a file's name.

The syntax of the RENAME command is:

```
RENAME old-fn old-ft old-fm new-fn new-ft new-fm [ ( option:
options:
[ NOTYPE | TYPE ]
```

The command renames the source file to have the name of the destination file. The TYPE option is similar to the TYPE option in the ERASE command: if you include the TYPE option, the RENAME command lists the files as it changes their names.

You can use an equal sign (=) in the destination file name to indicate that the component is the same as in the source file name. For example, to change the name of a file on your A-disk called "SOUND EXEC" to "MUSIC EXEC," use the command:

```
RENAME SOUND EXEC A MUSIC = =
```

To rename all the files whose filename is "SOUND" to have the filename "MUSIC", the command would be:

```
RENAME SOUND * A MUSIC = =
```

This command can be a bit dangerous if you change the filetype of a file to one that has special meaning to CMS commands. For example, if you change the filetype of COBOL file to EXEC and accidentally try to execute the file, you will get many error messages before CMS gives up.

TYPE Command

The TYPE command displays a file on your screen. Although it is convenient for short files, it is inconvenient for longer files.

Using XEDIT to browse through a file is much more convenient that using the TYPE command. XEDIT has two major advantages over TYPE:

- You can go backwards and forwards in the file with XEDIT. If you read a paragraph in a text file, then go on to the next screen, then want to go back and reread the paragraph, it is simple with XEDIT and impossible with TYPE.

- You can search for particular words in XEDIT. If you are looking through a long memo for a particular item, you can use XEDIT's search function to find a word in the file.

The general form of the TYPE command is:

```
TYPE fileid [ startline [ endline ] ]
```

Usually, you simply give the file name, such as:

```
TYPE PROFILE EXEC
```

If you know that you want to see only particular lines in a file, include the numbers of the first and last lines you want to see. For instance, to see from the 19th line through the 28th line of the file JERRYBOB MEMO A, use the command:

```
TYPE JERRYBOB MEMO A 19 28
```

If you want to see everything in the file after the 19th line, do not include the ending line number:

```
TYPE JERRYBOB MEMO A 19
```

LISTFILE Command

You used the LISTFILE command in Chapter 3 to list the files on your minidisk. The LISTFILE command has the same inherent problems that the TYPE command has: If the list is long, you must press the CLEAR key for each screen and you cannot go back to the previous screen to see earlier parts of the list. The next command in this section, the FILELIST command, is much more convenient than the LISTFILE command.

The basic syntax of the LISTFILE command is:

```
LISTFILE [ fileid ] [ ( options ]
options:
[ HEADER | NOHEADER ]
[ FORMAT ]
[ ALLOC ]
[ DATE ]
[ LABEL ]
```

As you saw, the LISTFILE command by itself lists the filenames, filetypes, and filemodes of the files you specify. If you give no fileid, the LISTFILE command lists all the files on your A-disk.

The options give you more information about the files. It is useful to include all the options:

```
LISTFILE (HEADER FORMAT ALLOC DATE LABEL
```

The LISTFILE command lets you abbreviate this to:

```
LISTFILE (LABEL
```

The output is:

```
FILENAME FILETYPE FM FORMAT LRECL  RECS BLOCKS  DATE      TIME     LABEL
LASTING  GLOBALV  A1 V         18    12      1 7/12/88 12:58:37 JSANT
PROFILE  EXEC     A1 V         63    12      1 6/19/88 14:44:43 JSANT
PROFILE  OLDEXEC  A1 V         80    10      1 6/19/88 14:41:16 JSANT
```

The FORMAT option lists whether a file has fixed-length or variable-length blocks and lists the LRECL and number of records in the file. The ALLOC option lists the number of blocks allocated to the file, while the DATE option lists the date and time the file was last updated. The LABEL option lists the disk label.

FILELIST Command

The FILELIST command is much more flexible than the LISTFILE command. Instead of simply listing the files for you like the LISTFILE command, the FILELIST command lets you interact with the list of files. You can go forward and backward, sort on different fields, examine the files in the list, and so on.

The basic syntax of the command is simply:

```
FILELIST [ fileid ]
```

If you do not include a fileid, FILELIST assumes "* * A".

Like the HELP command, the FILELIST command is based on the XEDIT editor. Your interactions with FILELIST are with the cursor control keys (⬆, ⬇, ⬅, and ➡) and with the PF keys. The FILELIST screen looks like this:

```
SANDY      FILELIST A0   V 108   Trunc=108 Size=3 Line=1 Col=1 Alt=0
Cmd   Filename Filetype Fm Format Lrecl    Records      Blocks    Date      Time
      PROFILE  OLDEXEC  A1 V        80        10           1    6/19/87  14:41:16
  ‾   PROFILE  EXEC     A1 V        63        12           1    6/19/87  14:44:43
      LASTING  GLOBALV  A1 V        18         6           1    7/12/87  14:51:39
      SAMPLE1  XXXX     A1 V        25         1           1    8/18/87  17:33:12
      SAMPLE2  XXXX     A1 V        25         1           1    8/18/87  17:33:24
      SAMPLE3  XXXX     A1 V        25         1           1    8/18/87  17:40:55
      REMIND   SCRIPT   A1 V        80       312           2    9/13/87  08:34:15
      REMINDA  SCRIPT   A1 V        80       691           4    9/13/87  09:12:53
      REMINDB  SCRIPT   A1 V        80        44           1    9/13/87  09:14:00
      REMINDC  SCRIPT   A1 V        80       103           1    9/13/87  09:14:43




1= Help      2= Refresh  3= Quit    4= Sort(type)  5= Sort(date)  6= Sort(size)
7= Backward  8= Forward  9= FL /n  10=            11= XEDIT      12= Cursor

====>
                                                        X E D I T  1 file
```

The first line is the name of the file that FILELIST has set up to keep the listing. The second line on the screen is a header for the list of files. The bottom line (====>) is an area where you can enter commands, as you will see soon. The two lines above this are the functions of the PF keys. They are:

PF1   Help — Gives help with the FILELIST command.

PF2   Refresh — Updates the screen to reflect changes. This is useful if you use FILELIST to erase or rename files.

PF3   Quit — Leaves FILELIST and goes back to CMS.

PF4   Sort(type) — Sorts the list by filetype. This is convenient if you want to see all of your EXEC files together, all your NOTE files together, and so on.

PF5   Sort(date) — Sorts the list by date on the files, latest dates first. This is useful if you are searching for a file you changed recently but you don't remember its name.

PF6   Sort(size) — Sorts the list by size of the file. This is useful if you run out of disk space and you want to see which is the largest file you can erase.

PF7   Backward — Scrolls back one screen.

PF8   Forward — Scrolls forward one screen.

PF9   FL /n — Advanced command, not necessary to know.

PF10   Not assigned.

PF11   XEDIT — Edits the file at the cursor. This is one of FILELIST's best features. If you want to look through many files on your minidisk, give the FILELIST command, move the cursor to any file you want to look at, and press PF11. When you quit from XEDIT, you are back in the FILELIST screen. You can then choose another file to look at from the list.

PF12   Cursor — Switch the cursor from the command line to the last position on the screen, or vice versa.

After FILELIST executes a command on a file (such as XEDIT using PF11 or a command that you type in), it puts an asterisk in the command area. This helps you remember which files you have already worked on. For instance, if you are using FILELIST to browse through many files with similar names, it is convenient to see which ones you have already looked at.

The FILELIST command makes performing the same command on many files easy. For example, suppose you want to erase the file "REMINDA SCRIPT"; you would simply put the cursor at the first column of the line with the file, type ERASE, and press the ENTER key:

```
 SANDY      FILELIST A0   V 108   Trunc=108 Size=3 Line=1 Col=1 Alt=0
 Cmd     Filename Filetype Fm Format Lrecl     Records    Blocks    Date      Time
         PROFILE  OLDEXEC  A1 V       80         10         1    6/19/87 14:41:16
         PROFILE  EXEC     A1 V       63         12         1    6/19/87 14:44:43
         LASTING  GLOBALV  A1 V       18          6         1    7/12/87 14:51:39
         SAMPLE1  XXXX     A1 V       25          1         1    8/18/87 17:33:12
         SAMPLE2  XXXX     A1 V       25          1         1    8/18/87 17:33:24
         SAMPLE3  XXXX     A1 V       25          1         1    8/18/87 17:40:55
         REMIND   SCRIPT   A1 V       80        312         2    9/13/87 08:34:15
 ERASE_REMINDA    SCRIPT   A1 V       80        691         4    9/13/87 09:12:53
         REMINDB  SCRIPT   A1 V       80         44         1    9/13/87 09:14:00
         REMINDC  SCRIPT   A1 V       80        103         1    9/13/87 09:14:43




 1= Help      2= Refresh  3= Quit    4= Sort(type)  5= Sort(date)  6= Sort(size)
 7= Backward  8= Forward  9= FL /n   10=            11= XEDIT      12= Cursor

 ====>
                                                   X E D I T  1 file
```

When you press ENTER, the command is carried out, and the screen is updated:

```
 SANDY      FILELIST A0  V 108   Trunc=108 Size=3 Line=1 Col=1 Alt=0
Cmd    Filename Filetype Fm Format Lrecl    Records      Blocks   Date      Time
       PROFILE  OLDEXEC  A1 V         80         10           1  6/19/87 14:41:16
       PROFILE  EXEC     A1 V         63         12           1  6/19/87 14:44:43
       LASTING  GLOBALV  A1 V         18          6           1  7/12/87 14:51:39
       SAMPLE1  XXXX     A1 V         25          1           1  8/18/87 17:33:12
       SAMPLE2  XXXX     A1 V         25          1           1  8/18/87 17:33:24
       SAMPLE3  XXXX     A1 V         25          1           1  8/18/87 17:40:55
       REMIND   SCRIPT   A1 V         80        312           2  9/13/87 08:34:15
*      REMINDA  SCRIPT   A1 ** Discarded or renamed **
       REMINDB  SCRIPT   A1 V         80         44           1  9/13/87 09:14:00
_      REMINDC  SCRIPT   A1 V         80        103           1  9/13/87 09:14:43




1= Help      2= Refresh   3= Quit    4= Sort(type)  5= Sort(date)  6= Sort(size)
7= Backward  8= Forward   9= FL /n   10=            11= XEDIT       12= Cursor

====>
                                                     X E D I T  1 file
```

Note the asterisk in the command area of the file you operated on.

Although FILELIST makes it convenient to give a command whose operand is a file name (since you don't need to type the file name), it goes even further. You can repeat a single command on many files by entering an equal sign (=) in the command area. For instance, to delete REMINDB SCRIPT and REMINDC SCRIPT, type "ERASE" next to the first file and simply an equal sign by the second:

```
 SANDY      FILELIST A0   V 108   Trunc=108 Size=3 Line=1 Col=1 Alt=0
 Cmd     Filename Filetype Fm Format Lrecl    Records    Blocks   Date      Time
         PROFILE  OLDEXEC  A1 V        80        10          1   6/19/87 14:41:16
         PROFILE  EXEC     A1 V        63        12          1   6/19/87 14:44:43
         LASTING  GLOBALV  A1 V        18         6          1   7/12/87 14:51:39
         SAMPLE1  XXXX     A1 V        25         1          1   8/18/87 17:33:12
         SAMPLE2  XXXX     A1 V        25         1          1   8/18/87 17:33:24
         SAMPLE3  XXXX     A1 V        25         1          1   8/18/87 17:40:55
         REMIND   SCRIPT   A1 V        80       312          2   9/13/87 08:34:15
 *       REMINDA  SCRIPT   A1 ** Discarded or renamed **
 ERASE REMINDB  SCRIPT   A1 V        80        44          1   9/13/87 09:14:00
 =_      REMINDC  SCRIPT   A1 V        80       103          1   9/13/87 09:14:43




 1= Help      2= Refresh  3= Quit    4= Sort(type)  5= Sort(date)  6= Sort(size)
 7= Backward  8= Forward  9= FL /n  10=            11= XEDIT       12= Cursor

 ====>
                                                          X E D I T  1 file
```

When you press the ENTER key, the ERASE command is performed on both files:

```
 SANDY     FILELIST A0  V 108  Trunc=108 Size=3 Line=1 Col=1 Alt=0
 Cmd    Filename Filetype Fm Format Lrecl      Records     Blocks   Date       Time
        PROFILE  OLDEXEC  A1 V       80         10            1    6/19/87 14:41:16
        PROFILE  EXEC     A1 V       63         12            1    6/19/87 14:44:43
        LASTING  GLOBALV  A1 V       18          6            1    7/12/87 14:51:39
        SAMPLE1  XXXX     A1 V       25          1            1    8/18/87 17:33:12
        SAMPLE2  XXXX     A1 V       25          1            1    8/18/87 17:33:24
        SAMPLE3  XXXX     A1 V       25          1            1    8/18/87 17:40:55
        REMIND   SCRIPT   A1 V       80        312            2    9/13/87 08:34:15
 *      REMINDA  SCRIPT   A1 ** Discarded or renamed **
 *      REMINDB  SCRIPT   A1 ** Discarded or renamed **
 *      REMINDC  SCRIPT   A1 ** Discarded or renamed **




 1= Help      2= Refresh  3= Quit    4= Sort(type)  5= Sort(date)  6= Sort(size)
 7= Backward  8= Forward  9= FL /n   10=            11= XEDIT       12= Cursor

 ====>
                                                       X E D I T  1 file
```

In many cases, you want to use commands longer than the few characters in the command column. FILELIST lets you type right over the file name. In this case, you can use the slash (/) symbol to refer to the fileid on the line you are on.

For example, to rename SAMPLE1 XXXX to SAMPLE1 YYYY, enter:

```
SANDY      FILELIST A0   V 108   Trunc=108 Size=3 Line=1 Col=1 Alt=0
Cmd    Filename Filetype Fm Format Lrecl    Records    Blocks    Date      Time
       PROFILE  OLDEXEC  A1 V        80        10         1    6/19/87 14:41:16
       PROFILE  EXEC     A1 V        63        12         1    6/19/87 14:44:43
       LASTING  GLOBALV  A1 V        18         6         1    7/12/87 14:51:39
rename / = YYYY =_        A1 V        25         1         1    8/18/87 17:33:12
       SAMPLE2  XXXX     A1 V        25         1         1    8/18/87 17:33:24
       SAMPLE3  XXXX     A1 V        25         1         1    8/18/87 17:40:55
       REMIND   SCRIPT   A1 V        80       312         2    9/13/87 08:34:15
*      REMINDA  SCRIPT   A1 ** Discarded or renamed **
*      REMINDB  SCRIPT   A1 ** Discarded or renamed **
*      REMINDC  SCRIPT   A1 ** Discarded or renamed **




1= Help      2= Refresh  3= Quit    4= Sort(type)  5= Sort(date)  6= Sort(size)
7= Backward  8= Forward  9= FL /n  10=             11= XEDIT      12= Cursor

====>
                                                    X E D I T  1 file
```

When you press ENTER, the file is renamed.

Since you have deleted many files and renamed others, it is probably a good idea to update the screen with the PF2 key. The result is:

```
SANDY      FILELIST A0   V 108   Trunc=108 Size=7 Line=1 Col=1 Alt=0
Cmd    Filename Filetype Fm Format Lrecl     Records      Blocks   Date      Time
_      PROFILE  OLDEXEC  A1 V        80         10           1   6/19/87 14:41:16
       PROFILE  EXEC     A1 V        63         12           1   6/19/87 14:44:43
       LASTING  GLOBALV  A1 V        18          6           1   7/12/87 14:51:39
       SAMPLE1  YYYY     A1 V        25          1           1   8/18/87 17:33:12
       SAMPLE2  XXXX     A1 V        25          1           1   8/18/87 17:33:24
       SAMPLE3  XXXX     A1 V        25          1           1   8/18/87 17:40:55
       REMIND   SCRIPT   A1 V        80        312           2   9/13/87 08:34:15




1= Help      2= Refresh  3= Quit    4= Sort(type)  5= Sort(date)  6= Sort(size)
7= Backward  8= Forward  9= FL /n  10=             11= XEDIT       12= Cursor

====>
                                                          X E D I T  1 file
```

You will find that, as you get more and more files on your minidisk, the FILELIST command will become more valuable to you. It is a good way of viewing all the files on your disk in different orders (using PF4, PF5, and PF6) as well as for being able to hop into and out of XEDIT to determine what various files contain.

FORMAT Command Ⓦ

The FORMAT command erases all the information on your minidisk and prepares it to receive files. As you were warned in Chapter 3, you should use the command carefully since it removes all the files from your minidisk. You should always check with your system administrator before you format your minidisk. He or she may have a suggestion for formatting your disk according to your company's standards.

The commands you use to format different minidisks are different. The following syntax only formats your A-disk:

```
FORMAT 191 A [ ( LABEL ]
```

The LABEL option lets you specify the label to go on the disk; the FORMAT command asks you to specify the label (which must be six or fewer characters).

SORT Command

The SORT command lets you sort the lines in a file. This is not often used, but can be very handy if you are making a long list (such as a telephone directory) and want it sorted. The XEDIT command has a sorter that is useful if you only want to sort part of a file.

The syntax is:

```
SORT fileid1 fileid2
```

fileid1 is the file to be sorted, and fileid2 is the new, sorted file. The file names for fileid1 and fileid2 must be different, and you must include filename, filetype, and filemode for each file. You can use equal signs (=) in fileid2 to indicate parts that are the same as in fileid1. When you give the sort command, you are prompted:

```
DMSSRT604R ENTER SORT FIELDS:
```

You can enter one or more pairs of columns in the records. For instance, assume your file looks like this:

```
Essler, Anthony       x1174
Pequeno, Lilly        x1136
Goff, Harry           x1244
Rust, Denise          x1107
```

If you wanted to sort the file by name, you would enter the columns as:

```
1 22
```

The resulting file would look like this:

```
Essler, Anthony       x1174
Goff, Harry           x1244
Pequeno, Lilly        x1136
Rust, Denise          x1107
```

You might also want sort the file by extension numbers. The columns you would enter at the prompt would be:

```
23 27
```

The resulting file would look like this:

```
Rust, Denise          x1107
Pequeno, Lilly        x1136
Essler, Anthony       x1174
Goff, Harry           x1244
```

You can even sort by more than one set of columns. For example, if some people in the list had more than one extension, it would be nice for the list to be sorted first by name, then by extension. The columns would be specified as:

```
1 22 23 27
```

COMPARE Command

If you have two files you think are the same or very similar, you can use the COMPARE command to find the differences. Any lines in the two files that are not identical are displayed. The syntax is:

```
COMPARE fileid1 fileid2 [ ( COL startcol [ finishcol ] ]
```

The file names for fileid1 and fileid2 must be different, and you must include filename, filetype, and filemode for each file. You can use equal signs (=) in fileid2 to indicate parts that are the same as in fileid1. If you want to only compare certain columns, you can specify them in the COL option.

The COMPARE command tells you which files it is comparing and prints pairs of unmatched lines. For example, when comparing PHONES LIST A with PHONES LIST B, you might see:

```
DMSCMP179I COMPARING 'PHONES LIST A' WITH 'PHONES LIST B'.
Hardford, Chris       x27
Hardford, Chris       x32
DMSCMP209W FILES DO NOT COMPARE
```

MAKING SETTINGS AND GETTING INFORMATION

Like all operating systems, CMS provides commands that allow you to tailor the system to your specific needs. For example, in Chapter 2 you saw how to change the amount of information you get in error messages. CMS also gives you information about your system resources.

The commands in this section are:

- INDICATE — Tells you about the amount of system usage
- SET — Lets you set system settings
- QUERY — Displays the system settings
- SYNONYM — Allows you to use different names for CMS commands
- DEFINE STORAGE — Lets you change the amount of virtual storage available to you
- TERMINAL — Lets you set characteristics about your terminal

Note that the QUERY command is actually two commands: CP QUERY and CMS QUERY. Likewise, the SET command is both CP SET and CMS SET. They are mixed in this book since the settings you can see and set are similar.

INDICATE Command

The INDICATE command tells you how busy your system is. It is the only command available to you that lets you "take the system's temperature" to tell how hard it is working.

Its syntax is:

```
INDICATE LOAD
```

The output looks like this:

```
CPU-097%  Q1-05  Q2-20  STORAGE-074%  EXPAN-014
PAGING-0203/SEC  STEAL-000%  LOAD-000%  SWAPPING-0247/SEC
```

The relevant information here is the number after "EXPAN." The rate of "expansion" in the elapsed time of a job compared to the job running on the computer by itself. Thus, "14" indicates that the average program is taking 14 times longer to run than it would if there were no other programs running.

Each site has its own guidelines for acceptable amount of machine load. For instance, many system administrators would feel that having an expansion of over 20 for a long period would indicate that something is wrong with the system or the way it is being used. Regardless of what the "average" expansion of your system is, you can use this as an indicator of how heavily used your system is and have more information on why the system may seem to be running fast or slow.

SET Command

The SET command lets you set up how CMS acts. There are dozens of options for the SET command. If you find yourself repeating a particular SET command over and over, you may want to make an EXEC file with the command so you can issue it more quickly.

RDYMSG   Tells CMS which kind of ready message to display (as you saw in Chapter 2). The options are:

```
RDYMSG LMSG
RDYMSG SMSG
```

ABBREV   Allows you to use system and user synonyms. These are described in detail later in this section under the SYNONYM command. The option's syntax is:

```
ABBREV ON
ABBREV OFF
```

IMPEX   Generally, it is convenient to run EXECs by simply typing their name, just like CMS commands. In a few cases, however, you may want to not have this happen; for example, if you want to be sure that when you type a command name, only a CMS command executes, not an EXEC. The IMPEX option (which stands for "implicit EXEC") lets you control whether CMS looks for EXECs when you give a command:

```
IMPEX ON
IMPEX OFF
```

IMPCP   This is similar to IMPEX. Usually, you want to run CP commands just as if they were CMS commands. This option lets you tell CMS whether or not to look implicitly for CP commands when you give a command:

```
IMPCP ON
IMPCP OFF
```

If you set IMPCP off, to give a CP command you must preface it with "CP." For instance, the INDICATE command covered earlier in this section is really a CP command. If you set IMPCP off, you would have to preface the command with "CP," as in:

```
CP INDICATE LOAD
```

MSG
As you will see in the next section, you can send messages to other CMS users (and they can send them to you) with the TELL command. These messages appear on their screens immediately after you send them. Getting a message can sometimes be a nuisance, however, such as when you are intently working under a deadline.

The MSG option lets you prevent these messages from appearing on your screen. Its syntax is:

```
MSG ON
MSG OFF
```

ON tells CMS to let messages come through, and OFF prevents you from receiving messages. The SET MSG OFF command also prevents messages from the spooler (described in Chapter 8) from appearing on your screen.

EMSG
Error messages are usually important since they tell you if a command completed and, if it didn't, why not. The syntax is:

```
EMSG TEXT
EMSG ON
EMSG OFF
EMSG CODE
```

TEXT indicates that only the text of the message is displayed; CODE indicates that only the error code is shown. OFF turns off all error messages, and ON turns on both the text and the error code. You can find out more about it from the HELP command (as you saw in Chapter 2). Thus, you should generally set EMSG to ON.

WNG
Tells CMS to allow or prevent warning messages from the system operator or system administrator to appear on your screen. Since warnings are rare, and are often important when they do appear, you should generally leave this set on. The syntax is:

```
WNG ON
WNG OFF
```

It is important to read any warning message carefully. They often tell you about critical conditions that may affect your work.

IMSG
Like other types of messages, informational messages can be turned on or off. These informational messages are often helpful as you learn more about CMS. The syntax is:

```
IMSG ON
IMSG OFF
```

PF   CMS allows you to create your own meanings for the PF keys. This is very useful for commands that you give often. For instance, if you give the FILELIST command many times a day, it is much easier to press one PF key than it is to type in the name. This is especially true for long commands.

The syntax for this option is:

```
PFnn [ DELAYED | IMMED ] [command]
```

The "nn" can be any number from 1 to 12 (or to 24, if you have a 3270 terminal with 24 PF keys).

For example, you might set PF5 to give the command "FILELIST * SCRIPT B" with the command:

```
SET PF5 IMMED FILELIST * SCRIPT B
```

DELAYED and IMMED indicate what happens when you press the PF key. DELAYED means that CMS simply types out the command on the screen, but doesn't execute it; IMMED means that the command is executed when it is typed. If you use DELAYED, you can edit the command line on the screen with the editing keys, just as if you had typed out the line yourself (CMS leaves the cursor at the end of the line). Using IMMED is like saying, "Type the command and press the ENTER key," meaning that you do not want to edit the command first.

Using the DELAYED option has many uses. For instance, imagine that you have many minidisks attached and you regularly give the FILELIST command for different disks. The following command sets up PF6 to give the delayed command "FILELIST * * " (note the extra space after the second asterisk):

```
SET PF6 DELAYED FILELIST * *
```

When you press PF6 after giving this command, you can then simply type the single-letter filemode for the minidisk you are interested in and press ENTER. This way, you don't have to have a different PF key set for each FILELIST command you might give.

There is a special command for the PF option that you will also find very useful. When you associate the RETRIEVE function with a PF key and press that PF key, CMS redisplays the last command you typed. This is handy for the situation where you mistype a command and press ENTER. Instead of having to retype the whole command, press the designated PF key; you can now edit the line and try again. By convention, most people make PF1 the RETRIEVE key:

```
SET PF1 RETRIEVE
```

The RETRIEVE function saves many of your previous commands (usually at least five). To repeat the command you gave three commands ago, press the designated PF key three times.

If You Are Familiar With Other Computers

The RETRIEVE function is similar to the F3 key in MS-DOS, except that the RETRIEVE function remembers more than just your last command. It is also similar, although not nearly as useful, as the history feature of many UNIX systems.

To reset a PF key to not do anything, don't include a command at the end. For instance, to reset PF6, give the command:

```
SET PF6
```

You will find many other uses for the PF option. As you use CMS more in your daily work, you will find certain commands that you use often; these are good candidates for PF keys.

QUERY Command

Like the SET command, there are dozens of options for the QUERY command. It is likely that you will find at least a few of them useful in your daily work. If you find yourself repeating a particular QUERY command over and over, you may want to make an EXEC file with the command so that you can issue it more quickly.

The following list gives the relevant options and their meanings. If no syntax is given, the option is used by itself. Most QUERY commands have a matching SET command, and the meanings of many of the responses to the QUERY command are described in the corresponding SET command.

RDYMSG — Tells the current form of the ready message. The response is either that the ready message is LMSG or SMSG. These indicate the long and short ready message formats you saw in Chapter 2.

LOGMSG — Prints the message you get when you log on. Since this often contains important information (such as system availability), it is important to read this message when you log on. You can use this command to remind yourself what the message said.

ABBREV — Indicates the status of whether synonyms are being interpreted, either ON or OFF (it is generally ON). This is described in more detail under the SYNONYM command.

IMPEX	Tells the status of the implied EXEC command interpreter, either ON or OFF (it is generally ON).
IMPCP	Indicates the status of the implied CP command interpreter, either ON or OFF (it is generally ON).
SEARCH	Displays the search order of your minidisks. The output is a list of minidisks in the order that they are searched (from first to last).
DISK {option}	Displays a great deal of information about the disk or disks specified. The information includes the unit number, the mode letter, the status, the number of cylinders, and so on.

The options for the QUERY DISK command are:

fm	Display information for the one disk.
*	Display information for all disks.
R/W	Display information for all disks to which you can write information.
MAX	Display information for the disk to which you can write information which has the most space available.

VIRTUAL STORAGE	Shows the size of your virtual storage.
LINKS cuu	Shows all users that are using a particular disk. See the LINK command for more information.
SYNONYM {option}	Displays the synonyms in effect. For more information, see the SYNONYM command later in this section. The options are:

```
SYNONYM SYSTEM
SYNONYM USER
SYNONYM ALL
```

ALL is the same as the combination of SYSTEM and USER.

PF	Shows how your PF keys have been set.
CMSLEVEL	Shows the name and version of CMS. The display looks like:

```
VM/SP RELEASE 5, SERVICE LEVEL 503
```

CPLEVEL	Shows the version of CP.
AUTOREAD	Tells whether AUTOREAD is on or off.
TIME	Shows the time and date as well as how long you have been logged on and how much processor time you have used.
TERMINAL	Displays the current terminal settings. See the TERMINAL command later in this chapter for more information.

VIRTUAL DASD	Shows the status of all of your disks.
READER	Shows files in your virtual reader (described later in this chapter).
USERID	Shows your userid and node name. Node names are discussed in detail in the NAMES command.

SYNONYM Command

Some command names may not be easy for you to remember. Fortunately, with the SYNONYM command, you can use your own names. You can create a table of names that are the equivalent CMS command and use the names from your table. You can also include synonyms and abbreviations for your own EXECs in this table.

There are two types of synonyms: system synonyms and user synonyms. System synonyms are set by your system administrator. You set your user synonyms with the SYNONYM command.

The SYNONYM command is used in conjunction with the SET ABBREV command. The SET ABBREV command has one option: ON or OFF. Generally, it is set on. This lets you abbreviate CMS commands to their shortest unambiguous length when you enter them (these are shown in Appendix B). If you give the SET ABBREV OFF command, you cannot abbreviate any CMS command or any EXEC.

The syntax for the command is:

```
SYNONYM [ fn [ SYNONYM [fm ] ] ] [ ( options ]
options:
[ STD | NOSTD ]
[ CLEAR ]
```

The file name is the file that contains your synonym list (it must have a filetype of SYNONYM). It is conventional to use your userid as the filename for the synonym file.

The STD option indicates that standard CMS abbreviations should be accepted; NOSTD indicates that they shouldn't. The CLEAR command causes CMS to forget the previous synonyms you have set. If you give no options at all, the SYNONYM command lists both the system synonyms and your user synonyms.

Generally, you just give the command with the name of your synonym file:

```
SYNONYM FREDL
```

The format for each line in your synonym file is:

```
command synonym count
```

The command is the name of the command for which you want to create a synonym (either a CMS command, a system EXEC, or a personal EXEC), and the synonym is the new name you want (up to eight characters). The count is the minimum number of characters that you must enter for the synonym to be recognized by CMS.

Here are some examples of what you might have in your synonym file:

```
FILELIST FLIST 2
TELL TO 2
```

Assume you have these in the file SYNS SYNONYM, and give the command:

```
SYNONYM SYNS
```

From then on, you could simply type "FL" or "FLI" instead of "FILELIST" when giving the command.

If You Are Familiar With Other Computers

If you also use MS-DOS, you may want to include the following synonyms:

```
FILELIST          DIR 2
ERASE             DEL 2
```

If you also use UNIX, you may want to include:

```
FILELIST          LS  2
RENAME            MV  2
ERASE             RM  2
```

To see the list of system and user synonyms, either give the SYNONYM command with no arguments, or give the QUERY SYNONYM ALL command.

You can also use the SYNONYM command to make abbreviations for CMS commands. This, however, is not recommended, since your abbreviations might clash with the abbreviation of other CMS commands. Always make commands have names different from CMS names.

DEFINE STORAGE Command

The DEFINE STORAGE command lets you set the amount of virtual memory you can use, up to the limit set for you by your system administrator. You can specify the amount in K (thousands of bytes) or M (millions of bytes). Note that 1K is not 1000 bytes, but 1024 bytes; similarly, 1M is 1,048,576 bytes. These numbers arise from the way that computer memory is designed.

The syntax of the DEFINE STORAGE command is:

```
DEFINE STORAGE { nnnnnK | nnM }
```

To set your virtual memory to 2M, give the command:

```
DEFINE STORAGE 2M
```

When you give this command, you are put in CP mode. You must restart CMS with the command:

```
IPL CMS
```

TERMINAL Command

If you are using a non-3270 terminal, you will find that IBM's default choices for the way you interact with CMS are often inconvenient. The TERMINAL command lets you change these default choices. It also lets 3270 users change some important settings. You can see the settings with the QUERY TERMINAL command.

The syntax is:

```
TERMINAL option ...
Options:
[ CHARDEL { ON | OFF | c } ]
[ LINEDEL { ON | OFF | c } ]
[ LINEND  { ON | OFF | c } ]
[ TYPE { TTY | 3101 } ]
[ SCROLL { CONT | nn } ]
```

You can specify as many TERMINAL options as you want in a single command. The options are:

CHARDEL
The character delete symbol is used to tell CMS to ignore the previous character; it is really only of use on printing terminals. 3270 users should turn CHARDEL off since they can edit lines with the editing keys. Printing terminal users generally use the at-sign (@) as the character delete symbol. Thus, when CHARDEL is on, the line:

```
FILR@ELIST
```

is read by CMS as:

```
FILELIST
```

If you want to change the character delete character (this is rare), give the TERMINAL command with the new character, such as:

```
TERMINAL CHARDEL ~
```

LINEDEL
Like CHARDEL, the LINEDEL (line delete) symbol is only useful on printing terminals. It is normally the cent sign (¢). If you type a long line that you want CMS to ignore, instead of typing a string of @'s, you can simply type ¢ and start the line over.

LINEND
The line end character is useful for both 3270-type displays and printing terminals. The line end character lets you put many CMS command lines on a single terminal line. The standard line end character is the pound sign (#). Thus, the command:

```
LINK LBUTLER 192 AS 198 R # ACCESS 198 G
```

is equivalent to the two commands:

```
LINK LBUTLER 192 AS 198 R
ACCESS 198 G
```

TYPE   The default for non-3270 terminals is that they are set for TTY
                emulation. This prevents you from using any PF keys. Since most
                terminals attached to a mainframe running CMS can emulate PF
                keys, you generally want to set this option to 3101.

SCROLL   On printing terminals, there are no "screens," so you are spared
                having to press the CLEAR key each time 22 lines are printed. If,
                however, you want CMS to stop after a certain number of lines, you
                can use the SCROLL option to set that number (in this case, CONT
                means never stop). If you set a number, CMS prints:

                MORE

                after each screen full.

COMMUNICATING WITH OTHER USERS

Since there are many people who use CMS systems at the same time, it is often useful to
communicate with them. For example, you might want to access information on a co-
worker's disk, or send a note to someone about a meeting. CMS gives you many ways of
interacting with the other users on your system.

VM plays a large role in user-to-user communications. The very basic design of VM
prevents you from having almost any effect on another user. For example, you cannot run
a program that watches what another user is doing without that user's permission. And, if
regular security measures are in place, you cannot see the contents of another user's minidisk
without that person's permission.

As you saw in Chapter 1, your virtual machine is all your own. When you communicate
with other CMS users, you do so through very tightly controlled pathways. VM makes sure
that your communications do not adversely affect other users.

The three types of communication covered in this section are:

- Disk access — The ability to read from (and, in some cases, write to) minidisks
  owned by other users
- Immediate messages — Messages that appear on other users' screens the next time
  they press the ENTER key (but only if they are logged on)
- Electronic mail and file transfer — Notes and messages that are sent to other users
  so they can receive them at their leisure

The commands are:

- LINK — Lets you connect to another user's minidisks
- ACCESS — Establishes a filemode for a linked minidisk
- RELEASE — Disconnects you from a linked minidisk
- NAMES — Sets up a database of names of other CMS users

- TELL — Sends an immediate message to another user
- NOTE — Sends an electronic mail message to another user
- SENDFILE — Sends a file to another CMS user
- RDRLIST — Shows if you have files from another user waiting to be stored on your minidisk

The NOTE, SENDFILE, and RDRLIST commands use a facility called the *virtual reader* to store messages and files. The concept behind the virtual reader is obscure and has its roots in the days of card punches. Fortunately, you don't need to know anything about the virtual reader to use these commands; simply assume it is a holding area that each user has for files received from other CMS users. Virtual readers are covered in Chapter 8.

LINK Command

The LINK command lets you set up a link to another user's minidisk. It does not make the linked disk available; you need to follow the LINK command with the ACCESS command. Since these two commands are almost always given at the same time, it is likely that you will want to make an EXEC with them.

Many sites have their own EXECs set up to automatically link and access a disk. These EXECs check for the first available address, perform the LINK, check for the first available filemode, and perform the ACCESS. Ask your system administrator about whether your site has such an EXEC set up. If so, you may want to skip the following two sections, since they go into detail that is only necessary if you need to give your own LINK and ACCESS commands.

```
EXEC to LINK and ACCESS another user's disk:



```

Before you give the LINK command to access another user's disk, you must know:

- The userid of the user
- The user's *cuu* for the disk you want to access (this is also known as the disk's *virtual address*). An example of a cuu is "191".
- The virtual address you want to assign the disk to
- Whether the disk has a password
- Whether you intend only to read from the disk, or to write on it as well

One of the most confusing aspects of using the LINK command is the difference between the two cuu's. Each user has his or her own cuu set up; that is, a cuu is only relevant for one user. That is why you need to know the cuu of the user's disk to link to it (it is like a street address of a home). When you assign the disk your own cuu, it does not affect the other user at all.

Finding the user's userid is easy; simply ask him or her what it is. If the user doesn't know the virtual address of the disk you want to access, he or she can give the "QUERY DISK fm" command with the filemode of the disk. The second column of the "QUERY DISK fm" command gives the virtual address of the disk.

There are three types of passwords, as you will see later in this section. If the disk has a password for the method you intend to use, the disk's owner must tell it to you before you give the LINK command. All disk passwords are between one and eight characters long. If you do not know the disk's password, CMS does not let you access the disk.

The virtual address which you assign to the disk must be one not used by any other disk. To see the list of all virtual addresses for your disks, give the QUERY DISK * command. The output might look like:

```
LABEL  CUU  M   STAT  CYL TYPE BLKSIZE   FILES BLKS USED-(%) BLKS LEFT  BLK TOTAL
FILES  191  A   R/W     2 3380 4096          5        11-04       289       300
MAIL   19C R/R  R/O     4 3380 4096         32       420-70       180       600
SYSA   190  S   R/O    56 3380 4096        188      3987-47      4413      8400
CMSY   19E Y/S  R/O   260 3380 4096       1087     36334-93      2666     39000
```

This shows that cuu's 191, 19C, 190, and 19E are used. Note that cuu's are in hexadecimal notation. If you aren't familiar with hexadecimal, don't worry; simply assume it is a numbering scheme that has the digits 0 through 9 and the letters A through F. Since disk cuu's often begin with "19", and most other cuu's do not use "19" as the first two digits, you can choose any other hexadecimal number that begins with "19" as your unused cuu. In this case, you might choose "199".

Choosing the access method (whether you only want to read, or to both read and write) is a bit trickier. The decision is complicated by your having to know whether other people (including the disk's owner) are reading from or writing to the disk at the same time you are accessing it. A short scenario helps show why this is a concern.

Assume that Pat has a disk with a file that Jean wants to read. Jean accesses the disk and starts looking in the file with XEDIT. While Jean is reading the file, Pat starts to update the same file, changing part of the contents; this happens without Jean's knowledge. Many problems can arise:

- Jean might think that the information she is looking at is current, when in fact it is not.

- The copy of the file that Jean is viewing may change (such as if Pat deletes the first ten lines in the file), causing her to see a scrambled view when she looks back in the file.

- If Jean quits from XEDIT, then starts it again on the same file, she may see two very different files, depending on Pat's changes. This can cause her a great deal of confusion.

The situation is much worse if two people are both updating the file without each other's knowledge. The file can become badly corrupted and unusable. Thus, you should think carefully not only about what you want to do with a shared file, but also what others are doing with the file at the same time.

You must first choose if you want to read from, or write to, the other user's disk. Generally, you only want to read information from someone else's disk. If you want to give them information, you should send them the information with the SENDFILE command described later in this section. This greatly reduces the chance that problems like those just described can happen. Instead of updating a file, make a copy of it on your own disk, change the copy, and send the other user the updated version with SENDFILE.

If you are reading from a disk, you need to decide whether you only want to read from it if no one else is writing to it, or whether you are willing to risk reading from the disk while others might be writing to it. The latter situation is acceptable if you are sure they will not write in the files you are reading.

If you are writing to a disk, you need to decide whether you want to lock out other users from reading from the disk, or whether you are willing to let them read from the disk while you are writing to it (such as if you are sure they will read files you are not writing). Since this is someone else's disk, you should assume it is likely they will want to write to the disk and that this might cause a risk of damaging the files.

There are seven access methods for the LINK command that let you specify to CMS what to do when you want to link to a disk. The letters in the left column are used in the LINK command.

ACCESS	EXPLANATION
R	Link to the disk for reading, and only do so if no other user has linked to the disk for writing. This means that either no one is using the disk, or that everyone linked to the disk only has read access. If anyone has write access to the disk, the LINK command prints a message.
RR	Link to the disk for reading regardless of whether other people have write access. This is more prone to error than R access because someone may be writing in the file you are reading; however, it guarantees that the LINK command will be successful.
W	Link to the disk for writing, and only do so if no other user is linked to the disk. This assures you that no one is reading the disk, so you can change any file without worrying whether your changes can affect people linked to the disk. If anyone has read or write access to the disk, the LINK command prints a message.
WR	Attempt to link to the disk for writing (as in W access); however, if anyone is linked to the disk, you get read access instead of an error message.
M	Link to the disk for writing if no other user has write access to the disk. This means you can get write access when other users have read access; if you change files that they are reading, you can cause problems for them. If anyone has write access to the disk, the LINK command prints a message. If others are linked to the disk and you are linking with M access, you may want to use the TELL command to let them know you intend to write to the disk. You can find the userids of everyone using the disk with the "QUERY LINKS cuu" command.

MR	Attempt to link to the disk for writing (as in M access); however, if anyone has write access to the disk, you get read access instead of an error message.
MW	Link to the disk for writing regardless of whether someone else has write access. This access mode is exceptionally dangerous and should never be used without special advanced safeguards in place; it has a high probability of losing files and making files unreadable.

A disk to which you are linking can have three different passwords: one for R or RR access, one for W or WR access, and one for M, MR, or MW access. The disk password is set using your site's security program. If you want someone to link to your disk, set up read or write passwords on your own userid.

Depending on the reason for your linking to the disk, you will generally only use R, RR, and W modes. It is important to note that, when you get R access, you are assured no one is writing to the disk at that moment. However, someone else can get write access later and you not know it. Thus, R access is only slightly safer than RR access.

Similarly, if you link to a disk with write access and begin writing, you may harm other's work. Many people feel this is a major weakness in CMS disk security.

If You Are Familiar With Other Computers

Many multi-user operating systems normally give you much better control over reading and writing on your disks to prevent damage to your data.

You are now ready to issue the LINK command. Its syntax is:

```
LINK TO userid user-cuu AS your-cuu mode
```

The userid and user-cuu are the other person's userid and their cuu for the disk. The your-cuu is the unused cuu you want to assign to this disk, and the mode is one of the seven modes already described.

For example, you might give the command:

```
LINK TO PATJ 194 AS 199 RR
```

This tells CMS to link PATJ's 194 disk to your cuu 199 in read-only mode regardless of any users who have the disk linked with write access.

If there is a password for the mode you are requesting, CMS prompts you for that password. The prompt is one of the following:

```
ENTER READ PASSWORD:
ENTER WRITE PASSWORD:
ENTER MULT PASSWORD:
```

When you type the password, it does not appear on your screen (if you are using a 3270-type terminal). If you are on a printing terminal, CMS prints a row of dark characters under the prompt and positions the cursor at the first character.

If the link is successful, CMS tells you that you have linked the disk. If there are other users who also have links, CMS also tells you how many others have which kinds of links. For instance, if you chose RR access and others have read and write access, your message might look like this:

```
DASD 199 LINKED R/O; R/W BY LJONES; R/O BY 13 USERS
```

This message means:

- DASD is an old IBM term for disk (it stands for *direct access storage device*).
- 199 is your unused cuu to which you linked the disk.
- R/O stands for "read-only."
- R/W BY LJONES means that LJONES has linked to the disk for writing (R/W stands for "read-write," which is the same as write access).
- R/O BY 13 USERS means that 13 other users have read-only links to the disk.

There are many situations that can cause errors in the LINK command. The most common are incorrect spelling of the userid, giving an incorrect cuu for the user's disk, trying to link to a cuu you are already using, and giving the wrong password.

This discussion has centered on linking to someone else's disk. Of course, you may want someone to link to yours. Letting someone link to your minidisks is as easy as telling them your userid and the cuu of the disk they want to link to. If there is a disk password, you need to tell them that.

Having a disk password is always a good idea. It adds an extra layer of security to your work without adding any overhead. Talk to your system administrator about how you set disk passwords at your site before you let someone link to your disk.

ACCESS Command

Once you have linked a disk to a cuu, you want to give it a filemode so you can use it with normal CMS commands. The ACCESS command lets you do this. Its syntax is:

```
ACCESS cuu filemode
```

For example, if you have linked another user's disk as cuu 199, and want to use it as your D disk, give the command:

```
ACCESS 199 D
```

From that point on, you can use any CMS command with the disk by specifying it with a filemode of D.

RELEASE Command

When you are finished using a disk, you should issue the RELEASE command. This command makes the files unavailable to you. The main reason for using it is politeness: If you have attached the disk and someone tries to link with an access mode that requires no other users be linked, they will not be able to get the link. If you have released the disk, they will get access.

The syntax of the RELEASE command is:

```
RELEASE { cuu | filemode } ( DET
```

You can either specify your cuu or the filemode, and you should always use the DET option (which is what makes the disk available to other users). For example, to detach the disk in the example in the ATTACH command, you can either give the command:

```
RELEASE D ( DET
```

or

```
RELEASE 199 ( DET
```

Note that logging off automatically releases a disk, so you do not need to give the RELEASE command before logging off.

NAMES Command

The NAMES command maintains your own personal database of names, addresses, and phone numbers of CMS users. Its most useful feature is that every person in the database can have a nickname you can use in other CMS commands; you use the nickname instead of having to remember everyone's userids. The TELL, NOTE, and SENDFILE commands (described later in this section) use the database to determine which userid is associated with the nickname.

Another interesting feature of the database is that you can make group nicknames. For example, if you regularly send the same memo to six people you work with, you can give that group of people a nickname and tell the database that that nickname refers to each of those people. When you use the NOTE or SENDFILE commands with a group nickname to send the memo, it is automatically sent to each person in the group.

The screen used in the NAMES command is based on XEDIT (described in Chapter 6). Like the FILELIST and HELP commands, you do not need to know much about XEDIT to use NAMES, but you will find many useful extensions when you read Chapter 6.

The names database is kept in the file "userid NAMES", where "userid" is your userid. It is a text file, so you can look through it with XEDIT or the TYPE command, although it is much easier to view and modify it with the NAMES command.

If you are not familiar with databases, a quick introduction is in order. A database holds groups of information; each group of information, called a *record*, has a similar structure. Each record is made up of *fields*; a field is a small piece of information, such as a name or a phone number. Each record has the same fields (although the fields have different information in them). Illustration 4-1 shows a pictorial view of a database.

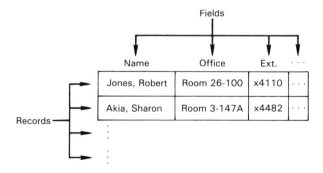

Illustration 4-1

In the names database, each record corresponds to a person or a group of people. The fields for each record are:

Nickname	Each record must have a nickname, which is used as the identifier for each record. The nickname can be up to eight characters long.
Userid	The userid of the person. Leave this field blank if this record is for a group of people.
Node	The node name of the computer on which this person has their userid. If it is the same as your computer, or if the record is for a group, you can leave this field blank.
Notebook	Generally, all notes that you prepare with the NOTE command (described later in this section) are kept in a single file called ALL NOTEBOOK. If you want to keep the notes sent to, and received from, this person in a different file, enter the filename in this field (the filetype is always NOTEBOOK).
Name	The person's name. This name is shown at the beginning of messages you send them, and you can feel free to show the name in any fashion you wish (last name first, first name first, or whatever). For a group, you may want to put a group descriptor in this field (such as "Accounts payable department").
Phone	The person's phone number.
Address	The person's address. You have up to four lines, and can format it any way you wish.
List of names	If this record is for a group, this list is each person in that group. There are three types of entries for this field:

- The person's userid (if they are on the same system as you)
- The person's userid, followed by "AT nodename," if they are on a different node of the network
- The person's nickname, if you have a separate entry for them in your database

Each name in the list of names is separated by a space.

When you run the NAMES command, your screen is set up so it is easy to enter and change the records. The NAMES screen looks like this:

```
 ====> SANDYL   NAMES    <========> N A M E S   F I L E   E D I T I N G  <====
Fill in the fields and press a PFkey to display and/or change your NAMES file.
Nickname: _        Userid:        Node:        Notebook:
                     Name:
                    Phone:
                  Address:
                        :
                        :
                        :
          List of Names:
                        :
                        :
                        :

You can enter optional information below.  Describe it by giving it a "tag".


Tag:              Value:
Tag:              Value:

1= Help      2= Add      3= Quit      4= Clear      5= Find      6= Change
7= Previous  8= Next     9=           10= Delete    11=          12= Cursor

====>
                                                    Macro-read 1 file
```

Fill in each field for the record and press the TAB key to go to the beginning of the next field. You can edit the text you enter with the cursor control keys and the editing keys you learned about in Chapter 2. When you finish filling in a record, press PF2 to add it to the database.

A couple of notes about filling in records:

- You can ignore the "Tag" and "Value" fields near the bottom of the screen; they are rarely useful.
- Do not use colons (:) in the text you enter in the fields. The NAMES program gets very confused if you have colons in the NAMES file.

The PF keys help you manipulate the database and enter information. Their uses in the NAMES program are:

PF1   Gives help on NAMES.

PF2   Adds the current record to the database.

PF3   Leaves the NAMES program.

PF4   Clears the fields. If you are entering more than one name in the database, press PF2 to save a record, then press PF4. This clears the information so you can enter the next person or group.

PF5	Finds a record in your database. Filling in any field on a clear screen and pressing PF5 causes NAMES to skip to the first record with that data. For instance, if you know someone's userid but not their nickname, enter their userid in the field and press PF5: NAMES displays that record.
PF6	Changes the record shown. Use this key instead of PF2 when you change information that is in the database, such as updating a telephone number or adding names to a group nickname.
PF7	Shows the previous record in the database.
PF8	Shows the next record in the database.
PF10	Deletes the record shown from the database.
PF12	Switches the cursor between the screen and the command line.

Changing records is just as easy as adding them. Using PF5, PF7, or PF8, find the record you want to change, use the editing keys to change it, then press PF6. If you are in CMS, you can give the NAMES command an operand of the nickname of the record you want to change, and it shows you that record first. Be sure to not change a record's nickname to one you have already used, since this can confuse the NAMES program.

When you start your database, you should definitely include a record for yourself. You can include any nickname, but be sure to have your proper userid. This record is used in the headings of letters that you send with the NOTE command, described later in this section.

The following is an example of a filled-in record for a person:

```
 ====> SANDYL   NAMES    <=========>  N A M E S   F I L E   E D I T I N G  <====
Fill in the fields and press a PFkey to display and/or change your NAMES file.
Nickname: MANUEL    Userid: MLOPEZ    Node:          Notebook:
                      Name: Manuel Lopez
                     Phone: x3-5902
                   Address: Advertising Dept.
                         : Room 5A
                         : Main Office
                         :
           List of Names:
                         :
                         :
                         :

You can enter optional information below.  Describe it by giving it a "tag".

Tag:              Value:
Tag:              Value:

1= Help      2= Add     3= Quit     4= Clear    5= Find      6= Change
7= Previous  8= Next    9=          10= Delete  11=          12= Cursor

====>
                                          Macro-read 1 file
```

Here is an example of a group list:

```
====> SANDYL   NAMES    <=========> N A M E S   F I L E   E D I T I N G  <====
Fill in the fields and press a PFkey to display and/or change your NAMES file.
Nickname: RADIOAD  Userid:        Node:        Notebook:
                   Name: Radio advertising group
                   Phone: x4-2700
                 Address:
                        :
                        :
                        :
           List of Names: MANUEL FRANK72 JLASTR
                        : VERA AT LONDON
                        :
                        :

You can enter optional information below.  Describe it by giving it a "tag".

Tag:              Value:
Tag:              Value:

1= Help      2= Add      3= Quit      4= Clear     5= Find     6= Change
7= Previous  8= Next     9=          10= Delete    11=        12= Cursor

====>
                                              Macro-read 1 file
```

TELL Command

The TELL command displays a message on the screens of one or more users. The message only appears if the user is logged on and receiving messages. The syntax of the TELL command is:

```
TELL name message
```

The name can be one of the following:

- A nickname from your names database.
- The userid of a person on your computer.
- The userid of a person on the network, followed by "AT nodename".

The message can be up to approximately 240 characters, depending on the length of the input field of your terminal (that is, you can enter up to the end of the input field).

If you use a nickname for a group of people, the message is sent to each person in the group. For example, you might give the following command:

```
TELL MANUEL Is the car loan ad running in Chapel Hill yet? I just heard
from them.
```

The TELL command first looks in your names database for a nickname of MANUEL; if it doesn't find it, it looks for a user whose userid is MANUEL. On MANUEL's screen, he would see:

```
MSG FROM SANDYL: Is the car loan ad running in Chapel Hill yet? I just
heard from them.
```

Users can prevent messages from appearing with the SET MSG OFF command. If they have done this, or they are not logged on, they will not get your message. The TELL command tells you the message did not get through and why.

Out of courtesy, you should probably not overuse the TELL command. Just as it is sometimes annoying to get many short phone calls when you are busy, it is also annoying to get many messages on the screen. Also, if you are not at your terminal, it is sometimes disturbing to come back to a screen full (or many screens full) of messages from various people.

Test the TELL command by sending yourself a message. Use the nickname you gave yourself in the NAMES command.

NOTE Command

A note is similar to a letter. You can include as much or as little information in it as you want. When you send the note with the NOTE command, the heading of the note is automatically set up like a memo (with your name, the recipient's name, and the date at the top). The note is sent to the recipient's virtual reader.

The NOTE command uses XEDIT to prepare the note. Thus, you should probably not use the NOTE command until you have read Chapter 6 and are comfortable with running XEDIT.

When you send a note, the NOTE command first sets up the letter. It then puts you into the XEDIT editor so you can compose the note. When you are finished, the NOTE command takes the file you have created and sends it to the people you specified.

Like the TELL command, the NOTE command uses the names database for translating nicknames into userids. It also uses the database for expanding userids into full names, if you wish. If there is an entry for userid in the database, it uses information from that record in the header.

The syntax of the NOTE command is:

```
NOTE [ name ... ] [ CC: name ... ] [ ( options ]
options:
[ NOACK | ACK ]
[ LOG | NOLOG ]
[ SHORT | LONG ]
[ PROFILE fn ]
```

The names you specify can be one of the following:

• A nickname from your names database (this can be a nickname for an individual or a group).
• The userid of a person on your computer.
• The userid of a person on the network, followed by "AT nodename".

Names that appear in the first group of names appear under the heading "To:" in the letter; names that appear after "CC:" appear under the heading "CC:". The options are:

NOACK   No acknowledgment is sent to you.

ACK   If you want to know when a person read the note you sent, you can give the ACK option. When the person reads the note, CMS sends a note back to you telling you the time they read the note you sent.

LOG
:   The NOTE command usually keeps a record of each note you send in the file called "userid NETLOG" (where "userid" is your userid). If you specify an acknowledgment, it appears in the log as well.

NOLOG
:   This tells the NOTE command not to log this note.

SHORT
:   The NOTE command can put a long or short heading in the note. The short heading contains your name, telephone number, userid, and the recipient's userid. It looks something like this:

```
Date: 17 April 1988, 4:27:32 PST
From: Manuel Lopez   x3-5902     MLOPEZ at ADMIN
To:   EBERRY
```

LONG
:   The long heading contains your name, telephone number, userid, node, and full address, and the recipient's name, telephone number, and userid. It looks something like this:

```
Date: 17 April 1988, 4:27:32 PST
From: Manuel Lopez   x3-5902     MLOPEZ at ADMIN
      Regional Manager
      Advertising Department
      Main Office, Room 5A
To:   Ellen Berry    x2-7166     EBERRY at ADMIN
```

PROFILE fn
:   The meaning of the PF keys in the NOTE environment is different than that of your standard XEDIT PF keys. If you want to use your own XEDIT profile instead of the NOTE commands profile, you must specify its name in this option.

When you enter the NOTE command, you are placed in XEDIT with the headings already prepared for you. You can add the text, edit the headings, and do whatever you would like to the text. When you are ready to send the note, enter the SEND command on the XEDIT command line. The note is logged and sent.

Notes on using the NOTE command:

- You do not need to make a group nickname to send a note to a few people. Simply list the names in the command line, such as:

```
NOTE BILLN JSAMUEL
```

- While you are editing a note, you can decide to add or delete names in the list you gave from CMS. To add names, enter the following command on the XEDIT command line:

```
NOTE name ... ( ADD
```

This lets you use nicknames just as you did on the command line.

To delete names, simply remove them from the list at the top of the file. Use the standard editing keys to remove the names you wish.

- The first line of your note contains options from the command line. It might look something like this:

```
OPTIONS: NOACK  LOG  SHORT  NOTEBOOK ALL
```

This line is not, of course, sent with the message. It is there for NOTE's convenience.

When you get familiar with XEDIT, you will see that using NOTE to send messages is quite simple. Some of XEDIT's features, such as split-screen editing and the ability to include other files in your note, make it an excellent environment for creating messages. These features combined with NOTE's capability to easily send to many people and to format the beginning of the note give you an excellent message-sending system.

SENDFILE Command

The SENDFILE command is similar to the NOTE command, except that you use it to send existing files instead of creating them from within the command. Use the SENDFILE command to send documents, reports, data files, or any other CMS files to other CMS users.

The syntax of the SENDFILE command is also similar to the NOTE command:

```
SENDFILE [ fn ft [fm] [ name ... ] [ ( options ]
options:

[ NOACK | ACK ]
[ LOG | NOLOG ]
[ NEW | OLD ]
[ TYPE | NOTYPE ]
```

If you give no arguments or options to the SENDFILE command, SENDFILE displays an interactive screen described soon.

You cannot use the * and % wildcard characters in the filename and filetype. The NOACK, ACK, LOG, and NOLOG options are the same as in the NOTE command. The names that you specify can be one of the following:

- A nickname from your names database (this can be a nickname for an individual or a group).
- The userid of a person on your computer.
- The userid of a person on the network, followed by "AT nodename".

The NEW option specifies that certain special information is added to the file (this is sometimes called the *NETDATA* format). That added information is removed when the user receives the file with the RDRLIST command described later in this section; the file that arrives is exactly the same as the one you sent. The RDRLIST command uses another CMS command, RECEIVE, to read the file. If, for some reason, the recipient does not have the RECEIVE command available (this is rare), you should use the OLD option; in this case, SENDFILE uses an older and less efficient format called *DISK DUMP* format to send the file.

The TYPE option tells SENDFILE to display information on your screen about the file sent and the recipient; this is often useful. Note that the TYPE option doesn't display the file on your screen. If you don't want to see the display (such as if you are sending dozens of files or a file to many people), use the NOTYPE option.

Like the NOTE command, SENDFILE puts the files in the recipients' virtual reader; they put the files on their disk with the RDRLIST command.

Giving the SENDFILE command with no arguments displays the following screen:

```
---------------- SENDFILE ----------------
File(s) to be sent    (use * for Filename, Filetype and/or Filemode
                           to select from a list of files)
Enter filename : _
      filetype :
      filemode :

Send files to  :

Type over YES or NO to change the options:

   NO    Request acknowledgment when the file has been received?

   YES   Make a log entry when the file has been sent?

   YES   Display the file name when the file has been sent?

   NO    This file is actually a list of files to be sent?

   1= Help          3= Quit          5= Send          12= Cursor

====>
                                        Macro-read 1 file
```

Fill in the filename, filetype, filemode (the filemode defaults to A), and the names of the recipients. You can use the * and % wildcard characters in the filename and filetype. Using these characters on this screen doesn't indicate that you want to send all files that match the specification. Instead, you are presented with a FILELIST screen that matches the specification, and you can choose which files you want to send from that screen.

The first three options correspond to the NOACK/ACK, LOG/NOLOG, and TYPE/NOTYPE options; the last option is meant mostly for advanced users who often send the same list of files. When you have filled in the screen, press PF5.

If you have named only one file (that is, haven't used wildcard characters), SENDFILE sends the file. If you have used wildcard characters, you see something like the following screen:

```
SANDYL     FILELIST A0   V 108   Trunc=108 Size=4 Line=1 Col=1 Alt=0
Cmd    Filename Filetype Fm Format Lrecl      Records       Blocks   Date      Time
_      REMIND   SCRIPT   A1 V          80         312            2   9/13/87 08:34:15
       REMINDA  SCRIPT   A1 V          80         691            4   9/13/87 09:12:53
       REMINDB  SCRIPT   A1 V          80          44            1   9/13/87 09:14:00
       REMINDC  SCRIPT   A1 V          80         103            1   9/13/87 09:14:43




1= Help       2= Refresh  3= Quit    4= Sort(type)  5= Sendfile    6= Sort(size)
7= Backward   8= Forward  9= FL /n  10=             11= XEDIT      12= Cursor
Type 'S' in front of each file to be sent and press Enter.
====>
                                                    X E D I T 1 file
```

Type an "S" in the CMD field for each file you want to send, then press PF5. You can use the rest of the FILELIST commands and options just as you normally would. When you press PF5, your files are sent and you return to the previous screen. If you want to stay in the FILELIST screen, instead of pressing PF5, simply press ENTER.

RDRLIST Command

When notes or files are sent to you, they arrive in your virtual reader. To get the files out of the virtual reader and on to your minidisk, use the RDRLIST command. The RDRLIST command is very similar to the FILELIST command; its screen looks like this:

```
SANDYL    RDRLIST   A0   V 108   Trunc=108 Size=2 Line=1 Col=1 Alt=0
Cmd    Filename Filetype Class User  at Node    Hold  Records  Date      Time
_      MANUEL   MAIL     PUN A MANUEL    ADMIN   NONE       7 08/01    10:13:58
       START    EXEC     PUN A LDUNNE    ADMIN   NONE       7 08/01    11:32:08




















1= Help      2= Refresh  3= Quit      4= Sort(type) 5= Sort(date) 6= Sort(user)
7= Backward  8= Forward  9= Receive   10=            11= Peek      12= Cursor

====>
                                                        X E D I T  1 file
```

Most of the PF keys are the same as the ones you are used to. The PF keys tailored for the RDRLIST command are PF9 (RECEIVE) and PF11 (PEEK). To move files from the virtual reader to your minidisk, put the cursor on the line with the file's name and press PF9. If you want to look in the file before you put it on disk, you can look at the first few hundred lines of its contents with the PF11 key.

You can receive many files at once by typing the RECEIVE command on the line of the first file, placing an equal sign (=) in the CMD field for each file, and pressing ENTER.

Files with filetype MAIL were sent with the NOTE command, and the RDRLIST command treats them in a special fashion. Instead of putting them on your minidisk, it appends them to your ALL NOTEBOOK file. This is quite useful for two reasons. If RDRLIST simply put the file on your disk, you could only have one note from each CMS user at a time, since all files from one user would have the same name. Also, this is a good method for keeping all your correspondence in one place.

There are many times when you want to replace a file on your disk with one from the RDRLIST command. For example, someone may be sending you an updated version of a group memorandum. Of course, it is a good idea to check the contents of the file in the list with the PEEK command (PF11) before you replace the file on your disk.

Replacing a file on your disk is not so easy in the RDRLIST command. To replace a file on your disk with one from the list, type the following line on the file's line and press enter:

```
RECEIVE / /nt ( REPLACE
```

This invokes the RECEIVE command with the correct arguments and the REPLACE option.

There are also many times you do not want to keep the file at all. Use the DISCARD command to throw away a file in the list. For instance, assume you have been away for a few days and you see the following in your RDRLIST screen:

```
 SANDYL    RDRLIST   A0   V 108   Trunc=108 Size=6 Line=1 Col=1 Alt=0
Cmd    Filename Filetype Class User  at Node    Hold  Records  Date      Time
 _     LDUNNE   MAIL     PUN A LDUNNE   ADMIN   NONE      7 08/01    10:13:58
       FINAL    REPORT   PUN A LDUNNE   ADMIN   NONE      7 08/01    10:14:02
       LDUNNE   MAIL     PUN A LDUNNE   ADMIN   NONE      7 08/04    14:32:17
       FINAL    REPORT   PUN A LDUNNE   ADMIN   NONE      7 08/04    14:32:55
       LDUNNE   MAIL     PUN A LDUNNE   ADMIN   NONE      7 08/05    08:14:19
       FINAL    REPORT   PUN A LDUNNE   ADMIN   NONE      7 08/05    08:16:19




1= Help      2= Refresh  3= Quit     4= Sort(type) 5= Sort(date) 6= Sort(user)
7= Backward  8= Forward  9= Receive  10=           11= Peek      12= Cursor

====>
                                                      X E D I T 1 file
```

There are three mail messages and three copies of the same file, sent on three different days. After you peek at the mail messages, you see that they preceded three drafts of the same report. If all you care about is the current draft, you want to discard the first two copies of the file and store the current one on your disk. You can do so in the following fashion:

```
 SANDYL    RDRLIST  A0   V 108   Trunc=108 Size=6 Line=1 Col=1 Alt=0
 Cmd    Filename Filetype Class User  at Node    Hold  Records  Date      Time
        LDUNNE   MAIL     PUN A LDUNNE   ADMIN   NONE      7 08/01   10:13:58
 DISCARDINAL     REPORT   PUN A LDUNNE   ADMIN   NONE      7 08/01   10:14:02
        LDUNNE   MAIL     PUN A LDUNNE   ADMIN   NONE      7 08/04   14:32:17
 =_     FINAL    REPORT   PUN A LDUNNE   ADMIN   NONE      7 08/04   14:32:55
        LDUNNE   MAIL     PUN A LDUNNE   ADMIN   NONE      7 08/05   08:14:19
        FINAL    REPORT   PUN A LDUNNE   ADMIN   NONE      7 08/05   08:16:19




 1= Help      2= Refresh  3= Quit      4= Sort(type) 5= Sort(date) 6= Sort(user)
 7= Backward  8= Forward  9= Receive  10=           11= Peek       12= Cursor

 ====>
                                                      X E D I T 1 file
```

When you press ENTER, the first two copies of FINAL REPORT are discarded:

```
 SANDYL    RDRLIST  A0   V 108   Trunc=108 Size=6 Line=1 Col=1 Alt=0
 Cmd    Filename Filetype Class User  at Node    Hold  Records  Date      Time
        LDUNNE   MAIL     PUN A LDUNNE   ADMIN   NONE      7 08/01   10:13:58
 *      FINAL    REPORT   has been discarded.
        LDUNNE   MAIL     PUN A LDUNNE   ADMIN   NONE      7 08/04   14:32:17
 *      FINAL    REPORT   has been discarded.
 _      LDUNNE   MAIL     PUN A LDUNNE   ADMIN   NONE      7 08/05   08:14:19
        FINAL    REPORT   PUN A LDUNNE   ADMIN   NONE      7 08/05   08:16:19




 1= Help      2= Refresh  3= Quit      4= Sort(type) 5= Sort(date) 6= Sort(user)
 7= Backward  8= Forward  9= Receive  10=           11= Peek       12= Cursor

 ====>
                                                      X E D I T 1 file
```

You can then receive the other files in the normal fashion.

FINDING OUT ABOUT OTHER COMMANDS

The IBM documentation describes dozens of other CMS commands. Some may be useful to you in different circumstances, especially if you are a programmer or work with the results of programmers' work. See Appendix D for suggestions about which IBM manuals will be most useful for you.

5

Introduction to CMS Applications and Utilities

The CMS commands you have seen so far help you use CMS. They don't do anything applicable to business (like accounting or graphics); they simply exist to make your interaction with the computer easier.

Of course, there is no reason to have a computer if all you can do with it is give commands that only relate to the computer. The main reason to use a computer is to use applications. You use CMS commands to support the application programs you are running.

Some people differentiate between "applications" and "utilities." In general, applications are programs that help you do business, and utilities are programs that help you run your computer. However, there is a very large overlap between the two categories, and it is usually not important to pigeonhole programs into one or the other category. For convenience, this book includes "utilities" as part of "applications."

This chapter gives an introduction to the main applications and programming languages sold or provided by IBM. Chapters 6 and 7 give more detail about the three that come as part of CMS: XEDIT, REXX, and EXEC2. Appendix A talks about applications sold by other companies.

There are many sources for applications:

- One of the biggest sellers of applications is IBM itself. Through its various departments, you can buy thousands of large and small CMS programs for a tremendous variety of tasks.
- There are also hundreds of companies that sell CMS applications. Some of these companies have only a single product, while others support dozens of programs.
- Colleges and universities also produce many CMS programs, and often give out their programs for free. Although many of these programs are mostly of use to other academics, some have wide use in the business community.
- Most companies that run CMS generate their own programs. These programs are specifically tailored to the needs of the company and are usually not available to other companies.

Note that commercial CMS applications vary widely in cost. IBM and CMS software companies often charge based on the size of the computer on which the application will be running. Some applications can cost hundreds of thousands of dollars.

By the way, you may notice that almost all IBM program names are acronyms. Many CMS users can rattle off all the acronyms as if they were common words. The more familiar you get with CMS, the more sense these acronyms will make to you.

COMMON IBM APPLICATIONS

IBM sells hundreds of CMS applications. The ones listed here are the most popular programs.

XEDIT (System Product Editor)

As you have seen throughout this manual, XEDIT is a very versatile program. It is much more than just an editor of text files. Many CMS commands, such as HELP and FILELIST, use XEDIT as an *environment*. An environment is a program that can be used as a base for other programs. XEDIT is similar to a food processor: You can add attachments to perform tasks (such as kneading dough or grating cheese) that are quite different from the ones it performs by itself.

Since these other programs use XEDIT as a base, they often act in a similar fashion. This makes learning to use them much easier. For instance, programs such as HELP and FILELIST use PF7 to move ahead one screen and PF8 to move back one screen. When you come across a new program that uses the XEDIT base, you can generally assume that PF7 and PF8 work the same way.

XEDIT is also extremely powerful. You can write XEDIT *macros*, which are similar to CMS EXECs. If you perform the set of XEDIT steps over and over, you can save those steps in a file and execute the file. Advanced users can make XEDIT macros that do incredible tasks in a single step.

If You Are Familiar With Other Computers

Very few operating systems come with a full-featured text editor as part of the package. Since XEDIT is part of CMS, and since XEDIT is very powerful and extensible, it has caused most other application developers to work with XEDIT in their products, or to at least mimic many of its capabilities.

REXX and EXEC2

IBM provides two *command interpreters* for CMS — REXX and EXEC2. A command interpreter is a program that lets you create lists of commands to run in sequence (these have been called EXECs in this book). You store these lists in files, then execute the commands in the list with the batch interpreter. Note that these command interpreters are different from the CMSBATCH command, which allows you to perform long automated tasks without using your terminal.

IBM's first CMS command interpreter was EXEC; they followed it with EXEC2. In 1983, they released REXX, which is significantly more powerful, and much easier to use, than EXEC2. Chapter 7 covers REXX in detail and EXEC2 lightly, since it is very likely you will only use REXX.

As you will see, REXX does much more than simply execute a list of CMS commands. It lets you decide which commands to run based on the results of previous commands. It also lets you construct lists of commands that act like programs. For instance, you can make an EXEC that runs a program, then asks you which of two programs you want to run next, based on the output of the first one.

PROFS (Professional Office System)

The PROFS system is IBM's foray into the office automation market. PROFS is a combined document-processing and electronic mail system. It also contains an integrated user interface that is different from CMS. If you are using PROFS, you will see that the PF keys have different meanings than in CMS, and you cannot reset their meaning. The PROFS screen design and the editor are also different from CMS's. You can run all CMS commands from within PROFS, but it is mostly used for people who don't use many CMS commands.

GML and DCF

IBM was one of the pioneers in advanced document processing. Much of this pioneering was done for their own in-house uses: With thousands of manuals to write and keep track of, IBM needed a consistent and powerful document system.

In the late 1970s, IBM developed the Generalized Markup Language, or GML. GML is a system for adding information to a document that aids in the formatting of the document. For example, there are ways of indicating which parts of the document are headings, which parts are lists, which parts are regular paragraphs, and so on. For example, the NAMES file uses GML tags.

GML is part of the Document Composition Facility, or DCF. Although using GML is sufficient for most people, some need more formatting control. DCF includes the SCRIPT language that lets you control the printing characteristics of each part of a document, such as which words are in italics or where to put lines on a page.

To create GML and DCF documents, you use XEDIT to make text files. These text files are then processed by programs to produce all the correct codes to make printers produce formatted pages.

If You Are Familiar With Other Computers

GML and DCF are two-step text processors. They do not show you what your document looks like as you are producing it. Most document products on microcomputers are *WYSIWYG* (what-you-see-is-what-you-get), which is often much easier to use than two-step text processors like GML. DCF is like SCRIPT and TROFF on UNIX systems.

SolutionPac for Publishing

IBM has bundled some special additions to GML into a special package that is aimed at book and magazine publishers. The additions make it easier to lay out the pages of magazines and to see the results of formatting changes. The SolutionPac also contains additional formatting styles that are specially tailored for publishers. It is a superset of GML and DCF with additional document viewing facilities.

ISPF

ISPF was developed for people who used the TSO operating system and have to start using CMS. ISPF mimics the TSO editing environment, which is especially useful for programmers. If you did not first use TSO, it is unlikely you will use ISPF.

SQL/DS

IBM's multi-user database management system for CMS is SQL/DS. It has many of the features that large database management systems from other vendors have, as well as using the new standard SQL for entering commands. Since databases are used so heavily, there is a great deal of competition in the database field. Many of IBM's competitors have products with features similar to SQL/DS. You should examine many database management systems before choosing one.

TSAF (Transparent Services Access Facility)

IBM included TSAF in version 5 of CMS. It allows applications running on different computers to communicate. It was designed to be used specifically by SQL/DS to create distributed database applications, but it can be used by many other programs as well.

RSCS (Remote Spooling Communications Subsystem)

RSCS is a network program that lets nodes on the network communicate. You use it to execute programs on nodes other than your own, or to check on the status of other nodes. It is also the principal method for submitting batch jobs on other computers. Almost every site that has networked VM machines has RSCS.

VTAM

VTAM allows users on networked VM computers to log on to different computers. For instance, if you have a userid on more than one computer, you can use VTAM to log on to each of your userids.

ICU

IBM's Interactive Chart Utility lets you create business charts and graphics if you have a graphics 3270. Business charts consist of pie charts, bar charts, and the like, that are based on data. The data is usually generated by other CMS programs. You can also create charts with words and simple drawings to produce slides and overhead transparencies. To use ICU, you need to have special graphics output devices, such as color printers and plotters, attached to your mainframe.

PROGRAMMING LANGUAGES

The following languages are all available from IBM. The only language that comes with CMS is Assembler, which is a smaller version of Assembler H (described soon). All of the programming languages have features that allow you to find problems in programs interactively.

COBOL

COBOL is still the most popular language in business computing. IBM has consistently put tremendous amounts of resources behind COBOL development, so that COBOL on IBM computers is considered the standard for COBOL computing.

Some younger programmers find that the COBOL language is not as easy to learn as other computer languages. Others contend that, once a COBOL program is written, it is often difficult to make changes to it without inducing new problems. Thus, many people learning computers have stayed away from COBOL in favor of other computer languages. However, since COBOL remains so popular, there is still a very strong demand for experienced COBOL programmers in large companies.

FORTRAN

FORTRAN was originally designed as the engineer's computer language. Its initial strengths were the ability to easily enter mathematical equations and perform steps in loops in a well-defined fashion. Like COBOL, many new languages have made giant improvements on these features, but, also like COBOL, FORTRAN is still well-entrenched in many circles. IBM's FORTRAN is especially strong on campuses and in manufacturing organizations.

PL/I

IBM invented PL/I as their all-purpose language in the late 1960s. Programs written in PL/I are easier to write and read than either COBOL or FORTRAN since it is easier to see each program's structure. For many years, IBM pushed PL/I as the programming language of the future, but it has not been as successful as IBM expected.

Pascal

Pascal is another modern, structured language that has become very popular on microcomputers; this has made it more popular on mainframes. IBM's Pascal compiler is used for many applications, especially finance.

BASIC

Due to BASIC's rampant popularity on microcomputers, IBM also developed a BASIC language for CMS. It is rarely used for any program development since most other languages are more efficient than BASIC. Also, REXX has as many, if not more, capabilities than BASIC and is supported much more heavily by IBM; also, REXX comes as part of CMS.

ASSEMBLER H

The ASSEMBLER H language is used to write programs that directly interact with the computer hardware. ASSEMBLER H programs are much harder to write and *debug* (assure that they are correct), but they run significantly faster than programs in any other language. To use ASSEMBLER H, the programmer must have an in-depth knowledge of how the hardware operates; other programming languages insulate you from this level of understanding.

LISP

The new field of artificial intelligence (AI) has spawned many programs for mainframes. LISP is one of the most popular languages for AI. LISP is structured very differently from other programming languages, and most people not interested in AI find it very hard to learn or use.

APL

For people who use matrix arithmetic a great deal, APL is an ideal language. It was developed specifically for matrix handling. Unfortunately, you need a special keyboard to program in APL.

GDDM

GDDM is not really a language, but a set of utilities that go with programming languages. It is IBM's base graphic language utility. GDDM lets the programmer create advanced graphics programs. GDDM is a method for making programs work with different graphics devices, such as printers, plotters, and 3270 terminals that have graphics attributes.

REXX

Although REXX was discussed earlier in this chapter as an application, it can also be viewed as a programming language. It offers programmers many of the best features of modern programming languages such as Pascal. Novice users can use REXX knowing almost nothing about programming; programmers can use it as a programming language coupled with the operating system.

6

Introduction to XEDIT

Throughout this book, you have been told that XEDIT is a wonderful editor that will be explained in Chapter 6. Hopefully, your anticipation has not turned to frustration. One of the reasons that this book has been promoting XEDIT so heavily is that it is one of the most useful features of CMS.

Although XEDIT is mostly used as an editor, advanced CMS users use it as a work environment. You have already seen many other CMS commands that work under XEDIT (FILELIST, HELP, and so on).

This chapter shows you how to use XEDIT and, by extension, how to use programs that use the XEDIT environment. The thrust of the chapter is on using XEDIT to edit your text files. Since XEDIT was really designed to be used with 3270-type terminals, all the examples are for 3270s. There is a section at the end of the chapter with a description of how to use XEDIT on ASCII terminals.

WHAT IS AN EDITOR?

An editor has three basic functions: creating text files, viewing text files, and modifying text files. Thus, an editor is a go-between for you and text files. This section explains concepts that are the same for all text editors. (Note that although XEDIT can edit nontext files, it is rarely used for this.)

You have already seen how to create text files: You start the editor, enter the editor's *input mode*, type in text, save the file, then quit from the editor. These steps are typical of creating files in all editors. When you are in input mode, everything you type is entered into the file. Thus, you can create long or short files using these steps.

Viewing a File

When you use an editor to view a text file, you do not change any of the text in the file. Instead, you use a limited number of editor commands to move around in the file. The steps are: You start the editor, use the editor's *movement* commands to see the various parts of the file, then quit from the editor.

As shown in Illustration 6-1, editors treat your terminal like a window in the file. Initially, the window is over the first part of the file, as shown in Illustration 6-2. When you give a command to move forward, the window slides down the text, as can be seen in Illustration 6-3. As can be seen in Illustration 6-4, each time you move forward, the window slides further down the text. If you give a command to move backward, the window slides up. For example, you have given two forward commands. If you now give a backward command, the window would be at the same position it was before you gave the second forward command, as shown in Illustration 6-5.

Thus, editors let you slide the window anywhere in the text. Most editors also have commands that let you quickly move the window to the beginning or the end of the file.

112

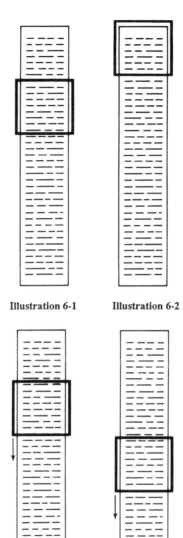

Illustration 6-1   Illustration 6-2

Illustration 6-3   Illustration 6-4

Editors also let you search for a particular part of a file. For example, you can tell an editor to show you the 50th line of a file; as can be seen in Illustration 6-6, the window automatically slides to show you that line, as well as the lines above and below it.

You can also give the editor a command that tells it to search through the file for the next instance of a certain set of characters (such as a word or a phrase). For instance, assume that the window is currently at the beginning of a long report, and you want to find the first

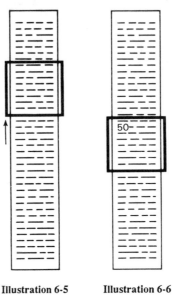

Illustration 6-5   **Illustration 6-6**

Illustration 6-7

time the word "salary" is mentioned. As shown in Illustration 6-7, when you gave the appropriate command, the editor would move the window to be over the line with that word. You can then ask it to repeat the find operation to look for "Salary" or use the other movement commands.

These commands do not affect the information in the file. They simply allow you to browse through the file in the same way you would look through a printed document.

> **If You Are Familiar With Other Computers**
>
> Computers with graphics interfaces, such as the Macintosh, let you move the window over the text by clicking at up and down arrows in the window. This makes moving over the text much more smooth than text-based editors. You can also jump to a part of the file by dragging a box in the border to the relative location in the file you want to view. For example, to see text about two-thirds of the way from the beginning of the file, you would drag the scroll box two-thirds of the way down the side of the window.

Changing the Contents of a File

Of course, the major task of editors is to change the text in a file. There are generally five distinct ways in which you modify text:

- delete
- add
- change
- move
- copy

Deleting text can be done in two fashions. The simple method for deleting small chunks of text is to place the cursor at the beginning of the text and remove characters to the right with the delete (*i*) key. The more complex method is to select the beginning and end of the area you want to delete and then delete the entire selected area at once. Note that deleting text does not leave a "hole" in your file: The text that was after the deleted section is moved so it is together with the text that was before the deleted section.

For example, assume you want to delete the second sentence in the following paragraph:

```
National Packaging has been very successful in attracting new
clients in the last two years. Our annual revenues have grown from
$7.3 million to $16.8 million since January 1986, and our profits
have grown from $1.1 million to $2.2 million. Our staff has
grown from 27 to 63.
```

When you remove the second sentence, the third sentence moves up:

```
National Packaging has been very successful in attracting new
clients in the last two years.
Our staff has
grown from 27 to 63.
```

When you add text, you choose where you want the text inserted and give the command to put you in insert mode. As you insert text, all text after the inserted text is moved so the inserted area does not "overlap" with the current text. For instance, if you add text after the first sentence in the previous paragraph, the second paragraph simply moves over:

```
National Packaging has been very successful in attracting new
clients in the last two years. This is some new text.
```

```
Our staff has
grown from 27 to 63.
```

Changing text is really a combination of deleting the old text and adding the new text. When you change text, the editor performs these two steps for you simultaneously.

To move text, you first select the beginning and end of the area you want to move, then select the spot you want to move the text to. Note that the destination is a single point in the text, not another area. The editor then deletes the selected text from its original position and inserts it beginning at the destination point. Copying text is very similar to moving it, except the editor does not delete the selected text.

Saving a File on Disk

When you are editing a file, you are not really changing the contents of the file on your minidisk. Instead, you are changing an *image* of the file that is in the computer's memory. The file on the minidisk still looks the same.

To have the changes you make to the image of the file be permanent, you must save the file image to disk. In XEDIT, you do that with the SAVE or FILE commands, as you will see soon. Until you do so, your changes are not on disk. Thus, if you are editing and your computer crashes, your work is lost unless you saved it to your minidisk (you will see later how to make XEDIT a bit safer than this).

XEDIT MACROS

Generally, you will use XEDIT for interactive editing. As you read this chapter, you will see that XEDIT has many commands. You can place those commands in a file and execute them without having to interact with XEDIT. XEDIT command files are often called *macro files*.

The PROFILE XEDIT file contains XEDIT commands, and has a similar use to your PROFILE EXEC file. Each time you run XEDIT, it first executes the commands in your PROFILE XEDIT file. You will see shortly that this is very useful since there are many commands which make using XEDIT much easier than it is normally.

STARTING AND STOPPING XEDIT

There are two common ways to start the XEDIT program: from the CMS command line and from the FILELIST program. From the command line, the syntax for the XEDIT command is:

```
XEDIT fileid [ ( options ]
options:
[ NOSCREEN ]
```

Although you used the NOSCREEN option earlier in this book, it was only there to prevent you from dealing with full-screen XEDIT before you had read this chapter.

When you run XEDIT, you must supply a fileid so XEDIT knows what file to edit. If you wish, you can give the name of a file that does not exist; XEDIT uses that name when it creates a new file for you.

Starting XEDIT from the FILELIST command is much simpler than from the CMS command line. In FILELIST, simply move the cursor to the line for the file you want to edit and press PF11, or you can enter "XEDIT" on the command line.

If you use XEDIT simply to view a file, and don't make any changes, you use the QUIT command to leave XEDIT. If you have edited your file, you have two choices for leaving from XEDIT. You can either quit the program without saving changes to the file, or save the changes to the file as you leave. While you are running XEDIT, the program monitors whether you give only viewing commands (ones which only move around in the file) or if you give editing commands (ones which change the file).

To leave XEDIT, you use three different commands:

- The QUIT command leaves XEDIT if you have only used viewing commands. If you have changed the file, the QUIT command does not work. This is a safety feature: You cannot accidentally use the QUIT command and lose all of the work you did changing the file. The PF3 key is the same as the QUIT command.

- The QQUIT (quick quit) command leaves XEDIT without saving your changes, even if you have made editing commands. This should be used cautiously, since you can lose your work if you accidentally use the QQUIT command before saving any changes you want. However, if you have made a mess of a file (such as by giving the wrong XEDIT commands), you can use QQUIT to get you back to where you started.

- The FILE command saves the changes to the file and leaves XEDIT. This is the equivalent of giving the "SAVE" command (to save the file on disk) followed by the "QUIT" command. If you have edited the file, this is the command to use to return to CMS or FILELIST.

While you are running XEDIT, you can always use its HELP command to get assistance. The XEDIT HELP command is structured just like the CMS HELP command, so you can use it to find command syntaxes and so on.

YOUR PROFILE XEDIT FILE

If you start XEDIT without having a good PROFILE XEDIT file, you may find that many of XEDIT's default settings are not to your liking. All users have preferences for how they want to interact with XEDIT. Fortunately, it is easy to create a good PROFILE XEDIT.

You may already have an PROFILE XEDIT file on your minidisk. Many system administrators give users an PROFILE XEDIT when they assign a userid. Use the LISTFILE command to see if the file already exists; if it does, check with your system administrator about adding the lines shown soon.

The macro listed next makes XEDIT much friendlier and easier to use. The examples in this chapter assume you have this PROFILE XEDIT file (or one that has these commands and others). The file looks like this:

```
/* Profile for XEDIT  */
SET ARBCHAR ON $
SET AUTOSAVE 10
SET CASE MIXED IGNORE
SET CMDLINE TOP
SET CURLINE ON 6
SET MSGLINE ON 3 3 OVERLAY
SET NONDISP |
SET NULLS ON
SET SCALE ON 3
SET SPAN ON BLANK 3
SET STAY ON
SET VARBLANK ON
SET WRAP ON
/* The next 4 lines display a line at the bottom of the XEDIT screen */
EXTRACT "/LSCREEN"
Lres = "1 = Help   3 = Quit   6 = ?   7 = Backward   "
Rres = "8 = Forward   9 = =   11 = Spltjoin"
SET RESERVED LSCREEN.5 NOHIGH Lres Rres
```

These commands are explained throughout this chapter.

If someone else at your site has already entered this PROFILE XEDIT from the book, you should get this person to send it to you with the SENDFILE command to save typing. You can then move it to your minidisk with the RDRLIST command.

To enter the PROFILE XEDIT yourself, you use the XEDIT NOSCREEN option one last time. From CMS give the command:

```
XEDIT PROFILE XEDIT A (NOSCREEN
```

During this process, if your screen fills up, remember to press the CLEAR key to continue.

After you give the XEDIT command, you see:

```
DMSXSU587I XEDIT:
```

Next, give the SET CASE MIXED command, then the INPUT command so you can add new text to the file:

```
SET CASE MIXED
INPUT
```

XEDIT tells you that you are in input mode:

```
DMSXMD573I Input mode:
```

Now, type the lines in the file exactly as they appear here. Press the ENTER key after you type in each line.

When you have entered these lines, press the ENTER key again (with no text in the user input area). XEDIT responds:

```
DMSXMD587I XEDIT:
```

Now give the FILE command to tell XEDIT you are done with this file. XEDIT saves the changes you have made and shows you the ready message to indicate you are now back in CMS. If you made errors when you were inputting the file, you can start over by using the QQUIT command and going through the steps again.

The next time you run XEDIT, the commands in this file are automatically executed.

XEDIT COMMANDS

When you enter XEDIT commands, you type in the command in the command area and press the ENTER key, just as in CMS. Pressing the ENTER key tells the computer to perform the command and update the screen. Throughout this chapter, when you are instructed to give a command, follow it by pressing ENTER.

You will also see a great similarity between XEDIT commands and CMS commands. XEDIT commands have arguments and options like CMS commands. Also, many XEDIT commands have the same names and uses as CMS commands; for instance, XEDIT has SET and QUERY commands.

On some computers, pressing the ENTER key or a PF key causes a major delay before you can enter more commands. This is usually due to many people using the computer's resources at the same time. Each time you press ENTER or a PF key, you are asking the computer to do a great deal of communications and processing. Thus, the fewer times you press these keys, the better. As you will see throughout this chapter, XEDIT lets you do a fair amount of editing before you have to press ENTER.

XEDIT'S SCREEN

To start experimenting with XEDIT, you will create a file. This gives you a good background in what XEDIT is and how to use it. From CMS, give the command:

```
XEDIT BUSINESS LETTER
```

You see:

```
 BUSINESS LETTER    A1  F 80   Trunc=80 Size=0 Line=0 Col=1 Alt=0
====> _
     |...+....1....+....2....+....3....+....4....+....5....+....6....+....7...


===== * * * Top of File * * *
===== * * * End of File * * *













1 = Help   3 = Quit   6 = ?   7 = Backward   8 = Forward   9 = =   11 = Spltjoin
```

You can move the cursor around on the screen with the cursor control keys. Note, however, that if you try to type in some restricted areas of the screen, your terminal does not let you. In fact, once you try this, your terminal won't let you do anything until you press the RESET key. This is a difficult feature of the 3270 terminal. The restricted areas of the XEDIT screen are:

```
 BUSINESS LETTER    A1   F 80   Trunc=80 Size=0 Line=0 Col=1 Alt=0
 ====>  _
        |...+....1....+....2....+....3....+....4....+....5....+....6....+....7...


 ===== * * * Top of File * * *
 ===== * * * End of File * * *








 1 = Help   3 = Quit   6 = ?   7 = Backward   8 = Forward   9 = =   11 = Spltjoin
```

The top line is the *status line*. This shows you the fileid of the file you are editing, the record format, and the LRECL.

The next line, marked with "====>", is the *command line*. This is similar to the command line you used in the FILELIST command. It was placed at the top of the screen instead of the bottom so that the home key ⏎ moves the cursor directly to the command line. XEDIT commands are similar to CMS commands, as you will see throughout this chapter.

The line after the command line is the *ruler* (also known as the *scale*). The ruler shows you the cursor column pointer, indicated by the vertical bar (|). It also shows you the number of each column on the screen, which is useful when you are entering tables. Also, if you get error messages or warnings (which are common in XEDIT), they appear on the ruler line and the two lines following it.

The set of five equal signs on the lines at the left of the screen is the *prefix area*. The prefix area is used for special XEDIT commands not given on the command line. The use of the prefix area is described in detail soon. When you are editing a file, there is a prefix line for each line of the file, as well as for the "Top of File" and "End of File" markers. Incidentally, the "Top of File" and "End of File" markers do not appear in your file; XEDIT shows you them so you can keep track of where you are.

If You Are Familiar With Other Computers

XEDIT does not have an automatic word-wrap feature due to the presence of the prefix area. If you type past the end of a line on the screen, your next characters appear in the prefix area of the following line, which can cause unexpected results.

There are two concepts you will find important as you read this chapter: the current line and the cursor column. Both of these are set when you give XEDIT commands. These are often important because the next command you give operates on the beginning of the current line or at the cursor column unless you specify otherwise. Even though you are using the full screen, these actions are left over from the days when everyone was using paper terminals.

For instance, the DELETE command deletes the current line (and makes the previous line the current line); thus, you had better be sure which line is the current line. Most 3270 terminals highlight the current line, and the ruler shows you the cursor column on the current line.

After you give a command, the current line is set to the last line acted on by the command. Often, the cursor column is the first column; however, some commands move the cursor column to some other position in the line.

When you are editing with XEDIT, you can simply move the cursor over text in the text area and type. For instance, if there is a word spelled incorrectly, simply move the cursor over it and retype it (you can use the delete and insert keys, Ⓘ and ⓐ, if they help). The next time you press the ENTER key, that change becomes part of the image of the file.

Entering Text

To start experimenting with XEDIT, you need text to work on. Your first task is to enter the following text. Use spaces, not the TAB key, or the cursor keys, for the date, the table, and the closing.

```
                            January 27, 1988

Cody Freeman, Vice President
Lincoln Union Bank
5512 South Market Street
Lincoln, CA  91422

Dear Ms. Freeman:

Thank you very much for talking with us the other day about our
request for an extension on our business loan. This letter
follows up on that meeting.

National Packaging has been very successful in attracting new
clients in the last two years. Our annual revenues have grown from
$7.3 million to $16.8 million since January 1986, and our profits
have grown from $1.1 million to $2.2 million. Our staff has
grown from 27 to 63.

We have reached the limits of our capacity at our present plant in
Lincoln. Due to limited processing, storage, and office area, we
need to move to larger quarters within 6 months in order to
continue growing. As you know, there is a good deal of vacant
manufacturing space available in North Lincoln.

We have found two different sites that would suit our needs quite well:

Site                   Size                 Cost
63 Industrial Way      85,000 sq. ft.       $5.5 million
5522 Grove Ave.        92,500 sq. ft.       $5.8 million

We believe that we can sell our current plant for $2.7 million.

Please let me know what you think of our loan proposal as soon as
possible. If you have any questions, feel free to call.

                            Sincerely,

                            Robert Vettner, President
                            National Packaging
```

Press the ⟨ key to move the cursor to the command line and give the INPUT command. This puts you in *input mode*, and the screen changes in many ways. You can now type text in. At the end of each line, press the TAB (➡) key; do not press the ENTER key at the end of each line. You can fix any typing errors by using the cursor control keys you learned about in Chapter 2.

The screen fills up when you enter approximately 20 lines. Press the ENTER key once; this moves the text up and gives you about half a screen of free space. When you have entered the entire letter, press the ENTER key twice: this takes you out of input mode and the screen looks as it did before (except you now have a file there). If you accidentally exit input mode before you are finished with the letter, give the INPUT command again.

The next step is to save the text on your minidisk. Press the ⟨ key to move the cursor to the command line and give the SAVE command. This stores the text on disk but lets you keep running XEDIT (as compared to the FILE command, which saves the text and leaves XEDIT).

You use this file for the examples in this chapter. Since many of the examples have you edit the text to try out XEDIT commands, you should make a copy of the file in case you accidentally save changes to the file. Use the CMS COPYFILE command to make a second copy of the file.

Instead of quitting from XEDIT, giving the command, and editing the file again, you can use XEDIT's CMS command. This command lets you give CMS commands while you are running XEDIT. On the XEDIT command line, give the command:

```
CMS COPYFILE BUSINESS LETTER A = BACKUP =
```

This works just as you would expect.

PREFIX COMMANDS

XEDIT's prefix commands are different from the ones you give on the command line. You give prefix commands by typing in the prefix area.

Most of the prefix commands are one character long; the character is typed directly over any of the equal signs. You can enter the prefix commands in upper or lower case, and they can appear over any part of the prefix area. Prefix commands are executed by XEDIT when you press the ENTER key or a PF key, not when you type them.

For example, the D prefix command deletes a line. To delete the third line of the file, you would enter a D over any of the equal signs on that line:

```
BUSINESS LETTER    A1  F 80   Trunc=80 Size=41 Line=0 Col=1 Alt=0
====>
       |...+....1....+....2....+....3....+....4....+....5....+....6....+....7...


===== * * * Top of File * * *
=====                                 January 27, 1988
=====
=d=== Cody Freeman, Vice President
===== Lincoln Union Bank
===== 5512 South Market Street
===== Lincoln, CA  91422
=====
===== Dear Ms. Freeman:
=====
===== Thank you very much for talking with us the other day about our
===== request for an extension on our business loan. This letter
===== follows up on that meeting.
=====
===== National Packaging has been very successful in attracting new
===== clients in the last two years. Our annual revenues have grown from
===== $7.3 million to $16.8 million since January 1986, and our profits
===== have grown from $1.1 million to $2.2 million. Our staff has
1 = Help    3= Quit    6 = ?    7 = Backward   8 = Forward   9 = =   11 = Spltjoin
```

When you press ENTER, the line is removed:

```
BUSINESS LETTER    A1  F 80   Trunc=80 Size=41 Line=0 Col=1 Alt=0
====> _
       |...+....1....+....2....+....3....+....4....+....5....+....6....+....7...


===== * * * Top of File * * *
=====                                 January 27, 1988
=====
===== Lincoln Union Bank
===== 5512 South Market Street
===== Lincoln, CA  91422
=====
===== Dear Ms. Freeman:
=====
===== Thank you very much for talking with us the other day about our
===== request for an extension on our business loan. This letter
===== follows up on that meeting.
=====
===== National Packaging has been very successful in attracting new
===== clients in the last two years. Our annual revenues have grown from
===== $7.3 million to $16.8 million since January 1986, and our profits
===== have grown from $1.1 million to $2.2 million. Our staff has
===== grown from 27 to 63.
1 = Help    3 = Quit    6 = ?    7 = Backward   8 = Forward   9 = =   11 = Spltjoin
```

Note that putting commands in the prefix area doesn't cause any action: You must press ENTER or a PF key for the prefix command to happen. Incidentally, if you enter a prefix command and change your mind before you press ENTER, you can simply move to the command and blank it out with the spacebar.

Another useful prefix command is I or A for inserting a blank line. To add a blank line after the fourth line:

```
 BUSINESS LETTER    A1  F 80   Trunc=80 Size=41 Line=0 Col=1 Alt=0
 ====>
         |...+....1....+....2....+....3....+....4....+....5....+....6....+....7...


 ===== * * * Top of File * * *
 =====                                    January 27, 1988
 =====
 ===== Lincoln Union Bank
 ===i= 5512 South Market Street
 ===== Lincoln, CA  91422
 =====
 ===== Dear Ms. Freeman:
 =====
 ===== Thank you very much for talking with us the other day about our
 ===== request for an extension on our business loan. This letter
 ===== follows up on that meeting.
 =====
 ===== National Packaging has been very successful in attracting new
 ===== clients in the last two years. Our annual revenues have grown from
 ===== $7.3 million to $16.8 million since January 1986, and our profits
 ===== have grown from $1.1 million to $2.2 million. Our staff has
 ===== grown from 27 to 63.
 1 = Help   3 = Quit   6 = ?   7 = Backward   8 = Forward   9 = =   11 = Spltjoin
```

When you press ENTER, XEDIT adds a blank line at that point. Incidentally, the A prefix command is identical to the I prefix command.

You can also precede prefix commands with a number to indicate how many times to perform them. For instance, to insert three blank lines after the "Sincerely," you would use:

```
=i3==                        Sincerely,
```

or:

```
=3i==                        Sincerely,
```

To delete the line and the following four lines, you would use "5D".

Some prefix commands consist of two letters: these are *block* commands. You put the double letters at the beginning and end lines of the block. For example to delete the paragraph that begins "National Packaging has," enter DD on the first and last lines:

```
===dd National Packaging has been very successful in attracting new
===== clients in the last two years. Our annual revenues have grown from
===== $7.3 million to $16.8 million since January 1986, and our profits
===== have grown from $1.1 million to $2.2 million. Our staff has
=dd== grown from 27 to 63.
```

This deletes the lines in the block.

The C and M commands copy and move lines in your file. They are used in conjunction with the F and P commands. Marking a line with an F indicates that the copied or moved lines will follow the marked line; marking a line with P indicates that the copied or moved lines will precede the marked line.

Using the F and P commands with C or M is fairly easy. For example, to switch the position of the paragraphs beginning "National Packaging has" and "We have reached," you would use the following prefix commands:

```
=mm== National Packaging has been very successful in attracting new
===== clients in the last two years. Our annual revenues have grown from
===== $7.3 million to $16.8 million since January 1986, and our profits
===== have grown from $1.1 million to $2.2 million. Our staff has
===== grown from 27 to 63.
=mm==
===== We have reached the limits of our capacity at our present plant in
===== Lincoln. Due to limited processing, storage, and office area, we
===== need to move to larger quarters within 6 months in order to
===== continue growing. As you know, there is a good deal of vacant
===== manufacturing space available in North Lincoln.
==f==
```

When you press ENTER, you see:

```
===== We have reached the limits of our capacity at our present plant in
===== Lincoln. Due to limited processing, storage, and office area, we
===== need to move to larger quarters within 6 months in order to
===== continue growing. As you know, there is a good deal of vacant
===== manufacturing space available in North Lincoln.
=====
===== National Packaging has been very successful in attracting new
===== clients in the last two years. Our annual revenues have grown from
===== $7.3 million to $16.8 million since January 1986, and our profits
===== have grown from $1.1 million to $2.2 million. Our staff has
===== grown from 27 to 63.
=====
```

To switch the position of two lines, use a single M:

```
=m=== 63 Industrial Way     85,000 sq. ft.     $5.5 million
==f== 5522 Grove Ave.       92,500 sq. ft.     $5.8 million
```

The following are the most useful prefix commands:

A	Add a line after.
C	Copy a line; must be matched with F or P.
CC	Copy a block of lines; must be matched with F or P.
D	Delete a line.
DD	Delete a block of lines.
F	Cause copy or move to happen following the specified line.
I	Insert a line after.
M	Move a line; must be matched with F or P.
MM	Move a block of lines; must be matched with F or P.
P	Cause copy or move to happen preceding the specified line.
"	Duplicate a line.

""	Duplicate a block of lines.
/	Set the current line to this line. Preceding the "/" with a number causes the column pointer to be moved to that column.
.	Make a label (described soon).
<	Shift a line left; characters shifted past the first column are lost. Preceding the "<" with a number indicates shifting the line by that many characters; "<5" shifts the line 5 columns to the left.
<<	Shift a block of lines left. This can be preceded by a number to shift the block by that many columns.
>	Shift a line right; lines shifted away from the first column are filled with spaces. Preceding the ">" with a number indicates shifting the line by that many characters.
>>	Shift a block of lines right. This can be preceded by a number to shift the block by that many columns.

Remember that prefix commands do not occur until you press ENTER. Thus, you can put many prefix commands on the screen and only press ENTER once. In fact, you can also put an XEDIT command on the command line and prefix commands in the command area; when you press ENTER, the prefix commands are executed first, then the command on the command line. This saves communication and processing time.

If you enter many prefix commands and decide you want none of them to occur, the fastest way to get rid of them is with the CLEAR key. This removes all changes you have made since the last time you pressed ENTER.

For instance, to change a block of 5 lines into blank lines, either:

• Use "I5" on the line before the block, "DD" at the beginning of the block, and "DD" at the end of the block, or
• Use "I5" on the line before the block and "D5" on the first line of the block

Another useful feature of the prefix area is that you can label lines. You will see later in the chapter how useful labels are as targets for commands. To set a label in the prefix area, start with a period (.) and follow it with up to four characters. For example, to put the label "beg" on a line, you would make the prefix area:

`.beg=`

There is an important aspect of using the prefix area. If you are in insert mode (that is, you have pressed the ⓐ key), you cannot enter prefix commands. This is due to one of the eccentricities in the design of the 3270 screen. If you try to type letters in the prefix area when you are in insert mode, your terminal simply beeps at you. You must press the RESET key to get out of insert mode so you can type the characters you want in the prefix area. Although all of these prefix commands can be performed using XEDIT commands from the command line, you will find it is much easier to use the prefix area.

XEDIT PF KEYS

As you saw in the HELP and FILELIST commands, XEDIT uses the PF keys extensively. These keys give XEDIT commands, some of which you are familiar with. The useful PF keys for XEDIT are:

PF1   HELP.

PF2   Add a line after the current line.

PF3   QUIT.

PF6   The ? command. This redisplays the previous command on the command line; that command can then be reexecuted by pressing ENTER. Pressing the PF6 key many times redisplays the preceding commands.

PF7   Go backward in the file one screen.

PF8   Go forward in the file one screen.

PF9   The = command. Reexecute the last command. Unlike PF6, this doesn't redisplay the last command: It simply executes it.

PF11   The SPLTJOIN command. This either joins two lines together or splits the current line apart. If the cursor is at the end of the line, this command joins the current line with the line after it (this may lose text at the end of the line, depending on the type of file you are editing). If the cursor is somewhere in the line, the command splits the line at the cursor position.

Remember that pressing a PF key has the same effect as pressing ENTER. Thus, if you have a command on the command line and/or prefix commands in the prefix area, pressing a PF key executes those commands as well.

COMMON XEDIT COMMANDS

If you have seen the XEDIT documentation, you know there are over 100 XEDIT commands. Like CMS, only a small number of them are useful for most people. This section leads you through the most useful commands.

SET Command

The SET command changes the way XEDIT looks. The SET commands in the PROFILE XEDIT file are all explained here, as are other set commands you might use. You may want to look at the PROFILE XEDIT as you read this section to see how the SET commands are used.

The most useful SET commands are:

ARBCHAR   This is the name for wildcard characters (which IBM calls "arbitrary characters"). The ARBCHAR function assigns a particular character to indicate any number of characters when you use XEDIT's search function. It is likely that you don't want to use *, even though this is the character used in CMS commands, because the asterisk

has special meaning in many types of text files; the standard choice
is the dollar sign ($).

```
SET ARBCHAR { ON c | OFF }
```

AUTOSAVE   The AUTOSAVE function automatically saves changes you
make to a file periodically. This is very useful if your computer
crashes often, and saves you from having to remember to give a
SAVE command to prevent you from losing work. Its syntax is:

```
SET AUTOSAVE [ n | OFF ]
```

The "n" is the number of changes you make before an automatic save is performed; 10 is a good number. OFF indicates you
are turning the AUTOSAVE mode off.

When XEDIT performs an automatic save, it tells you the
name of the file in the message area. If your computer crashes,
copy that file (usually called "100001 AUTOSAVE") to another
name and start editing that file. You can later replace the original
file with the saved file if you wish.

CASE   When XEDIT was designed, many programmers only wanted to
work with uppercase letters. Thus, XEDIT's default is to convert
all lowercase letters to uppercase. As you might imagine, this is a
very unpopular feature for anyone who uses XEDIT to write letters or memos. The CASE option lets you enter and search for
mixed-case letters. The syntax is:

```
SET CASE { MIXED | UPPERCASE } [ RESPECT | IGNORE ]
```

RESPECT tells XEDIT to always match case in search
commands; IGNORE indicates that case is not important in
search strings. Many users prefer to use the IGNORE option:

```
SET CASE MIXED IGNORE
```

CMDLINE   You can put the command line at the top or bottom of the screen.

```
SET CMDLINE [ BOTTOM | TOP | ON | OFF ]
```

BOTTOM puts the command line on the bottom line of the
screen; TOP puts it at the top. ON makes the bottom two lines the
command line, and OFF makes it so that there is no command
line at all.

CURLINE   You can tell XEDIT where on the screen to position the current
line. Initially, the current line is the middle of the screen, which is
inconvenient when you are adding text. Generally, setting it near
the top of the screen, a few lines below the scale, is best.

```
SET CURLINE ON { n | -n | M[ +n | -n ] }
```

n indicates the line number from the top of the screen; -n indicates the line number from the bottom. M is the middle of the screen; M+n means n lines below the middle of the screen, and so on.

MSGLINE
You can tell XEDIT where on the screen to position the message line. Initially, the message line is the second line of the screen. Generally, setting it to be on top of the ruler is best, since one-line messages do not cover up any of your text, and you do not need to be seeing the ruler all the time. You should generally allocate three lines for messages, since error messages often come in groups.

```
SET MSGLINE { ON placement | OFF }
placement:
{ n | -n | M[ +n | -n ] } } [ length ] [ OVERLAY ]
```

OFF indicates that no messages appear on the screen: Every error causes the screen to clear, which is very inconvenient. n indicates the line number from the top of the screen; -n indicates the line number from the bottom. M is the middle of the screen; M+n means n lines below the middle of the screen, and so on.

The "length" is the number of lines the messages can take up. If the messages are longer than this, they cause the screen to clear. You should generally use the OVERLAY option, since it allows you to put messages on top of the ruler without taking up blank space by itself.

NONDISP
This function chooses which character to show if you have non-displaying characters in your text file. It is rare that you will have non-displaying characters, but if you do, you want to see them so you can remove them. It is a good idea to choose a character to show that you are not likely to have in your file, such as the vertical bar (|).

```
SET NONDISP c
```

NULLS
An unfortunate choice for the default action of XEDIT was whether you can use the insert key ⓐ or not. Without going into the arcane reasoning behind this, you should assume that you always want to have NULLS set to ON (so you can use the insert key); the default is OFF.

```
SET NULLS { ON | OFF }
```

PFn
This lets you change the PF keys to be whatever you want. Note that XEDIT sets many of the PF keys for you, as shown earlier in this chapter. You can see the default settings by using the QUERY PF command.

The SET PFn syntax is:

```
SET PFn [ type ] [ string ]
type:
[ BEFORE | AFTER | ONLY | IGNORE ]
```

If you do not include any options, that PF key is made inactive. The four types are:

BEFORE	Execute the PF key before the command on the command line. This is the most common setting; it is also the default for all commands except "?" and "=".
AFTER	Execute the PF key after the command on the command line. This is rare.
ONLY	Only execute the PF key, and ignore whatever is on the command line. This is the default for the "?" and "=" commands.
IGNORE	If there is anything on the command line, ignore the PF key.

For example, to define PF 4 as the SAVE command, give the command:

```
SET PF4 BEFORE SAVE
```

RESERVED   The SET RESERVED command lets you reserve a line on the XEDIT screen and put text in it. This lets you put labels on the screen, but it also reduces the number of lines available for editing.

Its syntax is:

```
SET RESERVED placement { HIGH | NOHIGH } [text]
placement:
{ n | -n | M[ +n | -n ] }
```

HIGH indicates that the reserved line is highlighted; NOHIGH indicates no highlighting. The text can be any characters.

n indicates the line number from the top of the screen; -n indicates the line number from the bottom. M is the middle of the screen; M+n means n lines below the middle of the screen, and so on.

The SET RESERVED command at the PROFILE XEDIT adds a line on line 24 of the screen that reminds you of what some of the PF keys do. If you would rather have that line free for editing (increasing the information on the screen by about 5%), simply remove the last five lines from the PROFILE XEDIT file. Using a placement of 24 instead of -1 makes the reserved line disappear when you use XEDIT's screen splitting feature, described later in this chapter.

If you have put a reserved line on the screen and want to take it off, you must specify which reserved line to remove:

```
SET RESERVED placement OFF
```

SCALE

You can tell XEDIT where on the screen to position the ruler. Initially, the ruler is the middle of the screen, which is inconvenient when you are adding text. If you want it on at all, setting it near the top of the screen, directly under the command line, is best.

```
SET SCALE { ON placement | OFF }
placement:
{ n | -n | M[ +n | -n ] }
```

n indicates the line number from the top of the screen; -n indicates the line number from the bottom. M is the middle of the screen; M+n means n lines below the middle of the screen, and so on.

SCREEN

This option is used for editing many files at the same time, or editing two parts of a file at once. It is described later in this chapter in the section on splitting the screen.

SPAN

When searching for text, you often want to find a phrase. For instance, you might want to find the part of the sample business letter that contains the phrase "profits have grown." Note, however, that the phrase spans two lines:

```
National Packaging has been very successful in attracting new
clients in the last two years. Our annual revenues have grown from
$7.3 million to $16.8 million since January 1986, and our profits
have grown from $1.1 million to $2.2 million. Our staff has
grown from 27 to 63.
```

Of course, you generally do not know ahead of time that a phrase spans more than one line, but you would like XEDIT to search on multiple lines for the phrase.

The syntax of this command is:

```
SET SPAN { ON [ spec ] | OFF }
spec:
{ BLANK | NOBLANK } [ n | * ]
```

BLANK indicates that a blank can be inserted by XEDIT when it is searching more than one line; NOBLANK prevents this. For standard writing (as compared to computer programs), BLANK is much more common. The number corresponds to how many lines XEDIT should expect a phrase to be broken over; "*" indicates the whole file.

STAY When XEDIT searches for some text and doesn't find it, it normally makes the last line of the file the current line; this is rarely useful. Instead, you generally prefer for XEDIT to stay on the current line and tell you it could not find the text.

```
SET STAY { ON | OFF }
```

SYNONYM This is very similar to the SYNONYM command in CMS. It is useful in XEDIT for recognizing common mistypings of commands.

```
SET SYNONYM newname oldname
```

For instance, many people mistype the FILE command as "FIEL". If you have a synonym that equates FIEL to FILE, then you do not get an error message when you mistype it.

```
SET SYNONYM FIEL FILE
```

Note that you cannot have a synonym that ends in a number, since XEDIT does not recognize the number as part of the synonym.

VARBLANK Like SPAN, the VARBLANK function makes XEDIT's phrase searching more intelligent. With VARBLANK set on, XEDIT searches for phrases with a variable amount of blanks (spaces) between words. Thus, if you are searching for "profits have grown" and the phrase in the file happens to have two spaces between "profits" and "have," XEDIT still finds the phrase.

```
SET VARBLANK { ON | OFF }
```

VERIFY This function specifies whether XEDIT displays each changed line in the message area. On 3270s, there is rarely any use in having the changed lines displayed in the message area; on serial terminals, it is sometimes useful, but it can also be frustrating to have every change you make typed on your terminal.

```
SET VERIFY { OFF | ON }
```

OFF specifies that you do not want to see the changed lines in the message area; ON specifies that you do. The default for 3270s is OFF.

WRAP   If you are in the middle of a file when you give a search com-
                              mand, XEDIT normally stops when it gets to the end of the file if
                              it has not found the search text. Of course, if the text is earlier in
                              the file than your current location, this is terribly inconvenient:
                              You would rather have XEDIT wrap around to the beginning and
                              continue the search.

                              ```
                              SET WRAP { ON | OFF }
                              ```

QUERY Command

The QUERY command tells you about XEDIT's settings. The most useful query options
are:

ACTION   Tells you whether any editing commands have been performed on
                              this file. If no editing commands have been performed, you can leave
                              the file with QUIT.

LASTMSG   Displays the last message issued by XEDIT.

PF   Displays all 24 PF key settings. If you include a number, this displays
                              the setting for just that PF key.

RING   Displays the files in XEDIT's ring. This is described later in this
                              chapter in the section on editing multiple files.

In addition, you can check the current setting for the following SET commands:
ARBCHAR, AUTOSAVE, CASE, CMDLINE, CURLINE, MSGLINE, NONDISP,
NULLS, SCALE, SPAN, STAY, SYNONYM, VARBLANK, VERIFY, and WRAP.

STATUS Command

The STATUS command tells you the status of a host of options that you can set with the
SET command. It gives you all the information at once; some people feel that this is overkill,
but you may find it interesting. For example, the output might be:

```
APL OFF                   IMAGE ON                  SCOPE DISPLAY
ARBCHAR ON $              IMPCMSCP ON               SERIAL OFF 10 10
AUTOSAVE 10               LINEND ON #               SHADOW ON
CASE MIXED IGNORE         LRECL 80                  SPAN ON BLANK 3
CMDLINE TOP               MACRO OFF                 SPILL OFF
COLPTR OFF                MSGLINE ON 3 3 OVERLAY    STAY ON
CURLINE ON 6              MSGMODE ON LONG           STREAM ON
DISPLAY 0 0               NONDISP !                 SYNONYM ON
ESCAPE OFF /              NULLS ON                  TABLINE OFF -3
ETMODE OFF                NUMBER OFF                TERMINAL DISPLAY
FILLER                    PACK OFF                  TEXT OFF
FMODE A1                  PREFIX ON LEFT            TOFEOF ON
FNAME BUSINESS            RANGE :1 :41              TRUNC 80
FTYPE LETTER              RECFM F                   VARBLANK ON
FULLREAD OFF              REMOTE ON                 WRAP ON
HEX OFF                   SCALE ON 3                ZONE 1 80
SCREEN SIZE 24
```

```
MASK
TABS 1 5 10 15 20 25 30 35 40 45 50 55 60 65 70 75 80 85 90 95 100 105 110
VERIFY OFF 1 80
CTLCHAR OFF
COLOR ARROW        DEFAULT NONE HIGH PS0
COLOR CMDLINE      DEFAULT NONE NOHIGH PS0
COLOR CURLINE      DEFAULT NONE HIGH PS0
COLOR FILEAREA     DEFAULT NONE NOHIGH PS0
COLOR IDLINE       DEFAULT NONE HIGH PS0
COLOR MSGLINE      RED NONE HIGH PS0
COLOR PENDING      DEFAULT NONE HIGH PS0
COLOR PREFIX       DEFAULT NONE NOHIGH PS0
COLOR SCALE        DEFAULT NONE HIGH PS0
COLOR SHADOW       DEFAULT NONE NOHIGH PS0
COLOR STATAREA     DEFAULT NONE HIGH PS0
COLOR TABLINE      DEFAULT NONE HIGH PS0
COLOR TOFEOF       DEFAULT NONE NOHIGH PS0
```

Moving Around in the File

XEDIT makes it easy to scroll through a file. The TOP command moves the current line to the top of the file, and the BOTTOM command shows you the bottom. When you first run XEDIT, you are at the first line of the file.

You can page through the file with the BACKWARD and FORWARD commands. These commands move you a screen at a time. These are the same as the commands on the PF7 and PF8 keys.

The BACKWARD and FORWARD commands take numeric arguments if you want to go more than one screen at a time. For example, FORWARD 3 goes forward three screens.

To move in smaller increments than a full screen, use the UP and DOWN commands. These commands move a line at a time. You can also give them numeric arguments. For instance, DOWN 12 goes forward half a screen on 24-line screens.

Targets

A *target* is a method of specifying which line you want XEDIT to act on. Many commands take targets as arguments. For example, the DELETE command (which you will see soon) lets you specify a target as its argument; it then deletes all lines from the current line up to, but not including, the line with the target.

The search target lets you search for a string of characters. The first line on which that string appears after the current line is the line indicated by the target. The string must be preceded by a character not in the string; the standard character used is the slash (/). You can follow the string with the same character if you wish.

For instance, to find the target "the letter," use the target:

```
/the letter
```

To find the string on a line prior to the current line, precede the target with a minus sign:

```
-/the letter
```

Remember you can use the ARBCHAR character as a wildcard. If your ARBCHAR is $, the target:

```
/over$e
```

would match any of the following:

```
overtime
overdone
over the
over. Until he
```

and so on. Since you have set SPAN on in your PROFILE XEDIT, the matched text can be on up to three lines.

The second type of target is the line label. You saw how the . prefix command created a label for the current line; you can use that label as a target. Remember to always precede the label with a period, such as:

```
.beg
```

Some people like to use numeric targets, although they are not as common as search targets or labels. There are two types of numeric targets: *absolute* and *relative*. An absolute target specifies a line number based on the top of the file. Absolute targets are specified by a colon preceding the number. Thus, :27 indicates the 27th line in the file. A relative target specifies a line number based on the current line. Relative targets are preceded with a plus or minus sign. If the current line is the 22nd line in the file, -3 indicates the 19th line of the file and +4 indicates the 26th line of the file.

You can use the * character in relative targets to indicate the top and bottom of the file. -* indicates the line at the top of the file, and +* indicates the line at the bottom. Also, if you don't precede a number with a colon, plus, or minus, XEDIT assumes that you mean a relative line forwards from the current line.

You will see how to use targets in a variety of XEDIT commands throughout this chapter.

LOCATE Command

The LOCATE command finds the next line with the matching target. For instance, in the BUSINESS LETTER file, the command:

```
LOCATE :5
```

puts you on the fifth line. If you then give the command:

```
LOCATE /very
```

the current line is then at the tenth line.

The LOCATE command is special, in that you do not need to use the word "LOCATE": You can just specify the target. This is like having a "find the target" command without a command name. For instance, if you now give the command:

```
-3
```

you are on the seventh line.

Using the = command with the LOCATE command and search targets makes finding each successive instance of a word or phrase easy. Give the command:

```
/very
```

This puts you on the line beginning:

```
Thank you very much
```

Press the PF9 key (which is the same as the = command), and you are put on the line beginning:

```
National Packaging has been very successful
```

DELETE, COPY, and MOVE Commands

The DELETE command deletes the current line. If you include a target, it deletes all lines from the current line to that target, but does not delete the target line.

To delete three lines, you would give the command:

```
DELETE 3
```

To delete from the current line to line 20, give the command:

```
DELETE :20
```

To delete everything to the end of the file:

```
DELETE *
```

The COPY command copies a range of lines to a position after a line. Its syntax is:

```
COPY range-target after-target
```

For instance, to copy five lines to the line after line 26, give the command:

```
COPY 5 :26
```

The MOVE command is similar to the COPY command except it moves the lines instead of copying them. For instance, to move the current line down four lines, you would give the command:

```
MOVE 1 4
```

The COPY and MOVE commands bring up a great use for line labels. Instead of guessing how many lines you want to copy and the location of where you want to copy to, you can make your own standard labels. Three labels you might find handy are:

.BEG   The line you want to start copying or moving from.
.UPTO   The line up to which you want to select.
.AFT   The line after which you want the block copied or moved.

To see this, assume you want to move the first paragraph after the second. Use the .upto and .aft labels like this:

```
===== National Packaging has been very successful in attracting new
===== clients in the last two years. Our annual revenues have grown from
===== $7.3 million to $16.8 million since January 1986, and our profits
===== have grown from $1.1 million to $2.2 million. Our staff has
===== grown from 27 to 63.
.upto
===== We have reached the limits of our capacity at our present plant in
===== Lincoln. Due to limited processing, storage, and office area, we
===== need to move to larger quarters within 6 months in order to
===== continue growing. As you know, there is a good deal of vacant
===== manufacturing space available in North Lincoln.
.aft=
```

Assuming that the first line of the first paragraph is the current line, you could then give the easy-to-remember command:

```
MOVE .UPTO .AFT
```

The .beg label is also useful when the current line is not the one you want to start with. You can precede XEDIT commands with a target: This makes the target line the current line before the command is executed. Thus, even if you don't know where the current line is, set your labels as:

```
.beg= National Packaging has been very successful in attracting new
===== clients in the last two years. Our annual revenues have grown from
===== $7.3 million to $16.8 million since January 1986, and our profits
===== have grown from $1.1 million to $2.2 million. Our staff has
===== grown from 27 to 63.
.upto
===== We have reached the limits of our capacity at our present plant in
===== Lincoln. Due to limited processing, storage, and office area, we
===== need to move to larger quarters within 6 months in order to
===== continue growing. As you know, there is a good deal of vacant
===== manufacturing space available in North Lincoln.
.aft=
```

Give the command:

```
.BEG MOVE .UPTO .AFT
```

This is an easy, mnemonic method for copying and moving blocks of text.

CHANGE Command

The CHANGE command lets you change instances of one string of text to another. It is best suited for global changes (that is, making the same change throughout a file). If you want to make an individual change, it is often easier to simply make the changes directly on the screen.

For example, you might want to change the phrase "highly secret" to "very confidential." XEDIT lets you select the lines on which you make the change with targets.

The general syntax for the CHANGE command is:

```
CHANGE /from-text [ /to-text/ [ target [ count ] ] ]
```

For example:

```
CHANGE /highly secret/very confidential/ 5
```

The from-text and to-text are the strings to change from and to. If you don't specify a to-text, the from-text is simply deleted. The target indicates how far in the file to go. The count is the number of times in any given line to change the text.

The most common situation for which you use the CHANGE command is when you want to change all instances of one string to another. You would then use the commands:

```
TOP
CHANGE /from-text/to-text/ * *
```

The first * indicates you want to change throughout the file and the second * indicates you want to change the string each time it occurs on the line.

Note that the CHANGE command is not affected by the SET WRAP or SET SPAN commands. This means it only searches to the end of the file (necessitating a TOP command if you want to change the whole file), and it does not change phrases that span a line.

Splitting and Joining Lines with SPLTJOIN

Although XEDIT has SPLIT and JOIN commands, the SPLTJOIN command is easier to use, and it already exists as the PF11 key. The SPLTJOIN command looks at where the cursor is on the line:

- If it is at the end of the line, SPLTJOIN joins the two lines.
- If it is not at the end of the line, SPLTJOIN splits the line at the cursor position.

For example, use the following paragraph:

```
Cody Freeman, Vice President
Lincoln Union Bank
5512 South Market Street
Lincoln, CA  91422
```

If the cursor is after "President" and you press PF11, the next line is joined with the first:

```
Cody Freeman, Vice President Lincoln Union Bank
5512 South Market Street
Lincoln, CA  91422
```

If the cursor is in the middle of a line, such as before the zip code, pressing PF11 splits the line:

```
Cody Freeman, Vice President Lincoln Union Bank
5512 South Market Street
Lincoln, CA
91422
```

Moving Parts of Files

The GET and PUT command are powerful XEDIT commands that let you combine text files. For instance, assume you are editing a letter and you want to include a short data file you prepared earlier. With the GET command, you could simply specify where in your letter to insert the other file.

The PUT command puts lines from the current file in another file. Its syntax is:

```
PUT target [ fn [ ft [ fm ] ]
```

If the file you specify exists, the lines are appended at the end of the file. If the file does not already exist, XEDIT creates it. You can use an equal sign in the fn, ft, or fm to indicate that the filename, filetype, or filemode are the same as the file you are editing. Using the ".BEG" and ".UPTO" line labels makes using the PUT command easier.

For instance, if you want to put the labelled lines into a new file called SHORT HOLDER (or add the lines to the end of the SHORT HOLDER file), give the command:

```
.BEG PUT .UPTO SHORT HOLDER
```

If you want to put all the lines from the current line up to line 30 in SHORT HOLDER, you would use:

```
PUT :30 SHORT HOLDER
```

If you do not specify a file name, XEDIT stores the lines in a *temporary file*. This is very useful for transferring lines from one file which you are editing to another. You do not need to create a file to hold the lines and remember to erase the file later: You can use XEDIT's temporary file instead.

Once you put lines in XEDIT's temporary file, you can get them out with the GET command. The GET command has the following syntax:

```
GET [ fn [ ft [ fm ] [ first-line [ for-lines ] ] ] ]
```

If you do not use any options, the GET command inserts the lines from the temporary file at the current line. You will see more about this later in the chapter when you learn how to edit more than one file at a time.

Like the PUT command, you can use an equal sign in the fn, ft, or fm to indicate that the filename, filetype, or filemode are the same as the file you are editing. You can also use a * for the fm to have XEDIT search all available minidisks.

The first-line is the first record in the file to insert, and for-lines is the number of records to insert. If you do not specify for-lines, XEDIT inserts to the end of the file; if you do not specify first-lines, XEDIT inserts the whole file. The file is always inserted after the current line.

Thus, if you are editing BUSINESS LETTER and want to include all of the lines in the file called "SITES DATA", you would give the command:

```
GET SITES DATA
```

If you wanted to only insert lines 5 through 10 of SITES DATA, you would use the command:

```
GET SITES DATA 5 5
```

EDITING THE LETTER

You are now ready to experiment with the many XEDIT commands you have learned. Run XEDIT on the file to begin the lesson.

First, change the "two" to a "three" in the line:

```
We have found two different sites that would suit our needs quite well:
```

To do this, give the FORWARD command (or press PF8) to go to the second screen. Then, either:

- Move the cursor down to the beginning of the word "two", type "thr", press the insert key (ⓐ), and type "ee", or
- Give the command:

```
CHANGE /two/three/10
```

Next, add a blank line after the line that begins "5522 Grove Ave." The easiest way to do this is to put an "i" in the prefix area of that line and press ENTER.

Add text to the blank line. Move the cursor to that blank line and type:

```
173 Poplar Ave.       80,000 sq. ft.      $4.7 million
```

Now change all instances of "sq. ft." to "square feet". Give the commands:

```
TOP
CHANGE /sq. ft./square feet/* *
```

Feel free to experiment more with the commands you used. Remember not to save the changes you made to the file: Use the QQUIT command instead.

SPLITTING THE XEDIT SCREEN

So far, you have seen how XEDIT lets you view and edit a file. There are many situations when it would be convenient to view and edit two files at once. For example, you may want to take some text out of one file and put it in the middle of another file. Or, you might want to see how different parts of two files compare as you scroll through each. Fortunately, you can do this with XEDIT by splitting the XEDIT screen in two.

Two Views of One File

The simplest case is seeing two views of the same file at once. This is common when you are writing a long report or memo and want to view text you wrote before. For instance, if you are editing the body of a report and want to see how you worded an idea in the introduction, you could mark your spot with a label prefix command, go back to the introduction, note your wording, then use the label as a target to get back to your work. However, it would be much more convenient to split the screen into two views of the file and look at the introduction at the same time.

Splitting the screen is easy. The SET SCREEN command splits the screen into different screens, each with a command area and ruler. Its syntax is:

```
SET SCREEN { n | SIZE size1 [ size2 ... ] }
```

If you use n, the screen is split into n screens. Thus, to split the screen in two, use the command:

```
SET SCREEN 2
```

To go back to a single screen, use:

```
SET SCREEN 1
```

For example, if you are at the top of the business letter and give the SET SCREEN 2 command, you see:

```
 BUSINESS LETTER   A1  F 80  Trunc=80 Size=41 Line=0 Col=1 Alt=0
====>
      |...+....1....+....2....+....3....+....4....+....5....+....6....+....7...


===== * * * Top of File * * *
=====                                     January 27, 1988
=====
===== Cody Freeman, Vice President
===== Lincoln Union Bank
===== 5512 South Market Street
===== Lincoln, CA  91422
 BUSINESS LETTER   A1  F 80  Trunc=80 Size=41 Line=0 Col=1 Alt=0
====> _
      |...+....1....+....2....+....3....+....4....+....5....+....6....+....7...


===== * * * Top of File * * *
=====                                     January 27, 1988
=====
===== Cody Freeman, Vice President
===== Lincoln Union Bank
===== 5512 South Market Street
===== Lincoln, CA  91422
```

Note that your reserved line disappeared. Since you specified it was to appear on line 24, and there is no line 24 in the smaller screens, it does not get displayed when you split the screen. If you had reserved the line with a placement of -1, indicating one line from the bottom of the screen, it would have appeared at the bottom of both screens. Since you want all the space you can get when you split the screen, using 24 instead of -1 is more convenient.

Using the SET SCREEN SIZE argument lets you specify the number of lines in each screen. Although this is not common, you may want to have one of the screens larger than the other. For instance, to split the screens so the upper screen is 5 lines (the minimum) and the lower 19 lines, give the command:

```
SET SCREEN SIZE 5 19
```

(This only works correctly on terminals with 24 lines.) In the business letter, go back to a single screen (with SET SCREEN 1) and press PF8 to go one screen forward. Give the SET SCREEN SIZE 5 19 command. You see:

```
 BUSINESS LETTER    A1  F 80   Trunc=80 Size=41 Line=19 Col=1 Alt=0
 ====>  _
        |...+....1....+....2....+....3....+....4....+....5....+....6....+....7...
 =====
 ===== We have reached the limits of our capacity at our present plant in
 BUSINESS LETTER    A1  F 80   Trunc=80 Size=41 Line=19 Col=1 Alt=0
 ====>
        |...+....1....+....2....+....3....+....4....+....5....+....6....+....7...
 ===== have grown from $1.1 million to $2.2 million. Our staff has
 ===== grown from 27 to 63.
 =====
 ===== We have reached the limits of our capacity at our present plant in
 ===== Lincoln. Due to limited processing, storage, and office area, we
 ===== need to move to larger quarters within 6 months in order to
 ===== continue growing. As you know, there is a good deal of vacant
 ===== manufacturing space available in North Lincoln.
 =====
 ===== We have found two different sites that would suit our needs quite well:
 =====
 ===== Site                Size             Cost
 -==== 63 Industrial Way   85,000 sq. ft.   $5.5 million
 ===== 5522 Grove Ave.     92,500 sq. ft.   $5.8 million
 =====
 ===== We believe that we can sell our current plant for $2.7 million.
```

The top screen shows only two lines of the file because three are taken up by the file name, the command line, and the ruler.

When you have two or more screens, you can switch between them with the cursor control keys. Each screen is independent. This means that if you enter a command such as FORWARD and BACKWARD on the command line of one of the two screens, it only affects that screen. You can, however, enter commands on both command lines.

One very valuable use for splitting screens in one file is being able to see the results of a move that is more than one screen long. For instance, if you are moving a paragraph from the beginning to the end of a long file, it is nice to be able to see the results of the move (the deletion from the old location and the insertion in the new location) as they happen. To do this, split the screen so you can see the two locations, and use the MM and F prefix commands. When you press ENTER, you can see the results in both places.

XEDIT allows you to split the screen in three or four screens, but there is usually so little information on them that this is not very useful. Generally, two screens is enough for most people.

If you have an unequal split you use often (such as the SET SCREEN SIZE 5 19 just shown), you should save the command in your PROFILE XEDIT as a synonym so you can give the command easily. For instance, you might add the lines to your PROFILE XEDIT:

```
SET SYNONYM TWO SET SCREEN SIZE 5 19
SET SYNONYM ONE SET SCREEN 1
```

From then on, you can use your "new" TWO and ONE commands to split and unsplit the screen.

Editing Many Files

Editing two files in two screens is as simple as one. Once you have split the screen, using XEDIT's XEDIT command opens a new file in the current screen. For instance, if you are looking at BUSINESS LETTER in two equal screens (set up with SET SCREEN 2), and you want to look at a file called SITES DATA in the top screen, move to the command line for the top screen and give the command:

```
XEDIT SITES DATA
```

Your screen would show:

```
 SITES      DATA      A1  F 80   Trunc=80 Size=10 Line=0 Col=1 Alt=0
====> _
      |...+....1....+....2....+....3....+....4....+....5....+....6....+....7...


===== * * * Top of File * * *
===== Best sites so far:
=====
===== 63 Industrial Way      85,000 sq. ft.      $5.5 million
===== 5522 Grove Ave.        92,500 sq. ft.      $5.8 million
=====
===== Other sites of interest:
 BUSINESS LETTER    A1  F 80   Trunc=80 Size=41 Line=0 Col=1 Alt=0
====>
      |...+....1....+....2....+....3....+....4....+....5....+....6....+....7...


===== * * * Top of File * * *
=====                                January 27, 1988
=====
===== Cody Freeman, Vice President
===== Lincoln Union Bank
===== 5512 South Market Street
===== Lincoln, CA  91422
```

If you want to quit from both files at once, use the CANCEL command instead of two QUIT commands.

XEDIT can handle many files at the same time, even if they are not visible on the screen. If you use XEDIT's XEDIT command when two different files are visible, it displays the third one and puts the other one that was replaced in XEDIT's *ring*. The ring is a list of files that are active. Files are moved in and out of the ring as you close and open files from the screens.

For instance, assume you are editing BUSINESS LETTER and SITES DATA, and you want to start a new file called BANK IDEAS. While the cursor is in the screen with SITES DATA, give the command:

```
XEDIT BANK IDEAS
```

SITES DATA disappears from the screen, and a blank area for BANK IDEAS appears:

```
BANK      IDEAS    A1  F 80  Trunc=80 Size=0 Line=0 Col=1 Alt=0
====>  _
       |...+....1....+....2....+....3....+....4....+....5....+....6....+....7...


===== * * * Top of File * * *
===== * * * End of File * * *




BUSINESS LETTER   A1  F 80  Trunc=80 Size=41 Line=0 Col=1 Alt=0
====>
       |...+....1....+....2....+....3....+....4....+....5....+....6....+....7...


===== * * * Top of File * * *
=====                                  January 27, 1988
=====
_==== Cody Freeman, Vice President
===== Lincoln Union Bank
===== 5512 South Market Street
===== Lincoln, CA  91422
```

You can now input text into BANK IDEAS. When you are finished, give the FILE command. This saves the text and puts BANK IDEAS out of XEDIT's memory. Since SITES DATA is still in the ring, it reappears in the upper screen.

To find out about the files in the ring, use the QUERY RING command. This tells you the number of files and their names.

XEDIT MACROS

The sample PROFILE XEDIT contained mostly SET commands. This should not give you the impression that all XEDIT macros are simply lists of simple XEDIT commands that could be given from the command line. In fact, XEDIT has many commands that are only useful in macros. Using these commands requires an understanding of REXX, described in Chapter 7.

The first line of the PROFILE XEDIT is a comment; it is not executed by XEDIT. It is there to tell XEDIT to run REXX instead of EXEC2 (the reason for this is covered in Chapter 7).

The four lines at the end of the PROFILE XEDIT gave you a glimpse of what XEDIT macros can be used for:

```
/* The next 4 lines display a line at the bottom of the XEDIT screen */
EXTRACT "/LSCREEN"
Lres = "1 = Help   3 = Quit   6 = ?   7 = Backward   "
Rres = "8 = Forward   9 = =   11 = Spltjoin"
SET RESERVED LSCREEN.5 NOHIGH Lres Rres
```

The first of these lines, like the first line of the PROFILE XEDIT, is a comment and is only there to help you read the macro.

The EXTRACT command is only useful in macros. It is similar to the QUERY command in that it gives information about various settings. However, instead of displaying the information on the screen, the EXTRACT command makes the information available to XEDIT macros.

The result of the EXTRACT command is that XEDIT creates a *variable* that is used in the SET RESERVED command. A variable is a named place-holder in a program. You can put information in a variable using its name; you can later get the information out of the variable by referring to its name.

You can think of a variable like a mailbox with a name on it. You can say "put this message in the mailbox labelled Jones" or "tell me what is in the Jones' mailbox." These mailboxes are special in that they can only hold one object: Every time you put another object in them, the current object is lost. The contents of the mailbox changes, but the name on the mailbox always stays the same. In this case, the variable is called "LSCREEN.5" and, after the EXTRACT command is executed, it contains the number of lines on your terminal.

The next two lines (the ones that begin with "Lres =" and "Rres =") are REXX commands that define two more variables. In this case, the variables are used to hold strings of characters that will be combined into the line at the bottom of the screen. The last line is the SET RESERVED command. When REXX sees that line, it substitutes the values it knows for the variable names. Thus, when it sees "LSCREEN.5", it substitutes "24" (or whatever the length of your screen is).

You can now see the value of these lines. If you had simply had a line that read:

```
SET RESERVED 24 NOHIGH 1 = Help   3 = Quit ...
```

and you were on a terminal that had 36 lines, the reserved line would appear about two-thirds of the way down the terminal. With the macro, XEDIT determines where to put the line by looking at your terminal's characteristics first.

The lines can be used in other macros that you store in other files. The command you saw before to split the screen into two screens with a five-line screen at the top was:

```
SET SCREEN SIZE 5 19
```

This only works on 24-line terminals. You can use REXX's arithmetic capabilities to make a macro that always works. Enter the following lines in a file called TWO XEDIT:

```
/* Split the screen into two, with a screen with 5 lines on the top */
EXTRACT "/LSCREEN"
Lower = LSCREEN.5 - 5
SET SCREEN SIZE 5 Lower
```

The variable "Lower" holds the number of lines on your terminal, minus 5.

Another use for XEDIT macros is in saving beginning users from having to learn many XEDIT commands. For instance, the following macro indents a group of lines, starting at the current line. When you run the macro, it asks you how many lines you want to indent, and how many spaces. Using this information, it sets up the correct XEDIT command and executes it:

```
/* Indents text; prompts the user for number of lines and
    number of columns to indent */
say "How many lines would you like to indent?"
pull Nlines
if Nlines = "" then exit
say "How many columns would you like to indent the next" Nlines "lines?"
pull Ncols
if Ncols = "" then exit
SHIFT RIGHT Ncols Nlines
```

Note that this macro may truncate characters off the end of the indented lines, depending on the type of file you are editing. As you will see in Chapter 7, REXX's SAY command prints text on the screen, and the PULL command takes in variables interactively from the keyboard.

You can give this macro to other people to use. It is certainly easier for them to answer the questions than to search through the XEDIT documentation to find the proper command and figure out its syntax.

You now have two different types of commands in macros: XEDIT commands and REXX commands. In this book, XEDIT commands are shown in all capital letters; REXX commands are shown in all lowercase. REXX variables are shown in mixed case.

All XEDIT macro files must have filetypes of "XEDIT". Note that XEDIT requires you to name your macros carefully. If you give a macro the same name as an XEDIT command, XEDIT never executes the macro. Similarly, you cannot have a numeral in the macro's name, or XEDIT won't find it on your disk.

ADVANCED XEDIT TOPICS

The following topics are of interest to many fewer people than those in the earlier part of this chapter. They are described here both to show you some of XEDIT's interesting features and to give you an idea of some of the areas in which you might want to look further.

Giving CMS Commands

You can give CMS commands from within XEDIT. The CMS command lets you enter individual or groups of commands. You can execute CP commands if you have set IMPCP on. The CMS command's syntax is:

```
CMS [ command ]
```

If you include the command, it is executed immediately. If the command doesn't display any output, your screen stays as it is. If the command needs to display information (such as a QUERY command), the screen clears, the information is displayed, and you are left in MORE... mode. You then press the CLEAR key to get back to your XEDIT screen.

If you do not give a command on the command line, you are put in a mode where you can give CMS commands one after the other. The set of commands you can give is a subset of all CMS commands. You cannot execute the COPYFILE, FORMAT, or SORT commands, but can execute most others. To get back to editing your file, give the RETURN command.

For instance, to see the time, give the command:

```
CMS QUERY TIME
```

Excluding Portions of the Screen

XEDIT allows you to specify parts of your file that you do not want to see or edit. This can be useful if there are parts of your file you want to be absolutely sure you do not accidentally alter, or you do not want to see at all.

For example, if you have a data file which has special information in the first three lines that you never want to alter, you can use the SET RANGE command to prevent you from being able to see or edit them. The syntax of the SET RANGE command is:

```
SET RANGE top-target bottom-target
```

To prevent you from editing the top three lines, you would give the command:

```
SET RANGE :3 *
```

After you have given the SET RANGE command, XEDIT uses:

```
===== * * * Top of Range * * *
===== * * * End of Range * * *
```

instead of:

```
===== * * * Top of File * * *
===== * * * End of File * * *
```

No command you give affects the lines outside of the range, except FILE and SAVE. FILE and SAVE always save the entire file, even the lines you cannot see.

The SET SELECT, SET DISPLAY, and SET SCOPE commands allow you to hide and prevent from editing various lines in the file. They are fairly complicated and of limited interest, so they are not covered here. However, if you have a use for hiding lines that are not at the beginning or end of the file, you should read the XEDIT manuals for a description of these three commands.

The ALL command is a specialized version of the SET SELECT, SET DISPLAY, and SET SCOPE commands. It allows you to look at and edit a particular set of lines that match a repeating target. It is especially useful for examining every line that has a particular word or phrase on it. For instance, assume you have a long document that discusses the structure of your company. While you are writing it, the structure changes, and a particular department now has many fewer tasks. You want to find every instance in the document of where the department is mentioned.

The ALL command's syntax is:

```
ALL [ target ]
```

In this case, you would use the name of the department as the target. This would show you only the lines with that word on it, so you could decide which ones to change. To show all the lines in the file, give the ALL command with no target.

The SET VERIFY command (for which you saw a different use earlier in this chapter) prevents you from seeing particular columns, but it is different from the SET RANGE command in that it does not prevent commands from acting on those columns. It simply prevents you from seeing the columns.

For example, if you have a file whose lines are 90 characters long, but the first 10 characters are always uninteresting (such as all spaces), you can use the SET VERIFY command to hide the first 10 columns, showing you columns 11 through 90 instead. The syntax of the command is:

```
SET VERIFY { OFF | ON } [ start end ] ...
```

The start and end column pairs are the beginning and end columns for the columns you want to see. To only see columns 11 through 90, give the command:

```
SET VERIFY OFF 11 90
```

Color and Highlighting on 3270 Terminals

XEDIT allows you use the colors on 3270 color terminals. Many people find that using colors and highlighting on their screens is helpful, while others find it distracting. You can use these commands to experiment with the options available on your terminal.

The two XEDIT commands that affect color and highlighting are SET COLOR and SET RESERVED. You can use these commands whether or not your terminal supports the features: XEDIT ignores the parts you cannot use.

The SET COLOR command lets you set the color for each definable part of the screen. Its syntax is:

```
SET COLOR field [ color ] [ style ] [ HIGH | NOHIGH ] [ PS ]
```

The field is the part of the screen you want to modify:

ARROW	The pointing arrow (====>).
CMDLINE	The command line.
CURLINE	The current line.
FILEAREA	The text area.
IDLINE	The file data area (generally the first line of the screen).
MSGLINE	The message area.
PREFIX	The prefix area.
SCALE	The ruler.
STATAREA	The status area in the lower right corner of the screen.
TOFEOF	The "* * * Top of File * * *" and "* * * End of File * * *" messages.
*	All areas of the screen.

The color can be any of the following eight colors:

• BLUE
• GREEN

- PINK
- RED
- TURQUOISE
- WHITE
- YELLOW
- DEFAULT

The style is another form of highlighting. The four choices for style are:

- BLINK
- NONE
- REVVIDEO
- UNDERLINE

HIGH and NOHIGH indicate whether to use the terminal's highlighting capabilities; these are distinct from the color choices. Highlighted characters appear brighter than unhighlighted ones.

PS indicates the alternate character set you want to use in that area. The choices are PS0 and PSA through PSF.

Many terminals that do not have color have styles or highlighting. Extremely few terminals have alternate character sets.

By default, XEDIT only uses RED for the message line. None of the fields have default styles or alternate character sets. It uses the following defaults for highlighting for the fields:

ARROW	HIGH
CMDLINE	NOHIGH
CURLINE	HIGH
FILEAREA	NOHIGH
IDLINE	HIGH
MSGLINE	HIGH
PREFIX	NOHIGH
SCALE	HIGH
STATAREA	HIGH
TOFEOF	NOHIGH

For example, if you want to edit with black characters on a white background (like a normal piece of paper), you would give the command:

```
SET COLOR FILEAREA WHITE REVVIDEO
```

The SET RESERVED command lets you specify the same parameters as SET COLOR for the reserved line on the screen. Its full syntax is:

```
SET RESERVED place [ color ] [ style ] [ PS ] { HIGH | NOHIGH } [text]
```

Sorting

You learned in Chapter 4 how to use CMS's SORT command to sort an entire file. This is not always convenient, especially if you only want to sort part of the file. For instance, if you have a table in a report that you want to sort, you cannot use CMS's SORT command.

XEDIT's SORT command lets you choose which lines to sort, as well as the columns. It also lets you decide if you want the records in ascending order (A-Z) or descending order (Z-A). Its syntax is:

```
SORT target [ A | D ] col1 col2 ...
```

You can repeat the col1 and col2 specifications for each pair of sort columns. A and D specify ascending and descending. The SORT command sorts the lines from the current line up to, but not including, the target line.

XEDIT AND SERIAL TERMINALS

This chapter has been devoted to using XEDIT on 3270 terminals since XEDIT works much better on 3270s. You can use XEDIT on serial and asynchronous terminals, but only a small subset of the useful functions are available. Note that serial terminals connected to an ASCII cluster controller (such as the model 7171) can use the full set of XEDIT functions if the controller is correctly configured.

Most significantly, you cannot use prefix commands or most of the easy editing that you can with the cursor movement keys on the 3270. As it turns out, these are the most common actions used with XEDIT. Their replacements are not nearly as easy to use.

Note that some of the commands in your PROFILE XEDIT file are not allowed in terminal mode. Also, you want to set VERIFY on to see the changes to each line as you make them. If you are using a serial terminal, you should use the following shorter PROFILE XEDIT:

```
SET ARBCHAR ON $
SET AUTOSAVE 10
SET CASE MIXED IGNORE
SET NONDISP |
SET SPAN ON BLANK 3
SET STAY ON
SET VARBLANK ON
SET VERIFY ON 1 *
SET WRAP ON
```

When you use a serial terminal, you need a way to tell XEDIT which column in a line you want to edit. You can use the standard commands to set the current line, but the column pointer becomes much more important. The commands that shift the column pointer around in a line are:

CFIRST	Puts the column pointer at the beginning of the line.
CLAST	Puts the column pointer at the end of the line.

CLOCATE   Puts the column pointer at the part of the line identified by the *column target*. Column targets are similar to regular targets, but they only relate to positions in the column.

Once you have the column pointer where you want it, you need to use the column editing commands to change the text on the line. These commands are:

CAPPEND   Adds text to the end of the line, regardless of where the column pointer is.

CDELETE   Deletes from the cursor pointer up to, but not including, the specified column target.

CINSERT   Inserts characters at the column pointer.

CREPLACE   Replaces the text starting at the column pointer with new text.

Since you have no ruler on the screen, it is hard to tell where the column pointer is unless you have a very good memory. XEDIT puts an underline under the column with the column pointer if you have a typewriter terminal. This can be turned off with the command:

```
SET COLPTR OFF
```

The following is a sample terminal session. Start by entering the beginning of the BUSINESS LETTER file using the INPUT command. Note that this has three mistakes you will correct:

```
                                January 27, 1988

Cody Freeman, Vice President
Lincoln Union Bank
5512 South Market Street
Lincoln, CA  91422

Dear Ms. Fresman:

Thank you very much for talking with us the other day about
request for an extension on our business loan. This letter
follows up on that meeting.

National Packaging has been very successful in attracting new
clients in the last two years. Our annual revenues have grown from
$7.3 million to $16..8 million since January 1986, and our profits
have grown from $1.1 million to $2.2 million. Our staff has
grown from 27 to 63.
```

The first mistake is that the spelling of the name in the salutation is wrong. Go to the line by giving the LOCATE command:

```
/Ms. Fre/
```

Since you have VERIFY set on, XEDIT responds with the full line found:

```
Dear Ms. Fresman:
```

This puts the column pointer at the beginning of the salutation. You can now change "Fresman" to "Freeman" in one of three ways:

```
CHANGE /Fres/Free/
```

or

```
CLOCATE /sman/
CDELETE 1
CINSERT e
```

or

```
CLOCATE /sman/
CREPLACE e
```

You now need to add the word "our" at the end of the first line of the body. A good method would be:

```
2
CAPPEND  our
```

The fastest method for fixing the ".." in the second paragraph is simply:

```
CHANGE /.././ *
```

As you can see, this is not nearly as easy as cruising around the screen with the cursor control keys.

USING XEDIT COMMANDS IN OTHER UTILITIES

You can now see how useful knowing XEDIT is, even if you don't edit many files. Since the FILELIST and HELP commands are based on XEDIT, they respond to XEDIT's commands.

For example, the LOCATE command is very useful in the HELP command. You can search through a long help discussion for a specific word for which you are looking. It is also useful in the FILELIST command. If you have many screens full of files to sort through, you can search for characters in the file name; FILELIST makes the first found file the top line of the FILELIST display.

7

Introduction to REXX

By now, you are seeing how interconnected the parts of CMS are. By learning about XEDIT, you found out how to use HELP and FILELIST more effectively. You also saw some of the uses of REXX in the chapters on CMS commands and the chapter on XEDIT.

REXX (which is called the *System Product Interpreter* in IBM's documentation) runs EXECs for CMS and macros for XEDIT. You do not run the "REXX command"; instead, CMS or XEDIT runs REXX when it determines you want to run a command file you have named. Even though you don't invoke REXX directly, you should know how to use it, since REXX can make using CMS much simpler and less tedious.

You can think of REXX as a way of teaching CMS what you want to do. If you want to always give a group of commands together, you can put those in a file. When you tell CMS to execute that file, it executes all the commands sequentially. In this way, you have shown CMS once what you want to do many times.

If You Are Familiar With Other Computers

REXX is more advanced than most other command processors. The nearest equivalent to REXX is the C-shell in UNIX. REXX is significantly more powerful than the batch language on MS-DOS.

This chapter gives you a brief introduction to REXX. As you see how much REXX can do for you, you may want to learn more about REXX. For more information on REXX, two good choices are *The REXX Language: A Practical Approach to Programming*, by M. F. Cowlishaw (Prentice Hall, 1985) and *Modern Programming Using REXX*, by D. Gomberg and R. Ohara (Prentice Hall, 1986).

WHAT REXX CAN DO

Most of the EXECs and macros you have seen so far have been simple lists of commands. The main purpose of these has been to reduce typing (because you do not need to enter so many keystrokes) and increase reliability (because you do not need to remember command syntaxes once you have entered the command in the EXEC or macro).

In the PROFILE XEDIT in Chapter 6, you also saw another use for REXX: to prevent you from having to make decisions. In the SET RESERVED command, you want to use the number that is the length of the terminal. Of course, you could do this without REXX. You would give the QUERY LSCREEN command, look at the result, then use that result when you typed the SET RESERVED command. Instead of this, you used the EXTRACT command to save the result in a REXX variable, and used that REXX variable in the SET RESERVED command in the macro.

This shows an important use of REXX: to automate your work, even work that requires decisions. Computers are great at making decisions: they can compare two things and make a choice based on the comparison. The most common comparison you use is between a variable and a *constant*. A constant is a number or string of characters that never changes. For example, the number "5" is a constant. You might compare the number of pencils on the desk (a variable) to the number "5": Are there 5 pencils or not?

Comparisons can be more than yes/no questions; they can give greater-than and less-than results. These types of comparisons can be between two variables or a variable and a constant. For instance, you might ask, Which pile of rocks is bigger? Or you might ask, Does that pile have more than ten rocks in it?

You can use REXX to make such comparisons. For instance, in the INDENT macro in Chapter 6, the REXX "if" command compared the information typed on the line with the constant of nothing: if they typed nothing on the line, the macro performed one command, but if they typed anything else, it performed a different command.

REXX is also good at letting you decide how you want a command file to proceed while it is being executed. It is common to ask the user for input to a command file, then make a choice based on that input. You might ask, "How many times should I do this?" or "What name should I enter here?" or "Is this correct?" and so on. When you type in something and press ENTER, the REXX file can interpret what you type (by comparing it to what it expects in different situations) and act accordingly. For instance, if you ask the user whether to continue or not, the REXX file can look at the response from the user and determine if the user said "yes."

REXX LANGUAGE

The REXX language is fairly simple. You have already seen most of the parts of it in the EXECs and macros from the previous chapters.

There are many REXX commands (also called REXX instructions). These are similar to CMS commands: They take arguments and options. In this book, REXX commands start at the beginning of a line and exist on a line by themselves.

REXX files also can have *assignment* commands. You use an assignment command to set the value of a variable. An assignment command might be:

```
Highest = 5
```

In this case, the variable called "Highest" is set to 5. Using the mailbox analogy from Chapter 6, this is like saying, "Make the contents of the mailbox labelled 'Highest' the number 5."

REXX variables and constants can be either numeric or strings of characters. In the previous example, 5 is a numeric constant; thus, Highest becomes a numeric variable. An example of an assignment for strings is:

```
Answer = "Yes"
```

String constants are always expressed with either single or double quotes around them.

Assignment commands can have variables on both sides of the equal sign. For instance:

```
Highest = 5
Next = Highest
```

After these two lines execute, the variable "Next" equals 5. This is like saying "Make a copy of the contents of the mailbox labelled 'Highest,' and put that copy in the mailbox labelled 'Next'."

You can combine variables and constants into *expressions*. An expression can be formed in many ways. For numeric variables and constants, you can use standard arithmetic to make expressions. For example:

```
Highest = 5
Next = Highest + 3
```

After these two lines execute, the variable "Next" equals 8. "Highest + 3" is an expression that is made up of a variable (Highest), an arithmetic connective (+), and a constant (3).

You can make string expressions in a similar fashion. Putting two strings next to each other, separated by a space, makes an expression that evaluates to a single string: the first string, a space, and the second string. For example:

```
First = "XXX"
Second = "YYY"
Together = First Second
```

When you execute these lines, it is the same as:

```
Together = "XXX YYY"
```

You will learn about other connectives later in this chapter.

If a line in an EXEC has parts that REXX does not recognize, REXX assumes that the line is a command to be executed by CMS. Likewise, if a macro has a line with unrecognized parts, REXX assumes that line is to be executed by XEDIT. REXX executes the lines after substituting all the values of the variables. For example, look at the following EXEC:

```
Thefile = "BUSINESS LETTER"
XEDIT Thefile
```

REXX executes the first line, assigning the string "BUSINESS LETTER" to the variable called "Thefile". It then sees that the next line has something it doesn't recognize (namely, the XEDIT command). It substitutes the value of Thefile into the place of the variable, and comes up with:

```
XEDIT BUSINESS LETTER
```

It then causes CMS to execute that command.

There are a few more parts of the REXX language with which you should be familiar. You already know about comments: They are lines that begin with "/*" and end with "*/". The first line of any REXX file must begin with a comment, even if it is an empty comment:

```
/* */
```

You can put whatever you want between the beginning and end of the comment: REXX doesn't look at it. Generally, you want to put the name of the file and a short description of what it does, such as:

```
/* FILLER EXEC: adds appropriate names to text files */
```

REXX also has *functions* you can perform on variables or constants. A function is a procedure with arguments; functions are usually used just like expressions. The arguments to functions go between parentheses. For instance, the "length" function is used to find the length of a string.

```
Thefile = "BUSINESS LETTER"
Namelen = LENGTH(Thefile)
```

After these lines are executed, the variable Namelen would equal 15.

You can now understand better what the last four lines of the PROFILE XEDIT did:

```
EXTRACT "/LSCREEN"
```

The EXTRACT command puts values in variables. The variable is named the same as the argument to EXTRACT, followed by a period and a number. In this case, the variable LSCREEN.5 is assigned the number of lines on the terminal.

```
Lres = "1 = Help   3 = Quit   6 = ?   7 = Backward   "
Rres = "8 = Forward   9 = =   11 = Spltjoin"
```

These are two assignment commands that set string variables (note the double quotes at the beginning and end of the strings).

```
SET RESERVED LSCREEN.5 NOHIGH Lres Rres
```

REXX substitutes the value for the three variables (LSCREEN.5, Lres, and Rres) and tells XEDIT to perform the result:

```
SET RESERVED 24 NOHIGH 1 = Help   3 = Quit   6 = ?   7 = Backward
            8 = Forward   9 = =   11 = Spltjoin
```

That is really all there is to the structure of REXX files. Once you know a bit about the REXX commands, you can create your own REXX files.

To help you figure out what parts of a REXX line are doing, this book has a few standards for upper and lowercase:

- REXX commands are in all lowercase.
- REXX variable names are in initial capitals.
- CMS and XEDIT commands and arguments are in uppercase.

REXX does not require these rules; in fact, REXX doesn't notice case because it converts everything to uppercase unless you tell it not to. However, these rules help make REXX files easier to read.

REXX COMMANDS

Many REXX commands are quite simple to understand. Like CMS commands, the name of the REXX command always comes first, followed by its arguments. This section shows you how easy it is to understand most REXX commands.

SAY Command

The SAY command puts a message on the screen. Its syntax is:

```
say expression
```

For instance:

```
say "That number is too large."
```

This prints the string on the screen, without the quotes:

```
That number is too large.
```

As another example:

```
Highest = 6
say "The number is" Highest
```

This would display:

```
The number is 6
```

IF-THEN-ELSE Command

The IF command lets you make decisions in your REXX files. Its syntax is:

```
IF logical-expression THEN instruction [ ELSE instruction ]
```

The logical-expression uses REXX's comparative operators. The result of a logical expression is either true or false. The common logical operators are:

=	equals
¬=	not equals
>	greater than
<	less than
>=	greater than or equal to
<=	less than or equal to

For example, you might want to test whether a numeric variable called "Size" was greater than 5. The beginning of the IF command would be:

```
if Size > 5 then
```

When REXX evaluates an IF command, it first checks to see if the logical expression is true. If it is, REXX executes the instruction after the THEN. For example:

```
if Size > 5 then say "That is bigger than 5"
```

If Size was 5, it would display the string; if Size was 4, this line would not produce any output.

The ELSE option lets you do something different if the expression is false. It is given on the line following the IF command, although it is not a command by itself. For example:

```
if Size > 5 then say "That is bigger than 5"
        else say "That is not bigger than 5"
```

The IF command is incredibly useful in EXECs and macros. You saw one used in the INDENT macro: If the user pressed ENTER without typing in a number (indicating he or she didn't want to do that), the macro exited:

```
if Nlines = "" then exit
```

(The EXIT command is a REXX command that stops the EXEC or macro.)

PULL Command

The SAY command prints messages on the screen; the PULL command takes text typed by the user and puts it in variables. These are often used together, as you saw in the INDENT macro:

```
say "How many lines would you like to indent?"
pull Nlines
```

The syntax of the PULL command is:

```
pull var1 [ var2 ... ]
```

You can read in as many variables as you like and give them any name. When REXX reads the user's response, it converts it to uppercase and splits apart each word. The first word goes in var1, the second word goes in var2, and so on.

REXX's automatic conversion to uppercase is sometimes annoying. For example, consider this short EXEC:

```
/* Greeting EXEC */
say "What is your name?"
pull Name
say "Hello there," Name
```

Assume that a user runs this and responds to the query with "Jean". The third line would display:

```
Hello there, JEAN
```

This isn't terribly good-looking. You can use the PARSE PULL command instead of the PULL command if you don't want REXX to convert input to all uppercase. The EXEC would then be:

```
/* Greeting EXEC */
say "What is your name?"
parse pull Name
say "Hello there," Name
```

Using the PULL command and the IF command together gives you a great deal of flexibility. For example, the following EXEC prompts you for arguments to the RENAME command:

```
/* NEWREN EXEC: new interface for RENAME command */
say "Full name of the file to be renamed:"
pull fn1 ft1 fm1
if ft1 = "" then exit
/* If they left off the filemode, make it "A" */
if fm1 = "" then fm1 = "A"
say "Name you to which you want to change" fn1 ft1 fm1 ":"
pull fn2 ft2 fm2
if ft2 = "" then exit
if fm2 = "" then fm2 = fm1
/* If they left off the filemode, make it the same as before */
RENAME fn1 ft1 fm1 fn2 ft2 fm2
```

If the user doesn't enter the filename or filetype for either prompt, the EXEC exits. If they forget to enter a filemode in the first prompt, the EXEC supplies "A". In this case, the instruction after the THEN is an assignment. If they forget to enter a filemode in the second prompt, the EXEC supplies whatever they gave for the filemode in the first prompt. It then executes a CMS RENAME command with all the necessary arguments.

ARG Command

CMS and XEDIT commands can take arguments on their command lines: Why shouldn't EXECs and macros? REXX allows you to retrieve arguments on the command line with the ARG command. The ARG command acts very much like the PULL command, except that it fills variables from the command line instead of from the user's typing. Its syntax is:

```
ARG var1 [ var2 ... ]
```

The ARG command means you do not need to prompt the user for information all the time. For instance, you might want the NEWREN EXEC file just shown to take the first file from the command line instead of from the prompts. It would look like this:

```
/* NEWREN EXEC: new interface for RENAME command */
arg fn1 ft1 fm1
if ft1 = "" then exit
if fm1 = "" then fm1 = "A"
/* If they left off the filemode, make it "A" */
say "Name you to which you want to change" fn1 ft1 fm1 ":"
pull fn2 ft2 fm2
if ft2 = "" then exit
if fm2 = "" then fm2 = fm1
/* If they left off the filemode, make it the same as before */
RENAME fn1 ft1 fm1 fn2 ft2 fm2
```

The ARG command is especially handy in XEDIT macros. For instance, the following macro splits the screen into as many equal-sized windows as you specify on the command line, but first checks if those screens would be fewer than five lines long (the minimum). If they would be shorter than five lines, the macro splits the screen into as many screens it can. This macro is more convenient than the SET SCREEN's response when you try to split into more windows than allowed: SET SCREEN simply gives you an error message and doesn't do anything.

```
/* SSCR XEDIT: Splits the screen */
ARG Requirednum
if Requirednum = "" then Requirednum = 1
EXTRACT "/LSCREEN"
if Requirednum <= LSCREEN.5 % 5 then Nscr = Requirednum
    else Nscr = LSCREEN.5 % 5
SET SCREEN Nscr
```

The ARG command sets the variable Requirednum to the argument from the command line. The IF command checks whether an argument was given; if no argument was specified, the macro assumes an argument of 1. The EXTRACT command is the same as you have seen before.

The next IF command compares Requirednum to the integer part of the length of the screen divided by 5 (using "%" instead of "/" tells REXX to return only the integer portion of the result). If it was less than or equal to the number of screen lines divided by 5 (indicating the command will be successful), the variable Nscr is set to Requirednum; if it was greater than this number, Nscr is set to the largest value that will work. The SET SCREEN command is then executed.

REXX FUNCTIONS

Functions allow you to manipulate information in variables. They also let you get certain system constants. The form of a function is:

```
function( [ arg1 [ , arg2 ... ] ])
```

If a function takes more than one argument, they are separated by commas.

Some functions take no arguments: They are only used to get system information. For instance, the TIME and DATE functions do not need to have arguments. They return the current time and date:

```
say time()
say date()
```

Running this EXEC would display:

```
10:31:45
11 Jul 1988
```

Both functions can also take arguments that modify the displayed information. For instance, giving the TIME function the argument "H" causes it to return the number of hours since midnight.

```
say time("H")
```

would display:

```
10
```

REXX's string functions let you pick out parts of string variables and constants. This is useful if you know that parts of the strings in certain locations are useful.

The LEFT function returns the leftmost characters of a string. Its syntax is:

```
left(string, len)
```

For example:

```
Exstr = "This is the message"
say left(Exstr, 6)
```

would display:

```
This i
```

As you might have expected, the RIGHT function returns the rightmost characters in the string. The SUBSTR function is like the best of both LEFT and RIGHT: it returns characters from the middle of a string. Its syntax is:

```
substr(string, start-pos [, len ])
```

The returned string starts at the number specified in start-pos, and goes for the number of characters specified in len. If you don't specify len, SUBSTR returns to the end of the string. Some examples should make this clearer:

```
Exstr = "This is the message"
say substr(Exstr, 6, 5)
say substr(Exstr, 10)
```

This displays:

```
is th
he message
```

The LEFT function is useful for testing out a user's response to the PULL command. For instance, if you ask for a yes-or-no answer to a question, you might want the user to be able to answer "Y" or "y" or "YES" or "yes" or even "yeah." The following lets you do that:

```
say "Would you like to do that?"
pull answer
if left(answer, 1) = "Y" then say "OK"
```

The POS function goes one step further for you: It lets you search the whole string for a shorter string for which you are looking. It returns the position of the shorter string if it is found or 0 if it is not. Its syntax is:

```
pos(sought, string)
```

For example:

```
Exstr = "This is the message"
say pos("is", Exstr)
say pos("not", Exstr)
```

would display:

```
3
0
```

There are dozens of other REXX functions you can use. Most are of interest only to programmers.

QUOTING AND REXX

The most common problem with creating your own REXX files is when REXX does not respond the way you expected. The usual reason for this is that REXX interprets more than you had hoped for.

For instance, consider the following correct XEDIT command that might appear in a macro:

```
SET RESERVED -1 NOHIGH This appears at the bottom of the screen.
```

When REXX interprets the line, it looks for variables or REXX commands. Finding none, it still tries to do any "required" arithmetic. It sees the "-1" (which was meant to tell SET RESERVED to put the line on the bottom line of the screen) and tries to subtract it from the "variable" RESERVED. It gets confused (since RESERVED is not a REXX variable) and reports:

```
DMSREX476E Error 41 running LL XEDIT, line 2: Bad arithmetic conversion
```

To prevent this, you must put the -1 in quotes so REXX thinks it is a string constant to be passed with the command:

```
SET RESERVED "-1" NOHIGH This appears at the bottom of the screen.
```

Of course, this is an inconvenience. Quoting as much as you can prevents REXX from evaluating things you don't expect. The safest thing to do with commands to CMS or XEDIT that don't involve any REXX substitution is to quote the whole line; REXX does not, of course, pass the quotes with the command. For example:

```
"SET RESERVED -1 NOHIGH This appears at the bottom of the screen."
```

You must quote any line that has any symbol REXX looks for that you don't want interpreted. These include:

```
+  -  /  *  %  |  &  =  \  <  >  ;  (  )
```

Of course, this means you must quote a great deal: any CMS command with options, any XEDIT command with + or - arguments, and so on.

MAKE A DESK CALCULATOR

So far, you have only seen how to make REXX files that execute a line at a time from top to bottom. REXX has the capability of repeating lines based on criteria which you give. This, unfortunately, requires a fair understanding of programming and is beyond the scope of this book.

This section shows you a short, simple program that gives you a desk calculator you can use from either CMS or XEDIT. It involves some REXX programming, and is only briefly described. However, you should feel free to type it in and use it, regardless of whether or not you understand the programming in it. Save the file on your disk as CALC EXEC.

When you run the program, it prompts:

```
Type in an expression:
```

You can enter any arithmetic calculation you want. You should use parentheses to group parts of the calculation so REXX knows what to evaluate first. After each line you enter, REXX evaluates what you typed and displays the result. To exit from the calculator, press ENTER by itself instead of entering a calculation.

The EXEC is:

```
/* CALC EXEC: Simple calculator */
do until Expr = ""
  say "Type in an expression:"
  pull Expr
  interpret "say" Expr
end
```

For instance, you might enter the following (the lines you type are shown underlined):

```
Type in an expression:
34*55
1870
Type in an expression:
3*(11.5+7.22)
56.16
Type in an expression:
```

A brief explanation of the program is that it performs a loop of instructions (those that are indented) until a particular condition is met. The DO command in the second line tells REXX to do everything until the END command until the value of Expr is "". As you saw earlier in this chapter, the value of a variable in the PULL command is "" when the user presses ENTER without entering anything on the command line. Thus the DO-UNTIL-END command loops until the user presses ENTER without anything else in the command line.

The INTERPRET command on the fifth line simply makes a string of its arguments and executes that string. In this case, the string becomes a SAY command followed by a mathematical expression.

INTRODUCTION TO EXEC2

The EXEC2 language is a weak cousin to REXX. EXEC2 was CMS's command processor for many years, though, so it is likely that you will find many EXEC2 files on your system. This chapter gives you a very brief introduction to EXEC2 so you can read those files.

EXEC2 has many features in common with REXX. You can write EXECs and macros with EXEC2. It has variables and assignments, as well as looping procedures. It also has functions. However, it is not nearly as easy to write programs in EXEC2.

Each variable name and command in EXEC2 begins with an ampersand (&). This identifies each keyword to EXEC2 for its processing of the file. Each EXEC2 file must start with the "&TRACE" command. This identifies the file as an EXEC2 file.

EXEC2 comments are any lines that begin with an asterisk (*). Thus, a typical comment might be:

```
* This EXEC indents lines.
```

Most of the EXECs and macros you have seen can be easily converted to EXEC2 format. For instance, the PROFILE XEDIT file would look like this:

```
&TRACE OFF
*  Profile for XEDIT in EXEC2 format
SET ARBCHAR ON $
SET AUTOSAVE 10
SET CASE MIXED IGNORE
SET CMDLINE TOP
SET CURLINE ON 6
SET MSGLINE ON 3 3 OVERLAY
SET NONDISP
SET NULLS ON
SET SCALE ON 3
SET SPAN ON BLANK 3
SET STAY ON
SET VARBLANK ON
SET WRAP ON
* The next 5 lines display a line at the bottom of the XEDIT screen
TRANSFER LSCREEN
&READ VARS &X1 &X2 &X3 &X4 &X5
&LRES = &STRING OF 1 = Help   3 = Quit   6 = ?   7 = Backward  8
&RRES = &STRING OF = Forward   9 = =   11 = Spltjoin
SET RESERVED &X5 NOHIGH &LRES &RRES
```

Note that the EXTRACT command had to be changed to two commands: TRANSFER and &READ. The TRANSFER command puts the values that EXTRACT would have been assigned in variables into a special area called the *stack*; the &READ VARS command reads information out of the stack and puts it in variables.

EXEC2 has more limited string handling than REXX. The string assignment lines have to be changed to include the &STRING OF function.

The INDENT XEDIT macro would look like:

```
&TRACE OFF
* Indents text; prompts the user for number of lines and
*    number of columns to indent
&TYPE How many lines would you like to indent?
&READ VAR &NLINES
&IF &NLINES = "" &EXIT
&TYPE How many columns would you like to indent the next &NLINES lines?
&READ VAR &NCOLS
&IF &NCOLS = "" &EXIT
SHIFT RIGHT &NCOLS &NLINES
```

The &TYPE command is the same as the REXX SAY command. Note that the &IF command has no "&THEN".

CONCLUSION

This chapter has only skimmed the surface of what REXX can do for you if you are willing to program. Programmers often find REXX to be a wonderful programming language due to its flexibility and ease of use. If you are tempted to learn to program, REXX is an excellent first language.

8

Advanced CMS Topics

This chapter covers the more advanced subjects which beginning and intermediate users should know a bit about but are not required for day-to-day use. The usefulness of the information in this chapter will depend on how much or how little you need to use the commands described.

Even though this chapter is called "advanced CMS topics," you should not feel that the information here is meant only for advanced users. Instead, think of these topics as introductions to some of CMS's features that require more technical discussion than the topics in the previous chapters.

The material in this chapter is presented so that, if you are in a situation where you need to know about a particular advanced topic, you have access to a good conceptual description of the topic and of the CMS commands that relate to it. For instance, most users never deal with tape drives. Thus, the basics of tape drives are discussed in this chapter.

VIRTUAL DEVICES

Even though CMS has progressed far from the early 1970s, its user interface still relies on some of its more technical underpinnings in ways that sometimes require all users to know about them. Wisely, IBM has taken steps to shield you from some of these technical details, but there are still areas where it helps to know why it is so. The most common technical concept you will encounter is *virtual devices*.

In Chapter 1, you saw that VM is designed so it looks to you as if you have your own computer. When you run programs, you don't need to worry if another user is going to take away some of your memory or disk space. For anyone (other than the system administrator) to get access to any of your resources, you need to give them explicit permission.

Why Virtual Devices Were Invented

When VM was designed, this nearly complete separation of users on multi-user computers was a fairly new concept. Most IBM users were on single-user systems: Only one program ran at a time. Each program was submitted to a batch processor which would execute job after job. Thus, no one's job could affect someone else's because there was only one job executing at any moment.

Many programs had been developed with this single-user concept in mind. If the program wanted to print some lines on the line printer, it would simply grab control of the line printer and send it information to print. If the program wanted to read or write to the disk, it would just start moving the disk head. Of course, if there are many people using the printer or disk, simply sending or receiving data could be disastrous, since other users could be using them as well.

Thus, the VM developers needed to find a way to let the existing single-user programs run safely without massive changes. It was important to be sure no user could affect the state of another user except in known, harmless ways. If Celia had a program that caused lines to be printed on the printer, it should appear to work without error, but not do anything that could affect someone else's printout.

Also, the VM developers worried about how users would perform the communications common at the time. For example, if you wanted a copy of Jim's file, the security rules built into most early operating systems didn't prevent you from reading it off his disk (possibly reading files you shouldn't) or him from writing it on yours (possibly damaging some of your important files). Thus, most people kept their files on separate disks they physically mounted when they ran jobs. You couldn't read from a disk that was not mounted.

Instead, he would run a program to cause the file to be punched out on punch cards (remember them?), and hand you the stack of cards. You would then put the stack in the card reader and run a program that indicated the cards should be read into a particular file.

The VM designers thought of a unique way to allow CMS users to communicate: Give each user his or her own disk, punch, reader, and printer. Since users had their own virtual machines, why not give them virtual devices as well? These virtual devices were operating system software that pretended to punch cards, read cards, and print files (virtual disks are another, much more complex topic).

Now, if you wanted to get Jim's file, he would punch it on his virtual card punch, and put it in your virtual card reader. You could look through the stacks in your virtual reader and decide which ones to load on disk.

Similarly, if your program gave a "print" instruction, it only printed on your virtual printer: You would have to later transmit the output of your virtual printer to a program that controlled the real printer and organized everyone's printing. The printer you send your virtual printer output to knows how to organize different users' printing requests using a *queue*. The queue is described in more detail later in this chapter.

Note that the reason you don't need to know about any of this (unless you are printing files) is that CMS now has commands that cover up all of this. The NOTE, SENDFILE, and RDRLIST commands use your virtual punch and reader in such a manner that you don't need to know about virtual devices at all. Also, many sites have added their own commands to handle these details.

Spooling

This brings up an interesting dilemma: If these virtual devices are just pretending to do the jobs requested, how do you actually get them done? This involves another concept called *spooling*. Spooling involves CMS commands that you use before and after the programs that send to and receive from virtual devices. When you spool a device, you specify how it will act and where the output of that device should go.

For instance, you may want to send the virtual cards produced by a program to another user. Before you start the program, you use the SPOOL command to specify the recipient of the cards. After the program is finished punching the cards, you use the CLOSE command to end the "stack" of cards so the stack gets sent. The CLOSE command puts a marker in the device that separates the blocks of information: Each block of information is called a *spool file*. The CLOSE command also causes the file to be sent to the other user. (Do not confuse spool files with files that appear on your minidisk.)

Thus, the SPOOL command doesn't send data to your virtual devices: It only specifies how the data should appear and where the result ends up. The most important information you give to the SPOOL command is the destination of the spool files in your virtual device. Usually, you spool your virtual punch to someone else's userid; this puts the spool files in their virtual reader. You also usually spool your virtual printer to the special userid SYSTEM. VM watches what is spooled to this userid and, based on the class, reroutes the spool file to the print queue for the appropriate printer.

Note that the spooling system is volatile. If the system crashes while you have information that is spooled, it may not be there when the system comes up again. You should not rely on the spooling system to hold valuable information that is not stored safely on disk somewhere.

The other parameters that you can set with the SPOOL command include:

Class   Spool files have *classes* associated with them. A class is just a letter identifier. Some programs which read from virtual devices require that the material they read have a particular class.

Cont   The CONT option lets you group spool files together. (Cont is short for continue.) This prevents the CLOSE command from indicating that the spool file has ended. Use the NOCONT option to reset this.

Copy   You can specify that the virtual device send out multiple copies of spool files. For instance, you might want five copies of a file printed.

Hold   Normally, if you have spooled a virtual device to a VM device, every time you use the CLOSE command, the spool file is sent. If you use the HOLD option, your device holds the files until you use the NOHOLD option.

As you can see, this material is not for users with weak stomachs. If you have to deal with any of this other than through the SENDFILE, NOTE, and RDRLIST commands, read the IBM manuals. You can experiment by spooling files to yourself; this lets you examine the effects of these parameters. Hopefully, the preceding explanation helps explain what some of the magic incantations are used for.

CMS Commands for Virtual Devices

The two commands you have seen so far are SPOOL and CLOSE. You use the SPOOL command differently for the virtual reader than you do for the virtual punch and printer. It is highly unlikely that you will use the SPOOL command for your virtual reader. In fact, the only command you will probably ever use with your virtual reader is RDRLIST.

The syntax of the SPOOL command for the virtual punch and printer is:

```
SPOOL { PUNCH | PRINTER } [ options ]
options:
[ TO { userid | SYSTEM | * } ]
[ CLASS c ]
[ CONT | NOCONT ]
[ COPY n ]
[ HOLD | NOHOLD ]
[ FORM form ]
```

The TO clause specifies to where the devices will be spooled. "TO *" indicates that it is spooled to your reader; this is sometimes useful if you want to modify the spool file and resend it. The FORM option is only used with virtual printers.

For example, to direct your virtual punch to the virtual reader in userid JCROSS, give the command:

```
SPOOL PUNCH TO JCROSS
```

Use the CLOSE command to close the spool file in your virtual punch or printer. Its syntax is:

```
CLOSE { PUNCH | PRINTER } [ PURGE ]
```

The PURGE option immediately kills the spool file so it is not sent to the destination assigned in the SPOOL command. Use the PURGE option if you have made a mistake and want to get rid of the unclosed spool file. If you have specified the CONT option in the SPOOL command, the CLOSE command has no effect.

Remember that these commands are not needed by most users: It is much easier to send files with the SENDFILE command. The SENDFILE command takes care of all the options and checking required for using the spooling system. It is also much easier to read files from your virtual reader with the RDRLIST command than the commands shown here.

You can use the PUNCH command to put a file in your virtual punch:

```
PUNCH fileid
```

You can also use a different pair of commands, DISK DUMP and DISK LOAD. They write and read specially-formatted cards. Their syntaxes are:

```
DISK DUMP fn ft [ fm ]
DISK LOAD
```

Most of the other commands that relate to the virtual devices are really only useful for the virtual printer, and are described next.

Printing Files

When you spool your virtual printer to SYSTEM and put a spool file there, CMS prints your file if it has the correct class. For example, if your system sends all class G files to a specific printer and your spool file has that class, it gets printed on that printer. If your spool file has a class that no printer uses, it just sits there and never gets printed.

Each printer has a print queue. Each spool file is put into the queue in the order that it arrived. This assures that each print job prints separately. While your spool file is waiting in the queue, you still have a chance to change some of its spool parameters or to cancel it altogether. The commands to do this are described soon.

If You Are Familiar With Other Computers

Many microcomputers have print queues (often called print spoolers). Instead of being for many users, these queues are used to organize printing from many programs.

You need to ask your system administrator about which printer is associated with which class. IBM printers use *carriage control* characters at the beginning of each line to tell the printer how to advance lines and pages. Without the correct carriage control characters, your file does not print correctly. As you might have guessed, the carriage control characters for each printer are different.

Some application programs put carriage control characters in the first position on the line for you, while others don't. The file you send to the printer must have the correct carriage control characters, however. The carriage control characters in older printers, such as the Model 1403, are readable characters. For instance, a "1" indicates to go to the next page and a "+" indicates to type over the line again. Other printers, such as the Model 3211, use unreadable characters for the carriage control characters.

To put a file in your virtual printer, use the PRINT command. Its syntax is:

```
PRINT fileid [ ( options ]
options:
[ { CC | NOCC } ]
[ LINECOUN n ]
```

If the file you are printing has carriage control characters (such as program listings), use the CC option. Otherwise, use NOCC; NOCC is the default.

Most sites have EXECs for adding carriage control characters to files in preparation for printing; ask your system administrator for the name of the EXEC you should use.

```
Name of EXECs for preparing text files:
Printer model              EXEC


```

Some printers have special forms. You must name the form you want to use in the SPOOL command with the FORM option. The name of the form you want is set up by the printer operator.

It is likely that you have a variety of printers at your site. Ask your system administrator about the printers you can use and the class and form to specify. Model 3800 printers have other options that you must specify in the SPOOL command; if you are using one, be sure to ask about any special options needed.

```
Printers available to you:
Location            Model        Class        Forms


```

You may also be able to print on printers at different nodes on your network. In this case, instead of having the SPOOL command send to SYSTEM, you send to RSCS. However, every spool file you want printed over RSCS has to have a special *tag* attached to tell RSCS which printer to use.

To attach a tag to all future files in your virtual printer, use the TAG command. When sending files over RSCS, the syntax of the TAG command used at most sites is:

```
TAG DEV PRINTER node-name
```

To clear the tag, give the command:

```
TAG DEV PRINTER
```

You should ask your system administrator about the remote printers available to you and any tags necessary.

```
Remote printers available to you:
Location            Type         Class       Forms      Tags


```

You can modify the order and attributes of your files waiting to be printed on your local printers (you cannot do this for remote printers unless you are using special software). To see the files you have waiting, use the QUERY PRINTER ALL command. This tells you the file number (often referred to as the *spoolid*), the size, and the relevant attributes. The files are shown in the order they will be printed.

The CHANGE command lets you change the attributes. Its syntax is:

```
CHANGE PRINTER id { CLASS c | COPY n | HOLD | NOHOLD }
ids:
spoolid
CLASS c
FORM form
ALL
```

Most of the time, you only change one file and you identify it by its spoolid. You can change all of the spool files with a particular class or a particular form with the CLASS and FORM options; you can change all of the spool files with the ALL option.

You can reorganize the order that the files are printed with the ORDER command. The syntax for this is:

```
ORDER PRINTER spoolid1 spoolid2 ...
```

The named spool files are put at the beginning of your list in the specified order. If there are spool files you did not name, they are placed after the named ones.

There are times you want to cancel a print request. For instance, you might realize after spooling a file that it is much larger than you thought. Or, you might want to change some information in the file before it is printed. To do this, use the PURGE command. Its syntax is:

```
PURGE PRINTER { spoolid1 spoolid2 ... | ALL }
```

You can only use the CHANGE, ORDER, and PURGE commands on your own spool files.

Spooling Your Terminal

There is a special case in the previous discussion of virtual devices. The SPOOL and CLOSE command let you spool output from your terminal to your reader. This is useful if you want to capture the contents of your screen in a file so you can review it later. The commands to do this are:

```
SPOOL CONSOLE TO * START
CLOSE CONSOLE
```

After you have closed the console spooling, the file appears in your virtual reader with no filename or filetype. You can use the RDRLIST command to look through the file or to save it on your minidisk. Note that XEDIT, HELP, RDRLIST, and FILELIST sessions are not saved in the console output.

You will see another method for saving information from your terminal later in this chapter in the section on windows.

TAPE DRIVES

For many users, saving files to tape and retrieving files from tape is a rare occurrence. Tape handling is a source of great frustration and confusion for many users. There are dozens of incompatible tape formats and methods for dealing with them.

If you are just reading and writing CMS files, CMS's TAPE command does that easily. However, if you need to read and write other formats (such as special labels or large block size), you have to use other commands. Those commands generally have many difficult options. If you need to read or write such a tape, talk to your system administrator to find the exact commands you need to use.

Tape drives are similar to old-style reel-to-reel audio tape. Before you can read from or write to a tape, a tape operator needs to load the tape reel on one hub of the drive, wind the tape forward so the end goes to an empty reel, then advance the tape to the beginning of the data. In addition, he or she needs to give a command to attach that tape drive to your userid so you can access it. (Note that some sites do not let users access tapes at all; only the tape operator can read and write tapes.)

> Your tape operator is:

> Command or method to communicate with your tape operator is:

Thus, before you read a file from tape or write a file to tape, you need to request that the tape operator do two things:

- Mount the tape — put the tape in the drive and advance it to the beginning of the data. If you are going to be writing to the tape, be sure to tell the tape operator before the tape is mounted. If the tape operator asks whether you want the ring in or out of the tape, answer "ring in" if you are going to write to the tape or "ring out" if not.
- Give you access to the tape drive — use a privileged command to attach the tape drive to your userid. When this is done, a message appears on your screen that says something like:

```
TAPE 181 ATTACHED
```

If any cuu other than 181 appears in this message, you must include that number as an option to every TAPE command. To avoid this, be sure to ask that the tape be attached as your cuu 181.

The TAPE command has many purposes. The various syntaxes are described in this section. Remember, these commands only work with tapes in CMS format. If you are trying to read a tape in some other format, you must use a series of other commands, as specified by your system administrator.

Writing to a Tape

The TAPE DUMP command writes files to a tape. Its syntax is:

```
TAPE DUMP fileid [ ( options ]
options:
[ cuu ]
[ TERM | DISK | PRINT | NOPRINT
```

The fileid can contain asterisk wildcards. The command normally displays the name of each file on your screen. If you are dumping many files, you might want to use the DISK option instead, which creates a text file called "TAPE MAP" with a list of the files dumped.

If you are writing files at the beginning of the tape, it is a good idea to use the TAPE REW command first, just in case it was advanced past the beginning of the tape. Then, give the TAPE DUMP command. For example, to write all your EXEC files at the beginning of a tape, give the commands:

```
TAPE REW
TAPE DUMP * EXEC A
```

If you are going to be putting other files on the tape, and you want to group these files together, give the TAPE WTM command. This writes a tape mark that separates groups of files. This tape mark is also called an *EOF mark*, which stands for "End Of File"; however, it marks the end of a group of files, not an individual file.

For instance, if you now wanted to put all your XEDIT macros on the tape (after your EXECs), you would give the commands:

```
TAPE WTM
TAPE DUMP * XEDIT A
```

You now have two sets of files, separated by a tape mark. (Note that you did not give a TAPE REW command again: This would have caused CMS to write over the first set of files.)

When you have written all the files you want on the tape, you should do something that is a bit strange: You want to write 50 tape marks on the tape. Use the command:

```
TAPE WTM 50
```

This is useful for an interesting reason. If someone got your tape, thinking that there were three tape marks on the tape, and wanted to read the fourth file, they might try to skip over three tape marks. When they give the command to do this (which you will see soon), the tape drive skips over your two marks, then unwinds the reel looking for the last tape mark. Finding none, it goes until the tape runs off the reel. Computer operators hate it when this happens. This wastes the operator's time as well as tape drive time. Thus, putting on a large number of tape marks after all the data can help prevent this situation.

Reading From a Tape

The TAPE LOAD command reads files from a tape onto your disk. Its syntax is:

```
TAPE LOAD fn ft [ fm ] [ ( options ]
options:
[ cuu ]
[ TERM | DISK | PRINT | NOPRINT ]
[ EOF n ]
```

This looks just like the TAPE DUMP command. CMS looks for the file you specify and dumps it to your A disk (or the disk you specify in fm). You can use asterisks to dump all files matching the specification. If you use the EOF option, CMS looks for the file up to the specified number of tape marks.

Thus, if you now want to rewind the preceeding tape and get all the files whose names are "PHONES" from either of the two sets of files, give the commands:

```
TAPE REW
TAPE LOAD PHONES * ( EOF 2
```

This loads PHONES EXEC and PHONES XEDIT.

If you had given the option as "EOF 4" and had not put the extra tape marks at the end of the tape, the tape would have gone off the reel, causing the tape operator to have to reload the tape (after wasting tape drive time).

Positioning the Tape

To skip from your current position on the tape to the next tape mark, use the TAPE FSF command. Its syntax is:

```
TAPE FSF [ n ]
```

You can use this command to skip over multiple tape marks. To go back to a previous tape mark, use the command:

```
TAPE BSF [ n ]
```

You can also use the TAPE SCAN and TAPE SKIP commands. These commands look for particular files or for a number of tape marks; as they skip, they list all the files. Their syntaxes are:

```
TAPE { SCAN | SKIP } [ fileid ] [ ( options ]
options:
[ cuu ]
[ TERM | DISK | PRINT | NOPRINT ]
[ EOF n ]
```

The difference between TAPE SCAN and TAPE SKIP is that TAPE SCAN stops just before the specified file, while TAPE SKIP stops just after the file.

You are more likely to use TAPE SKIP without a fileid to see the contents of each group of files. If there are a large number of files on the tape, the DISK option can be handy, since you can then scan the file named TAPE MAP later with XEDIT.

Tape Modes

Each tape has three values associated with it: its density, number of tracks, and tape recording technique. The TAPE commands use defaults that are set at your system for the tape drives. You only need know these values if you are reading a tape someone gives you that has values different from the standard.

The possible densities are 200, 556, 800, 1600, 6250, and 38K. The number of tracks can be 7, 9, and 18 (7 is rarely used anymore).

If you need to change the mode for the tape you are reading or writing, give the TAPE MODESET command before any other TAPE command. Its syntax is:

```
TAPE MODESET [ ( options ]
options:
[ cuu ]
[ 7TRACK | 9TRACK | 18TRACK ]
[ DEN density ]
```

When You Are Finished

When you are done reading and writing your tape, you should do three things:

- Rewind the tape with the TAPE REW command
- Detach the tape drive from your userid with the DETACH command
- Tell the tape operator you are finished

To detach the tape, give the DETACH command:

```
DETACH cuu
```

Then, either call or send a message to the tape operator (the person who mounted the tape for you) and tell him or her you are finished. This is important since tape drives are limited resources often needed by other users.

If your site prefers to have tapes *unloaded* instead of just rewound, use the TAPE RUN command instead of the TAPE REW command before you detach it. You can find this out from your tape operator.

```
When finished with a tape, use:
    ◯ TAPE REW
    ◯ TAPE RUN
    ◯ Other command:
```

IPLing YOUR VIRTUAL MACHINE

You may end up in CP mode by accident. For example, if you accidentally press the PA1 key (if you are not using windows), you interrupt CMS and go back to CP. Occasionally, a program gets so badly scrambled that it causes CMS to stop; for instance, you might see:

```
DMKDSP450W CP ENTERED; DISABLED WAIT PSW '00020000 5021F7E6'
```

In either case, you should first attempt to start CMS again with the BEGIN command:

```
BEGIN
```

If this doesn't work (and that will be obvious), you need to start CMS with the IPL command:

```
IPL CMS
```

CMS WINDOWS

Version 5 of CMS has a new feature called *windows*. CMS's windows allow you to see and retain messages separate from your commands and to give commands in a slightly more convenient fashion.

> **If You Are Familiar With Other Computers**
> CMS's windows are nothing like Microsoft Windows or the Apple Macintosh. They are not based on graphics since the standard 3270 screen does not support graphics. They do not add features popular in microcomputer windows like pull-down menus and dialog boxes.

As you have seen, when information leaves your screen, it is gone forever. For instance, if you give the TYPE command on a long file, once you have cleared the screen, you can't go back to see what it said. CMS does not attempt to save anything displayed earlier.

With windows, CMS makes much more information available to you. Instead of just your actual screen, you also have many *virtual screens*. These virtual screens hold various types of messages and warnings; your primary virtual screen is called your CMS virtual screen. When you start CMS windows, you are looking at your CMS virtual screen. Some advanced application programs also use these virtual screens. You can imagine these virtual screens as other display screens that are available to you as you work.

There is a difference between a virtual screen and a window. A window is a small view of a virtual screen, as shown in Illustration 8-1.

What you see on your terminal is a window into a virtual screen. This is like XEDIT using your terminal to show a piece of a file; you could move the view that XEDIT showed up and down the file. You can move the window up and down the virtual screen. As you might imagine, all windows must be smaller than your terminal.

Virtual screens can be much larger than regular screens. The size of the virtual screen is set with the DEFINE VSCREEN command. Note that some programs from other vendors do not work at all in virtual screens.

Windows can be different sizes and you can see more than one window at time. Imagine that you have, as shown in Illustration 8-2, a large window into one virtual screen and a small window into a different virtual screen. You could put the smaller window on top of the larger window. Your CMS window is the size of the entire terminal, but other windows, such as the message windows, are smaller. These smaller windows appear on top of the CMS window.

You can make windows appear and disappear, and move them around. You can also use commands to make the windows larger and smaller.

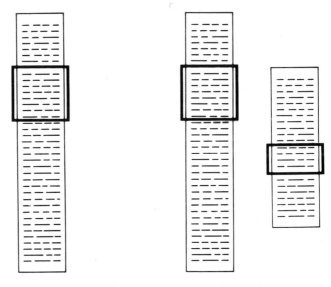

Illustration 8-1   **Illustration 8-2**

Full-Screen CMS

To start CMS windows, use the command:

```
SET FULLSCREEN ON
```

If you are going to use windows regularly, you should probably put this in your PROFILE
EXEC. Your screen now shows:

```
                         Fullscreen CMS              Columns 1-79 of 81
 Ready;
 —




















 PF1=Help       2=Pop_Msg    3=Quit       4=Clear_Top   5=Filelist    6=Retrieve
 PF7=Backward   8=Forward    9=Rdrlist    10=Left       11=Right      12=Cmdline
 ====>
  8:45:20  Message                        Enter a command or press a PF or PA key
```

This is the CMS window (actually, the window into your CMS virtual screen). It gives
you more capabilities than the regular CMS prompt.

The major part of the window is similar to the display area on your normal screen.
CMS displays information in this area. You can also give commands from this area, as well
as from the command line (the "====>" near the bottom of the window). As you can see,
the cursor is in the display part of the window. Any command you type appears there.

If you get a message (such as from the TELL command), it appears in the MESSAGE window. The MESSAGE window is a smaller window into the MESSAGE virtual screen. For example, if you send yourself a message with TELL, the MESSAGE window appears because there is something new in the MESSAGE virtual screen:

```
                        Fullscreen CMS                     Columns 1-79 of 81

Ready;
TELL * Here is a test message.




+------------------------------------------------------------------------+
|                               Messages                                 |
|                                                                        |
|   08:45:13 MSG FROM JSMITH: Here is a test message.                    |
+------------------------------------------------------------------------+




PF1=Help      2=Pop_Msg    3=Quit      4=Clear_Top   5=Filelist    6=Retrieve
PF7=Backward  8=Forward    9=Rdrlist   10=Left       11=Right      12=Cmdline
====>
 8:45:20  Message                        Enter a command or press a PF or PA key
```

The message window is smaller than the CMS window, and it appears on top of it. Since there is only one line of information in the window, CMS makes it a small window. If there were many messages (such as if many people had sent you messages with TELL), the MESSAGE window would only grow to eight lines, showing six messages. Imagine that you had gotten ten messages. Your terminal would show:

```
                           Fullscreen CMS                    Columns 1-79 of 81

Ready;
Tell * Here is a test message.



     +-----------------------------------------------------------------------+
     |                         Messages                        Lines 1 - 6 of 10 |
     |                                                                       |
     |   08:45:13 MSG FROM JSMITH: Here is a test message.                   |
     |   08:45:50 MSG FROM SAML: Is there something wrong with the phones?   |
     |   08:46:19 MSG FROM SARAH: My phone just went dead!                   |
     |   08:46:55 MSG FROM SAML: Now it's ringing with no one on the other end! |
     |   08:48:23 MSG FROM BROWN: Is the phone system messed up, Jim?        |
     |   08:48:44 MSG FROM SARAH: My phone is acting strange...              |
     +-----------------------------------------------------------------------+


PF1=Help       2=Pop_Msg    3=Quit        4=Clear_Top   5=Filelist    6=Retrieve
PF7=Backward   8=Forward    9=Rdrlist     10=Left       11=Right      12=Cmdline
====>
 8:50:37  Message                         Enter a command or press a PF or PA key
```

Note that the top of the MESSAGE window tells you that you are viewing lines 1 through 6 of the window, but that there are 10 lines to see. This lets you know to look further down in the window.

The easiest way to scroll the MESSAGE window forward is with the PA2 key. Note that even though the PF key labels at the bottom of the CMS screen say PF8 scrolls forward, you don't want to do that, since that scrolls the CMS window, not the MESSAGE window. The PA2 key always scrolls the top window forward.

If you keep pressing PA2, you see the other messages. When you press PA2 while you are looking at the last message, the window shrinks and finally disappears. There are other methods for scrolling the MESSAGE window, but they are not as convenient as using PA2. They are covered in the IBM *CMS User's Guide* (SC19-6210).

The other windows of interest are the CMSOUT and WARNING windows. The CMSOUT window appears anytime you give a CMS command in an non-CMS environment such as FILELIST or XEDIT. The WARNING window contains important warning messages from the system operator. The CMSOUT and WARNING windows act like the MESSAGE window.

If you have a smaller window on top of a larger one and you want to get rid of the smaller window, use the DROP WINDOW command. This puts it underneath the larger window. To bring it back up, use the POP WINDOW command.

WM Window

There is a special window you use to control other windows. The WM (window manager) window is accessed by using the PA1 key. It appears at the bottom of your screen and gives you options for scrolling the top window. Its actions are:

```
PF1=Help      2=Top      3=Quit      4=Clear  5=Copy   6=Retrieve
PF7=Backward  8=Forward  9=Maximize 10=Left  11=Right 12=Restore
====>
```

PF7, PF8, PF10, and PF11 scroll the top window, while PF4 clears it. PF2 goes to the top of the top window. PF5 makes a copy of the screen and saves it in the file called "COPY SCREEN". PF9 makes the window the size of the entire screen. When you are done with the WM window, PF3 clears it from your terminal.

One nice feature of virtual screens is automatic logging of everything that happens in the virtual screen. The CMSOUT, MESSAGE, and WARNING virtual screens are set up to save everything that appears in the virtual screens in files called "screenname LOGFILE" (such as "CMSOUT LOGFILE"). CMS appends new messages and warnings to these files automatically. The CMSOUT log file is a good alternative to the procedure for spooling your terminal that you saw earlier in the chapter.

Since these files can get quite large, you may want to delete them periodically, or at least edit out what you don't want. If you never look at the log files, you can prevent them from being created by adding the following commands to your PROFILE EXEC:

```
SET LOGFILE CMSOUT OFF
SET LOGFILE MESSAGE OFF
SET LOGFILE WARNING OFF
```

Using Windows

Many industry observers feel that IBM included CMS windows in preparation for advanced versions of OS/2, IBM's operating system for its new PS/2 personal computers. It is likely that PS/2s connected to CMS systems will interact with CMS windows in a much more useful fashion in the coming years.

RETURN CODES

Chapter 2 mentioned return codes, the numbers you see as part of the ready message. Now that you know much more about CMS commands, you can see more of the logic behind return codes.

IBM has set a standard for CMS return codes. The most common problems encountered by CMS commands use the same return codes. Knowing these, it is much easier to figure out what you did wrong if you get an error. Note that some return codes (especially 24) are used for many different meanings. The most useful information can be seen by using the HELP command on the error number displayed at the beginning of the error message.

CMS's common return codes are:

Code	Meaning
20	An invalid character was used in a file name.
24	An invalid option was given; a required argument was not supplied; a conflicting set of options was specified; or a prohibited set of options was specified.
28	The named file was not found.
36	The command tried to alter a disk that was read-only or the disk was not accessed.
100	The specified device is not attached; or there was a disk error on one of the disks used in the command.
100nn	Error from EXEC2. An error was encountered in an EXEC2 EXEC file.
200nn	Error from REXX. An error was encountered in an REXX EXEC file.

MACHINE AND SOFTWARE CONFIGURATION

Sometimes it is difficult to tell what version of various hardware and software you are running. If someone asks, it is useful to have the complete answer. The following, called ALLINFO EXEC, displays that information:

```
/* ALLINFO EXEC: shows relevant information */
QUERY CMSLEVEL
QUERY CPLEVEL
QUERY CPUID
IDENTIFY
```

The output looks like:

```
VM/SP RELEASE 4, SERVICE LEVEL 409
VM/SP RELEASE 4  HPO LEVEL 42, SERVICE LEVEL 408
GENERATED AT 03/12/88 10:29:33 PDT
IPL AT 04/01/88 08:04:02 PDT
CPUID = FF23140530900000
CHRISJ   AT LONDON   VIA RSCS      04/15/88 13:51:13 PDT      FRIDAY
```

IMMEDIATE COMMANDS

You got a brief view of immediate commands in Chapter 2 (using the HT immediate command to stop the TYPE command). Immediate commands are useful in many situations.

To give an immediate command, you must produce an attention interrupt to CMS or be holding in the MORE... state (such as when your screen fills up). To generate an attention interrupt on an ASCII terminal, press the Attention or the BREAK key.

The immediate commands are:

HT   Halts typing. This suppresses terminal output generated by any CMS command or program. The program continues to run, but output is not shown on the screen.

HX   Halts execution. This stops the currently-running program.

RT   Resumes typing. If you have halted typing with HT, and change your mind, you can use this command to start seeing messages and information on your screen again. You will miss all messages sent since you gave the HT command.

REXX has some additional immediate commands of interest to programmers.

TEMPORARY DISKS

Most sites allow you to create temporary disks that lose their information when you log off. These are useful if you are running programs that require extra space while they run, but you don't need to save the information after you log off; this is often the case for database management systems or programming language compilers. It is important to remember that you should not store any information on a temporary disk. When you log off, the disk is reused by other users. It is only useful for programs that need storage while they are running.

Setting up a temporary disk isn't always easy. Thus, many sites have standard EXECs for getting temporary disk space. Check with your system administrator on which EXEC you use to get temporary disk space.

```
EXEC to get temporary disk space:
```

If your site does not have such an EXEC, here are steps you need to follow to get yourself temporary disk space.

First determine the type of disk drive you are using. Give the command:

```
QUERY DISK *
```

In the column labelled "TYPE," you see the model number of the disk drive used for that disk. Popular types are 3380 and 3350. You need to use this type for the next step.

You next use the DEFINE command to set up the disk:

```
DEFINE disk-type AS cuu CYL n
```

The disk-type is the letter "T" followed by the model number ("T3380" or "T3350", for example). The cuu you choose must not be in use. The number of cylinders you specify should be enough for your application; 10 is a good estimate.

If there is no temporary space on any drives of that model, you get the message:

```
DMKDEF091E DASD cuu NOT DEFINED; TEMP SPACE NOT AVAILABLE
```

If there was more than one model of disk drives in the response to QUERY DISK *, try the DEFINE command with another model.

After you have the disk you must format it:

```
FORMAT cuu mode
```

Choose a filemode you do not currently have defined. You can now use the disk until you log off.

9

Different Versions of CMS

You probably noticed that this book refers to different versions of CMS (IBM calls these *releases*). For instance, there are some features in version 5 that do not exist in previous versions (such as windows). This is typical of operating systems.

Every operating system evolves. As it evolves, it gains new features; sometimes, old little-used features are discarded. The computer market demands that manufacturers improve software products fairly regularly to remain competitive with other products. Operating systems are not improved as often, however, because it is usually not very easy to move from one version of an operating system to the next.

There are tradeoffs for manufacturers and users using new versions of an operating system. Once users get settled with the features and performance of an operating system, they are often reluctant to try something new, especially if there are some restrictions and limitations for the new features. For example, if you regularly use a program under one version of CMS that does not run under a newer version, you might be hesitant to move to a new version.

When IBM revises CMS, it follows many guidelines, including:

- The vast majority of applications should work the same as they did in the previous version. Any programs that do not work the same should at least work, or have most of the program work. The exceptions here are a few special diagnostic programs that interact heavily with CMS's internals.
- CMS commands should work the same.
- All features added to CMS should be applicable to as many applications and commands as possible.
- No change should reduce CMS's future capability to interact with other operating systems on a network. In fact, as many new features as possible should be added to enhance CMS's connectivity.

Of course, these can't always be followed completely, but IBM has done a very good job of minimizing the changes that users see between versions of CMS.

Note the phrase "that users see." One of the reasons that it takes so long for sites to upgrade to new versions of CMS is that there are often hundreds of changes that affect system administrators and operators. Some are small but appear at important times; others are quite large. The amount of time and expense it takes to plan the migration from one version of CMS to the next is often many person-months. Thus, many sites do not upgrade quickly.

HISTORY OF CMS

CMS was originally designed at the IBM Cambridge Scientific Center in Massachusetts. As you saw in Chapter 1, CP stands for "control program." CMS's name is much more interesting: the initials stand for "Cambridge Monitor System." VM was designed as a response to the Multics operating system from General Electric.

In the late 1960s, the market for mainframes was much more volatile than it is today. As other manufacturers encroached on IBM's territory, IBM announced it was developing TSS (Time Sharing System). However, delivery of TSS was a long way off. So IBM released a multi-user option to its OS batch operating system. This option, called TSO (Time Sharing Option), was very slow and initially cumbersome.

IBM then added a hardware modification to the 360 mainframe that allowed the mainframe to segment memory much better. IBM then developed CP, which took advantage of this hardware modification (called a DAT for dynamic address translation). CP needed a better user interface, so CMS was developed.

In the early 1970s, IBM released its last public-domain version of the operating system called VM/370 Release 6 to its users. It still works, but it was not supported by IBM anymore.

Later, VM fell on hard times at IBM. IBM tried to get its users to move to other operating systems, such as MVS. VM development was moved from its headquarters in Burlington, Massachusetts to Poughkeepsie, New York. Many people on the VM development team left IBM during the move and took jobs at its Massachusetts neighbor, Digital Equipment Corporation. There, they helped develop the VMS operating system for DEC's VAX computer.

IBM made VM a tool to build MVS. Through this minor role, VM survived. Outside of the US, IBM could not get sites to switch from DOS (one of IBM's other batch systems) to MVS. Instead, many sites started running DOS in a virtual machine under VM. These customers became more and more reliant on VM for their day-to-day work. The customers using VM often pestered IBM to make it a more strategic product.

In the mid-1970s, IBM gave in and built VM a good user interface. IBM took VM tools from its various research centers all over the world and put together a real operating system that programmers and end-users could use. As VM again became popular in the data processing community, its support group was moved from Poughkeepsie to the programming labs at Endicott.

As this was happening, IBM was designing faster and bigger hardware at Poughkeepsie. VM was originally designed for smaller computers, and could not take advantage of the larger hardware. At customers' insistence, IBM made an upgrade option to VM called HPO (for high performance option). This allowed VM to run on IBM's most powerful mainframes.

CMS's first major enhancement was to allow it to use larger memory sizes (almost all of the changes discussed so far were to VM, not CMS). To do this, IBM had to change much of CMS. This new version is known as VM/XA SP (extended architecture system product), and runs on IBM's extended architecture machines, such as the 4381, 3081, and 3090.

"VM/370 Release 6"

Very few people use the public-domain version of VM/370. This is mostly due to IBM's lack of support for it. However, some sites still refuse to give it up.

The operating system comes with:

- Old CMS.
- An assembly language compiler.

- The capability of running OS/360 programs.
- A line-by-line editor.

It does not have most of CMS's better features, such as XEDIT, REXX, or the ability to communicate with other operating systems.

DIFFERENCES BETWEEN VERSIONS OF CMS

This section gives you an overview of IBM's changes between recent versions. IBM releases a new version of CMS approximately every two years.

Version 3 to Version 4

Version 4 was the first to allow the system administrator to load EXEC files into memory. This made commonly used EXECs run much faster and take fewer system resources.

The HELP command was significantly enhanced in version 4. For instance, HELP could now offer help on error messages. Sites were also given more capability to change HELP screens.

Version 4 also gave programmers access to a communications protocol called SNA (system network architecture). This allows CMS to communicatee much better with other IBM operating systems.

Version 4 to Version 5

The most obvious change to CMS in version 5 is the addition of windows. Even though they are of limited use, it is likely that they will make communication over networks easier. For instance, it is likely that many microcomputer operating systems will emulate CMS's windows for network communication.

Sites outside of the U.S. will use the new "national language support" facility to allow users to enter CMS commands and receive CMS messages in languages other than American English. This facility makes it easier for people using other languages to converse with CMS in their native language. This is further supported by the use of a "central message facility" that allows all programs to put their messages in text files that can be modified by sites.

If You Are Familiar With Other Computers

The national language support and central message facility are similar in concept to the resource system used on the Macintosh.

IBM enhanced CMS programs' ability to communicate. This means two people can be running programs on different machines that communicate in a standard fashion. In the future, this will allow programs on microcomputers that use the SAA architecture to work in concert with mainframe programs.

The logon procedure for users is slightly easier in version 5. When you get your system's logo on the screen when you first connect, you can log on directly from that screen instead of pressing the CLEAR key first.

The HELP command was enhanced to give you three levels of depth of help. In addition, the HELP command was again made easier to modify.

CMS IN THE FUTURE

CMS will clearly be an important operating system for many years to come. It enjoys a unique position at IBM: It is the only operating system to run on a very wide range of hardware. In addition, it is becoming even more popular among users. As personal workstations like the PS/2 become more popular, more people are going to be able to access IBM mainframes.

IBM has already stated what will be in version 6 of CMS. The most important features that will be added in version 6 will be the shared file system and interprogram communications. The shared file system will allow much better file-level security, including the ability to allow one person to safely write to a file while others read from it. Files will be able to be shared across VM systems, and there will be a facility for UNIX-like hierarchical directories. CMS programs will be able to communicate not only with each other (such as requesting and passing data or signalling when steps are complete), but also with programs running on other operating systems, such as IBM's OS/2 Extended Edition and DEC's VMS operating system. This will be performed through IBM's LU6.2 standard communications.

IBM will certainly make changes to CMS beyond version 6. It is likely that the windows introduced in version 5 will be significantly improved. Communications will also become easier, and users will not need to know as many arcane instructions (like the TAG command) when they communicate over a network. CMS is likely to be used by more and more people every year for the foreseeable future.

A

Commercial
CMS Applications

This appendix gives you a background in the types of application software that run under CMS. The CMS software market continues to grow as more mainframe sites adopt CMS for end-user computing and as more people adopt the System/370 architecture.

The 9370 will bring a large number of new users to CMS. Because of this growth, it is likely that many types of applications not available now will be available in the next few years. Also, since the 9370 is easily connected to PCs, many PC software applications will probably be converted to use the 9370 as a host system.

DATABASE MANAGEMENT SYSTEMS

Probably the most heavily used piece of software on most CMS systems is the database management system (DBMS). Almost every large company collects and analyzes most of its data using a DBMS. Even for small companies, a good, friendly DBMS is indispensable.

You saw an introduction to databases in the NAMES command in Chapter 4. Almost all DBMSs use the same structure for data, as shown in Illustration A-1.

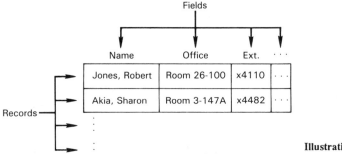

Illustration A-1

Each record consists of a fixed number of fields. Most DBMSs allow you to have as many records in your database as your minidisk can handle.

A DBMS lets you perform a wide variety of operations on databases. The general categories are:

- Adding and changing data
- Reporting on groups of data
- Searching for data that matches qualifications
- Relating databases

Adding data is fairly straight forward. Most DBMSs let a programmer design screens for data entry. For instance, a screen can be designed to look like the form from which data is taken. The screen that takes in data can be intelligent. For example, if you enter a person's city and zip code, the program can look up the zip code in a directory and warn you if it doesn't match the city you entered.

Changing data is similar to adding it. The program can display an entire record and let you choose which fields to change. Changing can also be intelligent: If you change the city but don't change the zip code, the program can warn you.

Reports from a database help you get a feel for important aggregate information. If you have a database whose records are sales, a simple report might be the sum of the sales. More complex reports can include subtotals (such as sales by region) or exceptions (such as all sales over a certain amount). DBMS report facilities usually let you format your reports in a variety of fashions.

When you prepare a report, it is usually valuable to present as much relevant information as possible. For instance, a report summarizing the quarter's sales might have subtotals for each salesperson, but not include the customer's names for each sale. A report showing the diversity of the customer base might show customer's names but not the amount of the sales.

Searching for specific data is an art, especially when using a very large database. Most DBMSs advertise their searching and sorting speeds, since these are the operations that take the most computer resources. For instance, if you want to create a report that shows all parts in an inventory that are low in quantity, you must first define "low." You start by viewing all records in the inventory database, then give a DBMS command to select only the records whose value in the "quantity on hand" field is equal to or below what you call "low." This leaves you with a subset of the records which you can then view or write a report about.

There are much more complex selections you can make. For example, you might want to give many criteria: select all records whose "quantity on hand" field is below 50 and whose "price" field is greater than $500. It is common to base a selection on a relationship between the fields in a record: select each record whose "quota" field is more than .75 times its "sales" field.

Once records are selected, you usually want them in a particular order. Sorting records is usually a time-consuming process. Thus, you try to sort as few records as possible. Instead of sorting and then selecting, it is much more efficient to select and then sort. You often do not sort on the fields that you used to determine the selection. For instance, you might select all sales over $100,000, and then show the data sorted by a salesperson.

To make selecting and sorting more efficient, DBMSs have special methods for *keying* specific fields. A key field is one where the DBMS keeps a compact representation of the field that is easier to select and sort. Keying takes extra resources, so not all fields in a database are keyed (in fact, usually only one is). For instance, in an employee database, if most of your selecting and sorting is done by name, it is likely that you want to key the name field.

In the early 1970s, a new concept became popular in DBMSs: *relational* databases. A relational DBMS is one which can relate the information in one database with that in others. For example, imagine you have two databases:

- A sales database whose fields include the amount of the sale and the name of the customer
- A client database whose fields include the customers' names and addresses

If you wanted to write a report that included each sale and include the names and addresses for the sales, you would have to get related information from both databases. The relationship between the two databases would be the customers' names.

Advanced DBMSs can relate records quickly and easily. Using relational databases can increase the security of your data. Fields can be spread into many databases, so people with low security authorization would only have access to less sensitive databases; people with higher security could view all of them.

FINANCE

IBM's dominance in the finance market has a self-perpetuating effect. Most major financial software runs on IBM mainframes, and much of it under CMS.

Much financial software is based around databases. Thus, many packages work in coordination with one or more DBMSs. Financial systems are often based around *transaction processing*. Transaction processing is more than just adding or looking at data: It is the updating of information already in the system.

Banks, of course, are heavily involved in transaction processing. Every time you write a check, the bank must not only note that the check is written, but also debit your account. A record is made for the check; its fields are your account number, the recipient bank, and the amount. This record is added to the bank's check data bank. However, the bank must do more than make a record of the check in its checks database: It must also update your record in the account balance database.

Transaction processing gets tricky in many ways that are not as important in DBMSs. For example, imagine that the financial program had finished adding the check to the checks database and was updating the record in the account balance database when the system crashes. Once it comes up again, the program must know what it was doing at the time of the crash; otherwise the account balance will not be updated.

Another problem with transaction processing is security. One of the reasons banks have so many computers is that the security necessary for financial transaction processing slows the software down significantly. There must be many safeguards to prevent unauthorized transactions (such as adding money to an account) from taking place.

Financial software is also used in securities (stocks and bonds) trading. The requirements for securities software is similar to bank software, except that the value of each transaction is often not as easy to determine as it is for banks. Thus, securities software must handle fluctuating values for securities as well as regular transaction problems.

Although most DBMSs put out reports, the reports for financial software are often very complex. For a manufacturing firm, a "snapshot" report of inventory is usually sufficient. For financial firms, however, reports often must show trends. Thus, instead of simply showing net balance, a financial package might have to show the fluctuation of net balances over various periods of time. This means keeping track of many more pieces of data and having many more methods for producing reports.

WORD PROCESSING

Chapter 6 showed you how to enter text in a text file with XEDIT. Although XEDIT is fairly easy to use, it cannot really be used for word processing due to its limitations.

For example, the following paragraph appeared in the sample letter from Chapter 6:

```
National Packaging has been very successful in attracting new
clients in the last two years. Our annual revenues have grown from
$7.3 million to $16.8 million since January 1986, and our profits
have grown from $1.1 million to $2.2 million. Our staff has
grown from 27 to 63.
```

If you wanted to change the second sentence to start, "our gross annual revenues", it would look like this:

```
National Packaging has been very successful in attracting new
clients in the last two years. Our gross annual revenues have grown from
$7.3 million to $16.8 million since January 1986, and our profits
have grown from $1.1 million to $2.2 million. Our staff has
grown from 27 to 63.
```

Note how that line is much too long compared to the other lines in the letter. Instead, you should *wrap* the words around to make the paragraph more even:

```
National Packaging has been very successful in attracting new
clients in the last two years. Our gross annual revenues have grown
from $7.3 million to $16.8 million since January 1986, and our
profits have grown from $1.1 million to $2.2 million. Our staff
has grown from 27 to 63.
```

Doing this by hand with XEDIT is fairly tedious.

Chapter 5 briefly described DCF, IBM's Document Composition Facility. DCF works in conjunction with XEDIT to make it easier to create documents. DCF produces good-looking output from text files. It is often called an *output formatter* because it makes the output of a printer visually structured in a nice fashion.

One of the main conveniences of using DCF is that you do not need to worry about wrapping the lines of your file. When DCF creates a paragraph, it automatically figures out how many words can fit on each line, and moves other words down to the next line. Even if your text file looks like this:

```
National Packaging has been very successful
in attracting new
clients in the last two years.
Our gross annual revenues have grown
from $7.3 million to $16.8 million since January 1986, and our
profits have grown from
$1.1 million to $2.2 million. Our staff has grown from 27 to 63.
```

the output will look good.

DCF can do much more than properly wrap paragraphs.

- It can add *styles* to characters. Styles commonly used in books and manuals are italic, boldface, and underlined. DCF determines whether the style you are requesting is possible on the printer you are using; if not, it makes its best guess about what to use instead.

- You can put headings and footings on each page. This is especially useful when writing manuals.

- If you want to refer to some other portion of your document, you can include *see references*. A see reference might look like this:

```
For more information on installing the program, see "Installation" on
page 42.
```

- A very advanced feature of DCF is *style sheets*. A style sheet is a specification of the elements in your document. For instance, every document has paragraphs. A paragraph can be formatted in many ways (such as justified or unjustified lines, a space before the next paragraph, the first line indented, and so on). There are many other style elements in documents as well, such as lists, chapter headings, examples, and so on. DCF lets you determine the format for each element once, and it automatically applies that to each part of your document you say has that style. This makes creating consistent formats quite easy.

There is much more to DCF than can be presented here. If you produce much printed output, you will probably find that DCF will help you.

ELECTRONIC MAIL

Most CMS users use the NOTE, SENDFILE, and RDRLIST commands to transmit messages and files to other users. NOTE and SENDFILE are *mail senders*, and RDRLIST is a *mail receiver*. These commands are only rudimentary electronic mail commands. Most commercial electronic mail systems, even ones on microcomputer networks, are much more advanced than these commands.

NOTE has features that most mail sending programs have:

- Send mail to more than one person by listing their names on the TO: and CC: lines.
- Send mail to groups of people (using the groups feature in the NAMES file).
- Include files and parts of files in your message (using XEDIT's GET command).
- Get optional acknowledgment for mail sent.

Other mail senders let you go much further than this, however. Here are some of the features of advanced mail senders:

- Specify a priority for the mail. This helps prevent clutter if many people are sending mail in a network.
- Put an expiration date on a message. Messages with short-lived value (such as meeting notices or lunch suggestions) automatically disappear after a deadline.
- Send header information with files. This lets the recipient know when the file was created and what type of information is in the file.
- Store mail groups in a central area. For example, if you have a mail group that is a department, every time a person is added to the department, only one file needs updating (instead of each person's NAMES list).
- Include graphics and sound in messages.

The RDRLIST command is barely acceptable for reading mail. For instance, the display you see does not tell you the subject of the mail or the contents of the file sent. Most mail readers are significantly more advanced, including features like:

- Allow automatic response to a message. Since most letters are part of an electronic mail conversation, it is handy to be able to compose a response to a letter as you read it and have it automatically sent to the person who sent the message to you. In the case of a letter sent to many people, you get the choice of sending your reply to just the writer of the letter, or also to all people who received the letter.
- Let you take parts of the original message and include them in your reply. The recipient can then see better the parts of the message to which you are replying.
- Display the subject matter and priority level in the reader. This allows you to discard junk mail without reading it.
- Give many options for storing mail, such as databases of messages that can be easily searched and sorted.
- Show highest priority messages first.
- Allow messages to be easily forwarded to another user. This is useful for people who are a central distribution point for messages (such as the receptionist for a sales force).
- View a file which is named in the message. For instance, a message may bring up an issue and state "please put your reply in the file called REPORT MSGS on the mail disk." Then, each person could read what others had said before they reply. This makes for a much more coherent reply.

GRAPHICS

The business data processing community has recently become enamored with graphics. There are two types of graphics that are common: charts showing pictorial representations of numbers, and presentation charts.

Pictorial representation of data allows the viewer to quickly compare values. The most common formats for these representations are pie charts, bar charts, and line charts. These are common for showing one-dimensional data.

For instance, assume you have data for the sales of the New York office for the four quarters of a year. A pie chart looks like the one shown in Illustration A-2.

Sales for New York

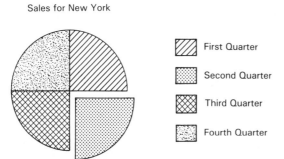

First Quarter

Second Quarter

Third Quarter

Fourth Quarter

Illustration A-2

Illustration A-3 shows what a bar chart looks like.

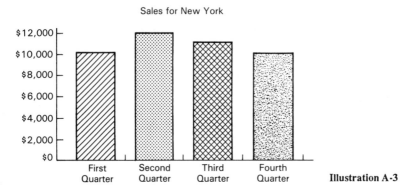

Illustration A-3

Illustration A-4 shows what a line chart looks like.

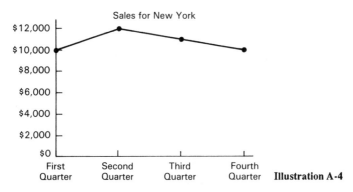

Illustration A-4

You can plot two dimensions of data at the same time. For instance, if you had the quarterly sales figures for New York, Detroit, and Boston, and wanted to compare them. A bar chart would look like the one shown in Illustration A-5.

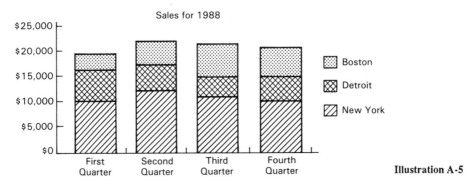

Illustration A-5

A line chart, which shows the relationships better, would look like the one shown in Illustration A-6.

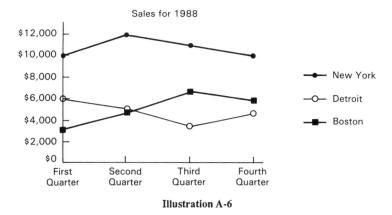

Illustration A-6

Presentation graphics allow you to make slides and overhead transparencies easily. You may want to include business graphics, or you might want to use mostly free-hand graphics and words.

Using presentation graphics with simple word charts can make them a great deal more interesting and can highlight points better. For instance, Illustration A-7 shows a plain word chart. Illustration A-8 is a more interesting version of the same chart with some embellishment.

New theme for campaign:

Efficient
telephone
communication

Illustration A-7

New theme for campaign:

Efficient
telephone
communication

Illustration A-8

SIMULATION

Financial simulation packages let you model what will happen in the future based on assumptions about the past. These packages are valuable in planning based on expected income and expenses.

Simulation programs let you link data from databases to equations of assumptions. If you are simulating the future sales of your company, an assumption might be, "The first quarter sales for next year will be up by the average increase in first quarter sales for the last three years." The program analyzes the increase in quarterly sales from the last three years and makes a projection for next year.

Another assumption might be, "If the increase in first quarter sales is greater than the decrease in fourth quarter sales for the preceding year, average the two to predict first quarter sales for next year." You can then use the simulation program to see the difference between the results of the two predictions.

Often, a company makes hundreds or thousands of such assumptions, and gives each assumption a certain amount of weight based on how true it was in the past. The simulation program can then put all the assumptions together to forecast the future. It can also simulate random events and show you the results with those events as part of the simulation.

Of course, the results of a simulation are no more accurate than the assumptions it is based on. Good simulation programs can back-track assumptions and compare them against the past so you can see if a particular assumption ever made sense.

STATISTICS

Many companies need to keep accurate statistics on their numerical data. Often, the types of statistics needed are much too complex to be handled by Database Management Systems. Thus, there are a variety of statistics packages available for CMS.

Statistics packages usually can read the numbers being analyzed from a variety of sources. Many of them include procedural languages, similar to programming languages, so you can specify the type of statistical report you want in very exact terms.

COMPUTER-AIDED INSTRUCTION

One of the biggest problems for most large companies is training new employees in using the company's computer system. Trainers are hard to come by, and scheduling someone to take a class is often difficult. Thus, many people have developed courses you can take at your terminal.

There are many ways in which a course can be presented by the computer. Universities have prepared *authoring* programs that make it easier to prepare computer-aided courses. Also, many software vendors have computer-aided training for people learning to use their products.

UTILITIES

Many software vendors have created CMS utilities to make running CMS easier and more efficient. These utilities often have the same functions as other CMS commands and IBM products, but have significant advantages.

One of the more popular utilities is system administration software. Little has been said about system administration in this book since it is well beyond the scope of most users. However, you can probably guess some of the potential headaches for a system administrator: backups, archiving, tape handling, security, batch scheduling, and so on. There are many packages that combine control of all these aspects of the system into one unified structure.

CMS is very secure for each individual user, but it is much less secure when users communicate or share data. In addition, there is no easy way to track and enforce password changes under CMS or to encrypt data stored on disk. IBM's optional security product, RACF, has a great deal of competition from other manufacturers.

Account management is especially important to firms that bill users for time and resources used. Many sites have a central computer facility that allows other departments to use its computers for a fee. To bill users, the system has to determine how much each person uses in disk space, CPU time, I/O time, and so on. There are many packages available that provide this data.

WHERE TO FIND MORE

The best sources of information about CMS software are the magazines that cover the mainframe markets. The two largest magazines in this category are *Datamation* and *ComputerWorld*. There are dozens of other smaller magazines as well.

Datamation often has articles about software and the software vendors. It also has extensive news analysis of the IBM market. *ComputerWorld* is more news-oriented, and has a tendency to write more about applications than *Datamation*. Both have advertisements for CMS software vendors every week. There are also many companies that rate and compare software; two well-known companies are Datapro and Auerbach.

You can also get a great deal of information from the two large IBM users' groups, SHARE and GUIDE. These groups hold regular seminars and meetings on a wide range of subjects. They both encourage users of commercial software to share their experiences. In the past, these two groups have competed for members, but they have recently tried to become more complimentary.

Some commercial vendors also have users groups for their software. The best of these groups are somewhat autonomous from the vendor so they can be critical when necessary. Even when these groups are quite close to the vendor, they often are of great value to their members.

B

CMS and CP
Command Reference

The underlined portion of the name in the syntax shows the minimum needed in the command name.

Command	Page	Type	Syntax
ACCESS	88	CMS	ACCESS cuu mode
CHANGE	176	CP	CHANGE PRINTER id { CLASS c | COPY n | HOLD | NOHOLD } ids: spoolid CLASS c FORM form ALL
CLOSE	176	CP	CLOSE { PUNCH | PRINTER } [PURGE]
COMPARE	73	CMS	COMPARE fileid1 fileid2 [(COL [mmm - nnn]]
COPYFILE	61	CMS	COPYFILE fileid1 fileid2 [(options] [NEWFILE | REPLACE] [NOTYPE | TYPE] [NEWDATE | OLDDATE]
DEFINE	188	CP	DEFINE STORAGE AS { nnnnnK | nnM } DEFINE disk-type AS cuu CYL n
DETACH	180	CP	DETACH cuu
DISK	173	CMS	DISK DUMP fileid DISK LOAD
ERASE	63	CMS	ERASE fileid
FILELIST	65	CMS	FILELIST [fileid]
FORMAT	72	CMS	FORMAT cuu mode [(LABEL]
HELP	34	CMS	HELP [topics | message-id]
HT	23	Imm.	HT
HX	188	Imm.	HX
IDENTIFY	187	CMS	IDENTIFY
INDICATE	74	CP	INDICATE [LOAD | USER]
IPL	25	CP	IPL CMS
LINK	79	CP	LINK [TO] userid cuu1 [AS] cuu2 [mode]
LISTFILE	50	CMS	LISTFILE [fileid] [(options] options: [HEADER | NOHEADER] [FORMAT] [ALLOC] [DATE] [LABEL] [BLOCKS]

LOGIN	24	CP	LOGIN userid
LOGOFF	42	CP	LOGOFF
LOGON	24	CP	LOGON userid
LOGOUT	42	CP	LOGOUT
NAMES	89	CMS	NAMES [nickname]
NOTE	94	CMS	NOTE [name...] [CC: name...] [(options] options: [NOACK | ACK] [LOG | NOLOG] [SHORT | LONG] [PROFILE fn]
ORDER	176	CP	ORDER PRINTER spoolid1 spoolid2 ...
PRINT	174	CMS	PRINT fileid [(CC | NOCC]
PUNCH	173	CMS	PUNCH fileid
PURGE	176	CMS	PURGE PRINTER spoolid1 spoolid2 ...
QUERY	78	CMS	QUERY option: options: ABBREV AUTOREAD CMSLEVEL DISK { fm | * | R/W | MAX } IMPCP IMPEX RDYMSG SEARCH SYNONYM { SYSTEM | USER | ALL }
QUERY	78	CP	QUERY option: options: CPLEVEL LINKS cuu LOGMSG PF READER TERMINAL TIME USERID VIRTUAL DASD VIRTUAL STORAGE
RDRLIST	99	CMS	RDRLIST
RECEIVE	100	CMS	RECEIVE spoolid [fileid]
RELEASE	88	CMS	RELEASE { cuu | mode } (DET
RENAME	63	CMS	RENAME fileid1 fileid2
RT	188	Imm.	RT
SENDFILE	96	CMS	SENDFILE [fileid] [TO { nickname | userid }
SET	74	CMS	SET options: options: ABBREV { ON | OFF } IMPCP { ON | OFF } IMPEX { ON | OFF } RDYMSG { LMSG | SMSG }

SET	74	CP	SET options: options: EMSG { ON | OFF | CODE | TEXT } PFnn [DELAYED | IMMED] [command]
SORT	73	CMS	SORT fileid1 fileid2
SPOOL	171	CP	SPOOL { PUNCH | PRINTER } [options] options: [TO { userid | SYSTEM | * }] [CLASS c] [CONT | NOCONT] [COPY n] [HOLD | NOHOLD] [FORM form]
SYNONYM	78	CMS	SYNONYM [fn [SYNONYM [fm]]] [(options] options: [STD | NOSTD] [CLEAR]
TAG	175	CP	TAG DEV PRINTER [node-name]

TAPE	177	CMS	TAPE BSF [n]
			TAPE DUMP fileid [(options]
			    options:
			    [cuu]
			    [TERM | DISK | PRINT | NOPRINT]
			TAPE FSF [n]
			TAPE LOAD fn ft [fm] [(options]
			    options:
			    [cuu]
			    [TERM | DISK | PRINT | NOPRINT]
			    [EOF n]
			TAPE MODESET [(options]
			    options:
			    [cuu]
			    [7TRACK | 9TRACK | 18TRACK]
			    [DEN density]
			TAPE REW
			TAPE { SCAN | SKIP } [fileid]
			[(options]
			    options:
			    [cuu]
			    [TERM | DISK | PRINT | NOPRINT]
			    [EOF n]
			TAPE WTM [n]

TELL	93	CMS	TELL { nickname | userid } message
TYPE	49	CMS	TYPE fileid [startline [endline]]
*	166	EXEC2	* text
/* */	158	REXX	/* text */

C

XEDIT
Command
Reference

The underlined portion of the name in the syntax shows the minimum needed in the command name. The types indicate whether the command causes the file to be edited or only changes the display.

Command	Page	Type	Syntax
ALL	149	Disp	ALL [target]
BACKWARD	136	Disp	BACKWARD [n]
BOTTOM	136	Disp	BOTTOM
CANCEL	145		CANCEL
CAPPEND	153	Edit	CAPPEND text
CDELETE	153	Edit	CDELETE
CFIRST	152	Disp	CFIRST
CHANGE	139	Edit	CHANGE /from-text [/to-text/ [target [count]]]
CINSERT	153	Edit	CINSERT text
CLAST	152	Disp	CLAST
CLOCATE	153	Disp	CLOCATE col-target
CMS	148		CMS [command-line]
COPY	138	Edit	COPY to-target dest-target
CREPLACE	153	Edit	CREPLACE text
DELETE	136	Edit	DELETE [target]
DOWN	136	Disp	DOWN [n]
EXTRACT	146		EXTRACT /operand ...
FILE	116		FILE [fileid]
FORWARD	136	Disp	FORWARD [n]
GET	141	Edit	GET [fileid [firstrec [numrec]]]
HELP	117		HELP
INPUT	123	Edit	INPUT [text]
LOCATE	137	Disp	[LOCATE] target
MOVE	138	Edit	MOVE to-target dest-target
PUT	141		PUT [target [fileid]]

```
QUERY            135                  QUERY option
                                      options:
                                      ACTION
                                      ARBCHAR
                                      AUTOSAVE
                                      CASE
                                      CMDLINE
                                      CURLINE
                                      LASTMSG
                                      MSGLINE
                                      NONDISP
                                      NULLS
                                      PF
                                      RING
                                      SCALE
                                      SPAN
                                      STAY
                                      SYNONYM
                                      VARBLANK
                                      VERIFY
                                      WRAP

QUIT             117                  QUIT

SAVE             116                  SAVE [ fileid ]

SET              129                  SET options
                                      options:
                                      ARBCHAR { ON c | OFF }
                                      AUTOSAVE [ n | OFF ]
                                      CASE { MIXED | UPPERCASE } [ RESPECT |
                                         IGNORE ]
                                      CMDLINE [ BOTTOM | TOP | ON | OFF ]
                                      CURLINE ON { n | -n | M[ +n | -n ] }
                                      MSGLINE { ON placement | OFF }
                                         placement:
                                         { n | -n | M[ +n | -n ] } [ length ]
                                            [ OVERLAY ]
                                      NONDISP c
                                      NULLS { ON | OFF }
                                      PFn [ type ] [ string ]
                                         type:
                                         [ BEFORE | AFTER | ONLY | IGNORE ]
                                      RESERVED placement { HIGH | NOHIGH } [text]
                                         placement:
                                         { n | -n | M[ +n | -n ] }
                                      RESERVED placement OFF
                                      SCALE { ON placement | OFF }
                                         placement:
                                         { n | -n | M[ +n | -n ] }
                                      SCREEN
                                      SPAN { ON [ spec ] | OFF }
                                         spec:
                                         { BLANK | NOBLANK } [ n | * ]
                                      STAY { ON | OFF }
```

```
                                      SYNONYM newname oldname
                                      VARBLANK { ON | OFF }
                                      VERIFY { OFF | ON }
                                      WRAP { ON | OFF }
```

SORT	152	Edit	`SORT target [A	D] col1 col2 ...`
SPLTJOIN	140	Edit	`SPLTJOIN`
STATUS	135		`STATUS`
TOP	136	Disp	`TOP`
UP	136	Disp	`UP [ n ]`
XEDIT	145		`XEDIT fileid`
?	129		`?`
=	129		`=`

Prefix commands:

A   Add a line after.

C   Copy a line; must be matched with F or P.

CC   Copy a block of lines; must be matched with F or P.

D   Delete a line.

DD   Delete a block of lines.

F   Cause copy or move to happen following the specified line.

I   Insert a line after.

M   Move a line; must be matched with F or P.

MM   Move a block of lines; must be matched with F or P.

P   Cause copy or move to happen preceding the specified line.

"   Duplicate a line.

""   Duplicate a block of lines.

/   Set the current line to this line. Preceding the "/" with a number causes the column pointer to be moved to that column.

.   Make a label.

<   Shift a line left; characters shifted past the first column are lost. Preceding the "<" with a number indicates shifting the line by that many characters; "<5" shifts the line 5 columns to the left.

<<   Shift a block of lines left. This can be preceded by a number to shift the block by that many columns.

>   Shift a line right; lines shifted away from the first column are filled with spaces. Preceding the ">" with a number indicates shifting the line by that many characters.

>>   Shift a block of lines right. This can be preceded by a number to shift the block by that many columns.

Display commands:

ALL
BACKWARD
BOTTOM
CFIRST
CLAST
CLOCATE
DOWN
FINDUP
FORWARD
LOCATE
TOP
UP

Edit commands:

ADD
CAPPEND
CDELETE
CHANGE
CINSERT
COPY
CREPLACE
DELETE
DUPLICAT
GET
INPUT
MOVE
SORT
SPLTJOIN

D

IBM
Manuals

IBM has dozens of manuals that relate to CMS. This appendix lists the major CMS-related manuals, gives their order numbers, and briefly describes each manual. They are listed in their approximate order of usefulness to beginning and intermediate users.

Note that IBM previously changed manual order numbers when it released new versions of software. Recently, IBM has done this less often. However, some manuals have changed order numbers with the release of CMS version 5.

Generally, you want to use the most recent version of the manual. If you need to order a manual for an older version, ask your system administrator.

Title	Number	Description
• *Quick Reference*	SX20-4400	Complete list of all CMS, CP, XEDIT, and REXX commands with complete syntaxes.
• *System Product Editor Command and Macro Reference*	SC24-5221	XEDIT command guide. Lists all XEDIT commands in alphabetical order. Useful if you use XEDIT heavily.
• *System Product Editor User's Guide*	SC24-5220	XEDIT user's guide. This gives a reasonable introduction to XEDIT.
• *CMS Command and Macro Reference*	SC19-6209	Alphabetical listing of CMS (not CP) commands. Very detailed and assumes a technical background.
• *System Product Interpreter User's Guide*	SC24-5238	REXX user's guide. Describes REXX as a programming language.
• *CP Command Reference for General Users*	SC19-6211	Alphabetical list of CP commands.
• *CMS Primer*	SC24-5236	Somewhat scattered introduction to using CMS. Not very useful after you have learned the basics of CMS.

• *CMS User's Guide*	SC19-6210	This manual is mostly for programmers. Although it has some introductory information, most of the book is only of use to programmers with a strong technical background. It has a detailed section on using tapes.
• *System Product Interpreter Reference*	SC24-5239	REXX reference. Good description of how REXX commands work.
• *Terminal Reference*	GC19-6206	Explains the differences between IBM terminals.

E

Checklists

This appendix is a collection of all the checklists in the book. You can fill these in as you fill in the ones in the chapters or as a compendium of the information that you might need to get from the system administrator.

Disks that are linked when you log on:

☐ Mine
☐ System
☐ Another user's (named _____)

Your system administrator is:

Your computer hardware is (check one):

☐ System/370
☐ System/370 Extended
☐ 9370
☐ XT/370 or AT/370
☐ Plug-compatible (non-IBM)

Your terminal is:

☐ 3270-compatible
☐ ASCII terminal
☐ Printing terminal

Your userid is (do *not* write your password):

Equivalent keystrokes for ASCII terminals:

3270 key   *Your keystrokes*

ENTER
PF1
PF2
PF3
PF4
PF5
PF6
PF7
PF8
PF9
PF10
PF11
PF12
Up   ⬆
Down   ⬇
Left   ⬅
Right   ➡
Tab   ➡
Back tab   ⬅
Return   ⬅
Home   ↖
Delete   🔲
Insert   🔲
ATTN
CLEAR
ERASE INPUT
ERASE EOF
RESET
PA1
PA2

You have automatic IPL:

☐ Yes
☐ No

To change your password:

Amount of disk space you have been allocated:

Amount of virtual storage you have been allocated:

Name of your node:

To get a list of all nodes:

EXEC to LINK and ACCESS another user's disk:

Name of EXECs for preparing text files:
Printer model   *EXEC*

Printers available to you:
Location   *Model*   *Class*   *Forms*

Remote printers available to you:
Location   *Type*   *Class*   *Forms*   *Tags*

Your tape operator is:

Command or method to communicate with your tape operator is:

When finished with a tape, use:
☐ TAPE REW
☐ TAPE RUN
☐ Other command:

EXEC to get temporary disk space:

Index

TEAR OUT THIS PAGE TO ORDER OTHER TITLES IN PRENTICE HALL'S MAINFRAME
SOFTWARE SERIES

QUANTITY	TITLE	TITLE CODE	PRICE	TOTAL
_____	Using VAX/VMS	93902-5	23.00	_____
_____	The CICS Companion: A Reference Guide to COBOL Command Level Programming	13446-0	22.00	_____
_____	Optimizing Performance in DB2	63823-9	40.00	_____
_____	CICS/VS Command Level Programming with COBOL Examples	13388-4	32.00	_____
_____	CICS/VS Online System Design and Implementation Techniques	13393-4	32.00	_____
_____	IMS/VS DB/DC Online Programming Using MFS and DL/1	45216-9	32.00	_____
_____	IMS/VS DL/1 Programming with COBOL Examples	45217-7	32.00	_____
_____	VSAM Coding in COBOL and VSAM AMS	94414-0	32.00	_____
_____	Fourth-Generation Languages, Vol. I	32967-2	47.00	_____
_____	Fourth-Generation Languages, Vol. II	32974-8	46.00	_____
_____	Fourth-Generation Languages, Vol. III	32976-3	46.00	_____
_____	SNA: IBM's Networking Solution	81514-2	48.00	_____
_____	VSAM: Access Method Services and Programming Techniques	94417-3	48.00	_____
_____	Data Dictionary: Implementation, Use, and Maintenance	19735-0	45.00	_____
_____	OS and VS Job Control Language and Utility Programs, Second Edition	64290-0	31.00	_____
_____	Structured Computer Project Management	85353-1	35.00	_____
			Subtotal	_____
		less discount (if appropriate)		_____
			Total	_____